What is
Digital Sociology?

What is Sociology? Series

What is
Digital Sociology?

NEIL SELWYN

polity

First published in 2019 by Polity Press

Polity Press
65 Bridge Street
Cambridge CB2 1UR, UK

Polity Press
101 Station Landing
Suite 300
Medford, MA 02155, USA

ISBN-13: 978-1-5095-2710-6
ISBN-13: 978-1-5095-2711-3 (pb)

A catalogue record for this book is available from the British Library.

Library of Congress Cataloging-in-Publication Data

Names: Selwyn, Neil, author.
Title: What is digital sociology? / Neil Selwyn.
Description: Cambridge, UK ; Medford, MA : Polity Press, 2018. |
    Includes bibliographical references and index.
Identifiers: LCCN 2018025187 (print) | LCCN 2018027027 (ebook) |
    ISBN 9781509527144 (Epub) | ISBN 9781509527106 (hardback) |
    ISBN 9781509527113 (pbk.)
Subjects: LCSH: Sociology. | Information technology–Social aspects.
Classification: LCC HM585 (ebook) | LCC HM585 .S458 2018 (print) |
    DDC 301–dc23
LC record available at https://lccn.loc.gov/2018025187

Typeset in 10.5 on 12 pt Sabon by Toppan Best-set Premedia Limited
Printed and bound in the United Kingdom by Clays Ltd, Elcograph S.p.A.

For further information on Polity, visit our website: politybooks.com

Contents

Preface

A print-based publication might seem a rather old-fashioned means of addressing the question of digital sociology. Indeed, tackling any question these days is increasingly unlikely to involve consulting a book. Instead most people's immediate approach to making sense of the question "What is Digital Sociology?" is likely to involve turning to Google (or perhaps Baidu, Yandex, DuckDuckGo and other alternative search engines). Some individuals looking for a deeper dive might check Wikipedia or perhaps search a bibliographic database for a couple of algorithmically recommended articles. In contrast, sitting down and methodically working your way through a 40,000-word book might appear a rather long-winded way of going about things.

This abundance of online information reflects the fast-changing nature of scholarship and knowledge. It also flags up the need for sociologists to pay serious attention to "the digital." Google, Wikipedia and similar information sources are not simply washing over academic disciplines such as sociology and leaving things unchanged. Instead, these technologies are significantly influencing the ways that knowledge is being developed and disseminated. As such, they are technologies that sociologists need not only to be making clever use of but also developing critical stances toward.

From this perspective, there is good reason to engage in "long-form" reading and writing around the question of digital sociology. While the internet is proving a flourishing forum for all manner of sociological conversations, it is telling that a specific sense of "digital sociology" has been most rigorously refined to date through full-length books. Sociological thinking around these issues was first captured in a prescient collection edited by Kate Orton-Johnson and Nick Prior (2013) – fifteen chapters that continue to provide a strong theoretical basis for anyone working in the field. Three years later, this was complemented by a wide-ranging survey of empirical and conceptual pieces edited by Jessie Daniels and her colleagues (2016), showcasing the diversity of "first-wave" digital sociology thinking and research across North America, Europe and Australasia. Published around the same time as these edited collections were sole-authored titles by Deborah Lupton (2014) and Noortje Marres (2017). Among other things, Lupton's book developed a great framework for making sense of digital sociology in terms of digital theory-building, digital methods and digital scholarship. Extending these themes, Marres provided a thorough grounding in the ontological and epistemological challenges thrown up by digital methods of social inquiry and analysis. These four books continue to be must-read references for anyone looking to venture into this area.

As these previous titles demonstrate, long-form books offer a welcome opportunity to slow down and take stock of what are rapidly evolving ideas. There is clear merit in continuing to blog, tweet, podcast and (un)conference about matters relating to digital sociology. Yet there is also clear benefit in engaging in uninterrupted, linear reflection that takes a little more effort and time. So this book seeks to provide a further opportunity to consider what it means to engage in sociological work that "relates to the digital ... is directed at the digital ... but also of the digital" (Carrigan 2015). There are a number of themes and principles underpinning our discussions. On the one hand is an awareness of what is taking place *outside* of sociology. It is important to remember that recent developments in digital sociology have not occurred in a vacuum. In this sense, care needs be taken in locating these ideas in relation to developments beyond the discipline. Indeed, one of the challenges when attempting to talk about digital sociology is the increasingly blurred distinction between straight-ahead sociological work and the mass of cognate work taking place across the digital humanities, new media studies, communications, design and computational subjects. As will be reiterated throughout this book, digital sociology is an inherently interdisciplinary endeavor that spans many different disciplinary boundaries.

On the other hand is the need to remember that this remains a book specifically about sociology. While reflecting on inter/intra-disciplinary cross-overs, we must not forget to emphasize what is inherently sociological about our interests. After all, this is a book concerned with digital sociology rather than "digital social sciences" or "critical digital studies." As such, it takes care to locate current concerns over digital sociology in relation to the "bigger picture" of sociology. One feature of this approach is a willingness to move on quickly from the surface-level features and novelties of the digital. If we are not careful, discussions of digital sociology can soon get bogged down in excessively descriptive and sometimes exoticized stories of how individuals now encounter and experience the digital. Examining the lived experiences of digitally mediated society is important but must be appropriately grounded in what might appear to be relatively dry issues of social structure, political economy, power relations, and so on. Thus while this book considers a range of current hot topics within digital culture and digital life, it does so within appropriately micro *and* macro levels of analysis.

If nothing else, this hopefully gives the book a longer shelf life than many other discussions of digital society. Rather than over-focusing on specific instances of how "the digital" is currently being experienced, this text is concerned primarily with enduring ideas and issues. The arguments, issues and ideas outlined here should remain relevant long after Twitter, Facebook, Mechanical Turk, and so on, have fallen out of fashion. Indeed, there is clear benefit to retaining a strong sense of history when talking about digital society – to remain mindful of where our current concerns sit within the history of sociological thought. In this sense, previous discussions of digital sociology have sometimes suffered from not being sufficiently grounded in the discipline's "pre-digital" work on technology. This book therefore takes care to foreground connections with nineteenth- and twentieth-century sociology – both as a rejoinder to ahistorical accounts of digital sociology and as a means of highlighting the strong connections with long-running concerns in mainstream sociology.

So, despite the definitive promise of its title, this short book does not set out to provide the final word on the subject. Instead, I hope that it offers an entry point to a burgeoning field of sociological activity and thought. For instance, there are many writers and theorists whom the book is able only to touch on in passing but are definitely worth engaging with in depth. Chapter 3's overview of digital methods skips through a range of different methods, each of which merits a full book in its own right. Chapter 4's indicative discussions of digital race and digital labor are intended to inspire readers to delve into *other* literatures on equally significant topics. There is plenty more to this area of sociology than can be squeezed into any single title. So I hope that this book will prompt readers to get thinking about the distinctively sociological things that still need to be said about the fast-changing "digital" conditions and circumstances in which many of us now live. Most importantly, it is intended to get readers thinking both about what the project of "digital sociology" is and about what it could be. Of course, as with most "What is?" questions in the social sciences, there are few specific straightforward answers to this book's title. Nevertheless, there are plenty of possibilities that warrant our sustained intellectual energy and attention.

Acknowledgments

Given the nature of this topic, much of the intellectual support from which I benefited during the writing of this book came online. I am particularly grateful for the tweets, blog-posts and other forms of digital writing shared by colleagues whom mostly I have never met, from places that mostly I have never been. None of the following people will be aware that they played an important part in the writing of this book, but they certainly deserve to be acknowledged regardless. These include digital scholars such as Karen Gregory, Jessie Daniels, Tressie McMillan Cottom, Frank Pasquale, Trebor Scholz, Mark Carrigan, Mercedes Bunz, Kate Crawford, Melissa Gregg, Nick Couldry, Dave Berry, David Beer, Lori Emerson, Antonio Casilli and the BSA Digital Sociology collective.

Other supportive people with whom I *have* interacted face to face include the likes of Luci Pangrazio, Jeff Brooks, Selena Nemorin, Deborah Lupton and Ben Williamson. Finally, I would like to thank all the staff at Polity for their help in seeing this book over the finish line. The initial idea and commission for the book came from Jonathan Skerrett, with additional editorial support from Karina Jákupsdóttir. Caroline Richmond provided excellent copy-editing and David Watson took care of the proof-reading – reminding me of the continued value of "traditional" publishing in a digital age.

1

Digital Sociology: Promises and Precedents

Introduction

For many people, the prospect of a "digital sociology" might well provoke questions of "why?" rather than "what?" Seasoned sociologists can be forgiven for responding to talk of digital sociology with a weary skepticism. After all, it could be argued that we live in societies blighted by the same basic social issues and problems that have persisted for many decades. From this perspective, it is not obvious why recent technological developments merit a particularly different approach to sociology. Even less jaded observers might be unconvinced of the need for a distinct "digital sociology." After all, surely anyone who is researching, writing and teaching about sociology today is engaged in digital sociology. Aren't all sociologists (at least implicitly) asking questions of digital processes and practices? Isn't everybody now making extensive use of digital technologies throughout their scholarship?

These are understandable reservations to have about a book titled *What is Digital Sociology?*. Yet these five chapters develop an argument that digital sociology is a more serious and substantial endeavor than might first appear. In essence, digital sociology is a call for taking a deliberate and

proactive "digital" approach toward *all* aspects of sociological work. This involves writing and researching aspects
of social life that are digital in nature as well as form. In
turn, this implies questioning the relevance of familiar social
methods and theory from "pre-digital" eras, while also striving to develop new ways of inquiring, thinking and knowing.
It also means pursuing digitally networked forms of scholarly
communication and interaction that are openly accessible,
shared and reconfigured.

So, while digital sociology should not be seen as a wholly
new (or superior) way of "doing" sociology, neither is it an
inconsequential footnote. Despite some appearances to the
contrary, digital sociology is not the brainchild of Twitter-
obsessed academics who (over)theorize selfies, memes and
other facets of internet culture. Instead, it marks a concerted
attempt by a broad range of sociologists to engage fully
with social settings that are now profoundly digital and
digitized. As this book will make clear, realizing such ambitions involves considerably more work than one might think.
Indeed, one of the central features of digital sociology is its
inherently interdisciplinary nature – pushing sociologists to
make connections with other areas that are already engaging critically in digital questions and digital settings. Digital
sociology challenges us to take ownership of ideas, methods
and techniques that have not traditionally been part of the
sociological toolkit.

The sales pitch for digital sociology is therefore straightforward enough – we need a discipline that is fit for the digitally
networked societies in which the majority of us now live. This
requires sociologists to develop ways of holding to account
the digital societies that we currently have, while also constructing plausible alternatives and advocating better futures.
Thus the ideas and arguments developed in this book should
be seen as enhancing (rather than undermining) established
forms of sociology. The idea of a distinct digital sociology is
certainly in keeping with sociology's standing as a "living,
evolving discipline" (Willis 1996: 107) that looks constantly
to question the new. As Dave Beer (2014: ix) suggests, the
most productive moments in sociology often occur when the
discipline "embraces its uncertainty and turns it to its advantage." When approached in these forward-looking terms,

then, there is surely much about "the digital" for sociologists to embrace.

Acknowledging the "digital society"

The case for a digital sociology certainly makes sense if we consider recent technological shifts in how much of the world now interacts and communicates. For example, we live in a world replete with personal digital devices. By 2017, the United States (population of 319 million) had an estimated 223 million smartphone users; worldwide numbers of smartphone users exceed 2 billion. In addition, laptops, tablets and other computing devices are used by a majority of people in developed regions. Crucially, almost all these devices are interconnected and networked. Nearly half of the global population (that is, 3.7 billion people) makes use of the internet – a proportion rising to around 90 per cent of adults in industrialized nations such as South Korea, Australia, Canada and the US (ITU 2017). While it is important to remain mindful of disparities in access and use, being online is an ordinary (rather than extraordinary) element of everyday life.

As a result, most people are now living large proportions of their lives through digital systems, services and applications. Communication with family and friends is increasingly mediated through text and video messaging. Information is commonly gathered through sources such as Wikipedia, social media news feeds, Google search results, online news sources and viral video clips from media organizations. Growing amounts of leisure and entertainment take place online – from the streaming of films and music to mass participation in online gaming and "e-sports." These practices all take place through global online platforms at massive scale. For example, Facebook boasts 2.17 billion monthly active users, followed by YouTube with 1.5 billion and WhatsApp with 1.3 billion (Statistica 2018). Google processes an average 40,000 search queries every second. Wikipedia is now available in over 280 languages, with the English-language version comprising nearly 5.5 million articles.

Such developments reflect the fact that contemporary society
is increasingly organized and administered through digital
systems, services and applications. Consider how citizens are
now likely to engage with education, health, legal and welfare
systems. What once were vast paper-bound bureaucracies are
now being reconfigured as vast digital bureaucracies. Digital
technology is now a key element of the democratic process,
as evident in recent national elections around the world. For
example, while ballot collections might still rely on paper
voting slips, much else of Donald Trump's rise to the US
presidency toward the end of 2016 related to social media,
email hacking and digital (dis)information. The cumulative
consequences of what might seem to be trivial digital practices can surprise even the most tech-savvy observers.

Significantly, these shifts are economic as well as civic
and cultural. Contemporary society is shaped by the digital
economy. The buying and selling of goods and services
increasingly takes place online, and financial trading is now
a wholly "virtual" affair. Consumers are engaged in online
banking and contactless payments. At the same time, many
forms of work and employment are digital in nature (if not
form). Amid these developments, the high-tech sector is a
dominant part of the global economy. The top three global
companies by the beginning of 2018 were all from the technology sector – Apple Inc. (with a market capitalization of
$880 billion), Alphabet Inc. ($820 billion) and Microsoft
($725 billion) (Neate 2018). Whereas financial reports in
the late twentieth century would celebrate the fortunes of
General Motors, Walmart and Exxon, now the talk is of
Facebook, Apple, Netflix and Google.

The need for a digital sociology does not stop at these
current trends. It is salutary to think beyond the current era
of smartphones, apps and websites and toward emerging
technological developments. The much anticipated Internet
of Things is beginning to take (actual) shape, with network-
connected sensors, processors and other electronics being
embedded in everyday objects – from refrigerators to clothing. The ability of "smart" objects to collect, receive and
process data looks set to alter significantly the relationships
that people have with the material environment, as "physical spaces" become overlaid with "code spaces." Indeed,

ongoing developments in artificial intelligence (AI) and "Big Data" processing have prompted growing debate over the significance of autonomous systems, algorithmic decision-making and a general blurring of humans and machines. While the precise nature and consequences of these developments remain uncertain, the ongoing digitization of society along such lines is set to continue for the foreseeable future.

Preceding sociologies of technology (a brief history)

If we accept that the digital is a recent development with significant bearing on contemporary society, then there is surely good reason for sociologists to be concerned with how their thinking, practice and craft might better reflect these changes. However, these current concerns need to be properly situated within the long tradition of sociological thought on technology. Before unpacking the ostensibly new turn of digital sociology, it is worth taking time to trace the origins of our current enthusiasms within preceding sociologies of technology. While these thinkers might not have been concerned with "digital" technology per se, there is clearly a lineage that our current discussions need to acknowledge and draw upon. Indeed, it could be argued that digital sociology continues a long history of sociological thought on technology. This can be grouped loosely into three phases of cognate work.

(i) Classical sociologists and technology

Digital sociology does not mark the first time that sociologists have turned attention toward technology. In fact, technology has been a sociological preoccupation since the beginnings of the discipline. Late nineteenth-century sociology emerged in response to economic and societal shifts that were entwined with the development of "new" technologies – not least the emerging industrial era, the rise of capitalism and the shift from religion to science. As such, it is worth remaining mindful of the "vibrant and consistent interest in technology among sociology's forefathers" (Gunderson 2016: 41).

Indeed, many of the early sociological thinkers had some thing to say about technology (often, more precisely, about "machines"). For example, Auguste Comte's description of phased societal progression was driven by his valorization of a final technocratic "scientific phase." This has prompted claims that Comte's writing from the first half of the nineteenth century "reads very much like elements of a Silicon Valley manifesto" (Quill 2016: 89), with irreconcilable social and political issues reduced to technical problems with technological solutions. In contrast to Comte's conspiratorial "technological optimism" (ibid.: 96) was the writing of Max Weber. While Weber is best known for his work on rationalization and the technocratic "iron cage of bureaucracy," he wrote widely on the development of industrial, military, architectural and musical technologies. For example, Weber was concerned by the reframing of military officers as "technicians" in an era of increasingly modern "mechanized" warfare. His studies on the development and diffusion of musical instruments (such as the piano) prefigured more recent trends to focus on mundane technological artifacts. Unlike Comte, Weber conveyed a deep ambivalence toward these innovations of his time, drawing attention to the compromised social conditions of technological development (Maley 2004).

While technological concerns were apparent in the work of many classical social theorists, the US sociologist Torsten Veblen has perhaps the strongest claim to advancing "a conscious and explicit sociology of technology" (Weinstein 1982: 46). Veblen was the original English translator of key German texts on "*Technik*," thus hastening the adoption among Anglophone writers of his preferred term "technology" rather than the more pointed European notion of "technique" (Morozov 2011). Veblen is credited as the first to challenge the notion of technological determinism – i.e. the commonsense presumption that technology is autonomous and drives history. Instead his work reasoned that institutional and corporate "vested interests" often acted to constrain the development of new technology – making it often more beneficial for institutions (and countries) to engage in forms of technological "borrowing" rather than innovation. As such, Veblen advanced a persuasive account of the social

nature of technology development and diffusion. As he reasoned, "the scope of the process is larger than the machine"
(Veblen 1904: 5).

Of course, the leading classical social theorist on technology is generally considered to be Karl Marx. The machines
of modern industry were a central element of Marx's account
of the economic system of capitalism. His work explored
the economic *and* social effects of technology – questioning
not only the economic impact of machines on prices, cost
and production but also the impact that machines had on
the social organization of work and workers' lives. Marx's
writing on technology remains compelling, and he evoca-
tively described steam-driven "cyclopean" machines operating amid the "giant" of modern industry. He also thoroughly
researched the history of technological development, engaging
closely with the work of engineers such as Charles Babbage
and looking back to the handicraft tools of the Middle Ages
and pre-industrialized manufacturing machines such as the
handloom. Throughout his writing, Marx refined the idea
that technologies are entwined with the social, economic and
political conditions of their times.

Marx's thinking gives sociology an enduring legacy of
framing technology in a double-edged manner. On the one
hand, much of his writing points to the ways in which
machines enabled and extenuated conditions of domination
and exploitation of workers by capital. He showed how the
increased automation of industrialized machines led to an
intensification of work, longer working hours, the deterio-
ration of working conditions and the displacement (if not
outright dismissal) of workers. As Marcuse (1964) notes,
Marx's work is especially perceptive in illustrating how domination is perpetuated *through* technology and *as* technology.
On the other hand, Marx also retains a sense of hope that
societies might be able to make use of these technologies in
alternative, more humane ways. Thus Marx draws attention
to the emancipatory potential of technology – writing on
occasion that technology offers an opportunity for superseding wage systems and establishing truly social systems of
production (Roth 2010). In this sense, Marx laid foundations for an even-handed critique of technology that has
persisted throughout many subsequent sociological accounts

of technology. As Matthewman (2011: 29) observes, Marx "had an admiration for the things that technology could do and contempt for what it was used to do."

(ii) Twentieth-century sociologists and technology

As sociology grew as a discipline across the twentieth century, so too did sociological accounts of the considerable technological developments of the time. One prominent voice in the first half of the century was William F. Ogburn – a US sociologist whose career returned regularly to questions of technology and change. By early twentieth-century standards, Ogburn was notable for his attention to cultural and societal aspects of technological development. He reasoned, for instance, that technological inventions did not result simply from creative individual genius of "great men." Instead, he described how the development of new technologies "are in large part culturally determined" (Ogburn and Thomas 1937: 91) – a fact demonstrated by the simultaneous emergence of similar technological "breakthroughs" by different "inventors."

Ogburn also explored the repercussions of technology development – proposing the idea of "cultural lag" whereby social life and institutions are seen to adapt more slowly to developments in "material culture" (notably the invention of technology). This lack of societal adjustment therefore resulted in social problems and disorganization. In this way, Ogburn pre-empted later popular ideas of technology "diffusion," "convergence," "innovation" and second-order effects of technological development. While Ogburn's writing could now be said to "read like a parody of technological determinism" (Volti 2004: 399), he nevertheless acknowledged the "complex of interconnections" between social institutions and technology (Ogburn 1936: 2). While limited, Ogburn's work laid the ground for more nuanced discussion of the role that technology plays in shaping aspects of society and culture.

Of course, Ogburn's implicit determinism and presumption of the benefits of technological invention prompted criticism from other sociologists. Around the same time, for example, Lewis Mumford was arguing for more politically nuanced understandings of societal adjustment to technology – often advocating for "change in a direction *opposite* to the machine" ([1934] 2010: 316). Mumford wrote of "technics" rather than technology, evoking the Greek notion of "*techne*" to position technological tools as part of broader social practices. This allowed him to distinguish between two opposing modes of technology. He described "polytechnics" as the combined use of small-scale and versatile tools and practices in ways that were "life-orientated" and concerned with addressing human problems. In contrast, "monotechnics" described the development of "mega machines" that are immensely powerful yet diminish humanity and human interests. For example, Mumford saw the dominance of road networks based around automobiles as leading to unacceptable environmental degradation as well as marginalizing more life-affirming forms of transportation (such as walking, cycling or public transport). As one of his enduring quotations puts it, "forget the damned motor car and build the cities for lovers and friends" (cited in Jackson 2011: 67).

Mumford's concerns over such "megatechnics" pointed to the environmental and ecological consequences of technology. He argued for restraint in order to reach a "dynamic equilibrium" between technological development and ecological, biological and human needs (thus establishing what he termed an "economy of plenitude"). Yet this stark outlook was not without hope. Mumford also argued that humans are defined by the limits of their bodies, minds and human nature – meaning that technology can never be all-defining. Because of this, he reasoned that humans will always retain a consciousness of technology and, with it, a possibility of redefining the role it plays in their lives. As Mumford concluded his 1970 book *The Pentagon of Power*: "for those of us who have thrown off the myth of the machine, the next move is ours."

Alongside sociologists such as Ogburn and Mumford, the twentieth century saw a succession of socially inflected accounts of technology from non-sociologists. In particular, a number of major twentieth-century philosophers addressed technological issues – from Heidegger's *The Question*

Concerning Technology to Lyotard's discussions of knowledge in an era of information-processing machines. One prescient approach is the work of Jacques Ellul. Over the course of seventy years, Ellul constructed an insightful yet bleak account of modern technological society and its diminished human freedoms. Rather than "technology," Ellul wrote of "technique" – i.e. "the totality" of technological artifacts and accompanying processes, practices, rules and institutions. For Ellul, "technique" constituted the system (and systemic logics) within which social life takes place. He reasoned that the emerging technological system of the twentieth century was predicated upon the valorization of efficiency. Thus all technologies are expected to contribute to increased efficiency – "the defining force of a new social order" (Ellul 1964: 17) that privileges characteristics of technical rationality and artificiality at the expense of interests related to "humanity" and "the natural world."

In this sense, Ellul bemoaned what he saw as an increasingly prevalent state of "autonomous technology" where technology becomes an end rather than a means. While the development of any new technology remains a socially influenced and contingent process, it is nevertheless embedded in the underpinning imperative of continued development of ever more efficient techniques. Thus the solution to any societal problem is always understood to be the production of new technology. In his later writing, Ellul (1990) referred to this as "the technological bluff," where people unquestioningly accept technological change as problem-solving and advantageous even when it acts to destroy values, ethics and other aspects of "humanness." Ellul therefore offered a "despair[ing]" (Feenberg 1995) view of the technological society being in constant "dialectic tension with human freedom" (Garrison 2010: 197). Crucially, he saw little hope of this tension being resolved. Ellul reasoned that people are either "fascinated" or "diverted" by technology and therefore have little desire and/or time to be critical. Thus the only ways that this impasse might change would require large-scale destructive war, the unlikely event of "God decid[ing] to intervene," or a sudden large-scale shift in human awareness of "the threat" of technological society (Ellul 1964: xxx).

(Iii) STS (science and technology studies)

These early accounts offer useful ideas, although all have clear limitations and gaps when set against the complexities of the contemporary digital age (see, for example, Ritzer 2013). Perhaps the closest twentieth-century precursor to digital sociology is the interdisciplinary field of "science and technology studies" (STS). STS emerged in the 1970s, bringing together a variety of academic areas interested in engaging critically with science, engineering and technology – the history of science, the philosophy of science, anthropology and public policy. Much early STS work drew on theory and method from the sociology of scientific knowledge to address the scientific controversies of the time. Concerns over the Cold War, nuclear power and emerging ecological crises provided early STS scholars with ample subject matter.

Despite its titular "T," STS has a long-standing ambivalence toward technology. Many STS scholars make no distinction between technology and science, preferring to talk in terms of "technoscience," where technology and science are understood as linked and developing in tandem. However, the 1980s saw a burgeoning interest in technology within some areas of STS – prompting pronouncements of a "turn to technology" and what Woolgar (1991: 21) described as "an almost indecent rush by some sociologists of scientific knowledge into the social study of technology." Underpinning this turn was growing recognition of a need to unpack the sociotechnical nature of technology. As Thomas Hughes (1983: 1) put it, this is the idea that "technological affairs contain a rich texture of technical matters, scientific laws, economic principles, political forces, and social concerns." During the 1980s and 1990s, sociologists working in STS set about addressing the ways in which social, political and economic factors influenced the technologies that ended up being developed and implemented in twentieth-century society, paying particular attention to the contested nature of technological design and uptake.

Against this background, STS has long posed a set of probing questions of technology that map onto current concerns of digital sociology. One ongoing issue is the (non-)

neutrality of technology, encapsulated in Langdon Winner's (leading) question "Do artifacts have politics?." Winner (1986) highlighted two ways in which this was indeed the case. On the one hand, he argued that technological artifacts can be designed and implemented (often unconsciously) to have particular social effects. Here he recounted a story of bridges on the Long Island Expressway being designed to be sufficiently low to allow passage for cars but not public buses. On the other hand, he argued that some technological artifacts can be "inherently political" in that they require specific social conditions and political arrangements to operate. Winner illustrated this with the example of nuclear power reactors requiring the existence of a strong centralized, authoritative state.

While influential, Winner's arguments attracted considerable pushback within STS circles. One prominent counterargument was the development of "social construction of technology" (SCOT) by other STS luminaries such as Wiebe Bijker and Trevor Pinch. It has subsequently been contended that "SCOT signals sociology's rediscovery of technology" (Matthewman 2011: 92). At the time, however, the idea of technology as socially constructed was seen simply as a necessary way of contesting technological determinist accounts of technologies having a fixed character, purpose and agency. Instead, SCOT promised a way of "opening up the black box" of technology (Pinch 1998). Key here was the idea of the "interpretive flexibility" of any technological artifact, especially during initial stages of technology design and use. From this perspective, there is no necessary or obvious way that any technological artifact should be designed or used. Indeed, designs and uses will vary between different groups and contexts and often result in conflict between competing views and ideas.

While describing technology as socially constructed, SCOT does not position technologies as permanently devoid of fixed meaning or actions. Instead, SCOT sees the diversity of interpretations of a technology as likely to diminish over time, often until its agreed meaning reaches a stage of "stabilization" and sometimes "closure." An alternative point of view is offered by a third reflexive strand of the STS turn toward technology – the idea of "technology as text." This developed the idea of interpretive flexibility further, challenging the idea that technologies can ever have stable or even "closed" attributes. Instead, as Steve Woolgar (1991) proposed, perhaps there is no "essence" of technology beyond the meanings that people ascribe to it. From this perspective, any technology needs to be understood in terms of its "essential indefiniteness" and indeterminacy.

While they are clearly not in full agreement, some important ideas recur throughout these approaches. First is an adherence to "symmetry" in telling all sides of the story of any technology. This involves recognizing that there is no one script or pathway that a technology will follow. Thus STS places great emphasis on giving equal consideration to dominant *and* peripheral opinions, successful *and* failed versions of the technology. This requires paying attention to all "relevant social groups" (from the most minor influences to the major shapers). Second is a disposition to be contrary and belligerent while also creative and well-humored. Indeed, Gunderson (2016: 46) describes the "aesthetic standard" in STS as including a "playful seriousness, attention to thick descriptions of the mundane, pleasure in subverting common assumptions." Third is an underlying interest in identifying alternatives – particularly in terms of working out how technology might better act in the public interest. A key STS interest lies with "deliberative democracy" – supporting the discussion and debate of significant science and technology controversies that affect wider society. Thus STS looks for ways that marginalized and excluded versions of what a technology could be are given greater prominence through representative means.

Previous "digital sociology" by another name

In terms of historical precedents, it is also worth acknowledging other prominent bodies of literature that precede and underpin the current digital sociology turn. As is evident from the previous sections of this chapter, one of the clear gaps in sociological discussion of technology throughout the most of the twentieth century was a lack of women's voices and critical

accounts of gender and technology. Thus second-wave feminism during the 1970s and 1980s prompted the emergence of
a "feminist technology studies," reasoning that "technology
itself cannot be fully understood without reference to gender"
(Cockburn 1992: 32). This work moved quickly from the
long-standing question of "women in technology" (more
pointedly, the *lack* of women in technology) into critiquing
the gendered ways in which dominant twentieth-century technologies were designed, perceived and experienced. Seminal
work included studies of domestic and reproductive technologies – problematizing the gendered assumptions underpinning
the social and cultural construction of these technologies,
practices and relations that surrounded them (see Stanworth
1987). Subsequent work focused on the gendered nature of
everyday computer and telecommunications use, alongside
the gendered nature of digital technology design, contexts
of use, stereotyping and identities of users (see van Zoonen
1992). While disagreements persist over the implications of
these analyses (i.e. whether masculinized technologies should
be reshaped or rejected outright), such work was key in shifting academic attention away from technological artifacts and
toward cultures and practices of use.

Alongside the consistent focus of these analyses on technology's role in reproducing patriarchy, the third wave of
feminism during the 1990s was notable in celebrating the
radical possibilities for destabilizing conventional gender differences (Wajcman 2009). Key here was Donna Haraway's *A
Manifesto for Cyborgs* (1985) – a hugely influential provocation on the social possibilities thrown up by the fast-dis-
solving boundaries between machines, humans and animals
implicated by advances in biotechnology and "cybernetic
organisms." Crucially, Haraway describes the cyborg as a
politicized entity, subtitling her manifesto "Science, Technology, and Socialist Feminism." This account is intended to
subvert meanings surrounding digital technology – putting
forward alternative views, language and practices. Haraway's
thinking kick-started a subsequent "cyber feminist" literature
through the 1990s where writers like Sadie Plant (1996)
argued that internet technologies were essentially female (i.e.
non-linear, self-replicating systems, weaving connections and
multitasking in intuitive ways). Moreover, emerging virtual

technologies were seen to provide women with opportunities for developing subjectivities free from embodied gender cues. As Plant (ibid.: 181) contended, "cyberspace is out of man's control." This work takes a provocatively optimistic (if not utopian) view of women assuming control and disrupting technology practices. It is also highly playful and creative – reveling in the uncertainly of cutting-edge technology development and bringing academics together with artists, designers, writers, software developers and activists.

Digital sociology also owes a debt to sociological commentary on the "information society," "knowledge society" and "post-industrial age" that flourished toward the end of the twentieth century. Here, a number of authors attempted to make sense of economic, occupational, spatial and cultural shifts relating to new information technologies – with many proclaiming the emergence of a markedly different era. Perhaps best known is Daniel Bell's description of "post-industrial society." Writing in the early 1970s, Bell explored the sociological implications of an economy predicated upon data processing and the production of ideas and knowledge. Bell's *The Coming of Post-Industrial Society* ([1973] 1999) pointed to the rising prominence of occupations in information work and anticipated the rise of "theoretical knowledge" – i.e. societies run on the basis of abstract models, frameworks and simulations facilitated by "intellectual technologies" (rather than empirical understanding and/or practical intuition).

While Bell was speculating largely on developments in mainframe computing and telecommunications, Manuel Castells's *The Information Age* trilogy in the second half of the 1990s offered an authoritative account of the social structures arising from the increased connectivity of the internet and worldwide web. Castells describes a burgeoning "information capitalism" unfettered by constraints of time and geography. In this sense, the network society is conceptualized as a "space of flows" rather than a "space of places." As is the case with macro-level analyses, such accounts of information-infused societies have obvious limitations. From Bell to Castells, accounts of a new form of information society arising from technological developments have understandably faced accusations of technology determinism. Fifty years after the publication of *The Coming of Post-Industrial Society*, these descriptions remain ideal types rather than accurate reflections of reality for most people around the world. Yet such writing certainly reminds us of the capacity of sociology to address grand economic, political and cultural implications of the digital age.

Finally, digital sociology also has clear affinities with the past twenty-five years of "internet studies." Since the early 1990s, internet studies have brought sociologists together with other disciplines concerned with social aspects of the internet. These include media and communications studies, cultural studies, economics, policy studies, law, psychology, information studies and computer science. Barry Wellman – one of the leading sociological lights in the field – described internet studies originating as a "user studies" off-shoot of the otherwise software-focused field of research into "computer-supported collaborative work." An initial feature of this social turn was internet studies scholars' exploration of "virtual community" and online identity (Turkle 1995; Rheingold 2000). Studies here explored how groups of users formed and interacted through the early listservs and bulletin boards of the 1980s and 1990s and later within "virtual worlds" and on social media. Over the past three decades, internet studies have continued to focus on "how community dynamics continued to operate on the internet ... and how intertwined offline relationships were with online relationships" (Wellman 2004: 125).

Other strands of internet studies have developed to explore issues of internet governance (focusing on areas of policy, law-making and regulation) and internet democracy (covering issues such as the online public sphere, e-democracy and civics). Perhaps the most enduring line of inquiry has been on everyday internet use. This includes studies exploring the use of the internet in domestic, workplace and other organizational contexts, corresponding with other work concerned with detailing patterns of internet non-use – i.e. so-called digital divides, gaps and inequalities (Norris 2001). During the 2000s, internet research burgeoned across media and communications studies, exemplified by the increasingly prominent Association of Internet Researchers led by scholars such as Nancy Baym, Alice Marwick, Kath Albury, Jean

Burgess and many others. Together, these approaches constitute a solid body of sociological work detailing "the rapidly changing dynamics of networked societies and the institutions and individuals within them" (Dutton 2013: 1).

So why "digital sociology" ... right here, right now?

In many ways, then, it could be concluded that there is nothing radically new about the idea of a digital sociology. Sociological questions have been asked of technology throughout the development of the discipline. Thus it is worth acknowledging that sociologists had established a good grasp of social, cultural, political and economic implications of technological change long before the advent of Facebook and Google. Current enthusiasms for digital sociology certainly echo previous sociological "turns" to technology over the past 100 years or so. In this sense our subsequent discussions need to remain mindful of those that have come before.

In particular, the "pre-digital" theorists and researchers just outlined provide digital sociology with a number of useful starting points. There is above all a variety of well-tested questions, existing methods and established approaches for digital sociologists to appropriate. For example, this previous work reminds us of the need to interrogate the transformative claims that are attached to any new technological development, be it optimistic claims of empowerment *and/or* dispirited accusations of disempowerment. From Karl Marx onward, there has been ongoing debate whether technology has essential qualities and characteristics or whether it is socially constructed. Moreover, if technology does not "determine" society, then what exactly is the relationship between social change and technology? These are long-standing questions that digital sociology needs to continue to address.

These previous analyses also provide a ready selection of pertinent issues, problems and areas of inquiry. For example, sociologists from Max Weber onward have been concerned with how technology is entwined with issues of efficiency, rationality, power and control. In particular, this focuses attention on the systems and structures that are associated with the development of new technology This also fore grounds the importance of the political economy of technology development and implementation – not least associations between technological progress and economic interests and ideologies. Conversely, work in the late twentieth century in feminist and internet studies draws attention to the entwining of technology with issues of identity formation and identity politics. This writing and research highlights the role of technology in the reproduction of inequalities and injustices. Echoing scholars such as Mumford and Ellul, it also points to the likely unintended consequences and hidden costs of technology use – ranging from ecological destruction to the diminishment of humanity and human freedoms.

Some of the work just outlined also demonstrates various approaches that technology scholarship can take, from the cyberfeminist interest in combining activism and art to the STS mindset of being playfully argumentative and belligerent. These precursors therefore suggest that there is little reason why digital sociology should not strive to be creative, transgressive *and* spiky. The fact that "technology" is a topic that lends itself to a degree of speculation and engagement with unknown futures means that digital sociologists have license to be a little off-kilter and playful in what they do and how they do it. This is a topic that lends itself to speculation, provocation and experimentation.

Finally, the body of preceding work also steers digital sociology toward a range of useful dispositions and ambitions. While writers such as Marx, Ellul and Winner were profoundly critical of what they perceived technology to be, they were not devoid of hope. However bleak, much of this previous work consoled itself by considering alternatives and thinking otherwise. Thus current digital sociologists are well advised to keep at least half an eye on "alternative technology," "responsible innovation" and "deliberative democracy." Although tackling what might seem to be all-encompassing conditions such as dataveillance and platform capitalism, digital sociology does not have to result in wholly dystopian, hopeless conclusions.

Current work in digital sociology therefore has much to learn from its heritage in this pre-digital sociology. These are themes that will be referred back to throughout this book. Nevertheless, it is perhaps fitting to conclude this opening chapter by acknowledging the aspects of digital sociology that *are* different, new and distinct from what has gone before. While digital sociologists are standing on the shoulders of giants, we need to be confident in the things that digital sociology can do that Marx, Weber, Ellul and STS do not. From this perspective, there are at least three lines of distinctiveness that spring to mind.

First, digital sociology allows us to make sense of very different technological conditions than those described by previous generations of sociologists. While continuities are apparent, the current wave of digital technologies is quantitatively and qualitatively distinct from the technological conditions that previous generations of sociologists have addressed. For example, there are significant differences in the nature and form of what is done with contemporary digital technologies and the pervasive manner in which they are coming to operate across most (if not all) spheres of life. There are also significant differences in scale and granularity. For example, the assemblages of digital tools, practices, processes and systems currently at large do not map seamlessly onto earlier analyses of the "mega machines" of the industrial age or the "mass consumption" of broadcast media. However prescient they might have been, Marx, Ellul and others were not contemplating AI or the Internet of Things in their arguments. Even the "internet" that Castells was writing about in the 1990s is a very different proposition to the online environments of today. Talk of the interconnected "open" potential of the "worldwide web" now seems an anachronism in our current era of proprietary platforms, tiered network access and closed apps. In short, digital sociology is addressing a very distinct technological landscape in contrast to the scholars of ten, fifty and 150 years ago.

Second, digital sociology allows us to redress specific blind spots in previous sociological work on technology. For instance, despite the example set by feminist writers, there is still plenty of scope to address issues of identity politics – not least how digital technology is entwined with issues of race, sexuality, disability and intersections therein. There is also a need to better address the computational basis of digital technology – not least the coded architectures of software, platforms and systems and the programmed nature of what digital technologies seem to "do" of their own accord. In addition, digital sociology is an opportunity to better address the intimate, personal and affective nature of contemporary technology use. With all facets of "the personal" being increasingly drawn into the digital devices and systems with which people interact, there is a need for scholarship that explores the issue of how we feel through technology and the intensity of experience as we encounter others online. Big ticket issues of society, economy and culture remain important, yet digital sociology can also be more introspective and intimate than previous sociological accounts of technology.

Third, digital sociology allows us to engage with digital technology on its own terms and in its own forms. As will be reiterated throughout this book, digital sociology is not simply the study of the digital as a topic; it also takes the digital to be an integral way of doing sociology. Digital sociology is practiced through digital resources. Sociologists can use an array of digital technologies to investigate, inquire, interact with and participate in their objects of study. They can now take advantage of an array of digital data and digital data analysis. Digital sociology is also performed through the media that it addresses, with sociological audiences and publics readily accessible through digital means. The notion of public sociology in the digital age has certainly moved on from acts of pamphleteering, giving public speeches and publishing journal articles.

Most excitingly, the current digital age could be seen as a time when ordinary people (and, by extension, sociologists) stand a realistic chance of "owning the means of production." Marx was not able to design, produce and distribute a socialist steam-powered mill. Yet it is not beyond the capacity of many sociologists to design and produce their own technologies, if only a simple website or app. Instead of striving only to imagine alternative technologies, it is now possible for sociologists to be involved in actually building and distributing them. Digital sociologists no longer have to speculate how things could be otherwise – they can make a tangible contribution to building (or more specifically coding) the future along different lines.

Conclusions

It is important to recognize that digital sociology is not a completely new or unprecedented development. Throughout its history, sociology has been a discipline that asks questions of the dominant technologies of the time. Yet digital sociology is clearly an important development in the sociology of the early twenty-first century. In short, it marks an opportunity for the discipline to look confidently beyond its roots in the industrial revolution and strive to make better sense of a post-industrial conditions that are now digitally distinct and often decidedly different. In this sense, the significance of digital sociology lies in its timing. This might not be a wholly new way of doing sociology, but it is a wholly necessary way of continuing to advance the discipline and maintain the relevance of sociological thought to contemporary society.

As such, digital sociology should be welcomed as a moment in the disciplinary development of sociology that sociologists of all dispositions can take full advantage of. This is perhaps the first time that sociological questions are being asked of the dominant technologies of the time by a generation of sociologists who are themselves immersed in the same technology. The theorists of the nineteenth and twentieth centuries had little first-hand experience of working with steam engines or nuclear reactors. In contrast, many of the leading digital sociologists are from a generation who were "born digital." As such, sociological work is increasingly assuming digital forms – these are times for blogging, tweeting and coding, as well as producing long-form monographs. In addition, it is significant that digital sociology comes at a time when sociological inquiry is being led by people who are not all white men. Given all these opportunities and openings, the next chapter will further explore the potential and promise of digital sociology. If we accept the basic premise of a digital sociology, then what might be the specific benefits of pursuing it? In short, "what can digital sociology do for us?"

2
Digital Sociology: Central Concerns, Concepts and Questions

Introduction

In many ways, the question of "What can digital sociology do for us?" is easily answered. In short, digital sociology allows us to make better sense of the digital world in which we live. To expand this a little, digital sociology provides a way of asking better questions of digital society – identifying problems, tensions and underlying issues that otherwise get glossed over amid the hyperbole that tends to cloud discussions of "new" technology. In doing this, digital sociology encourages a number of approaches that are worth further reflection. This chapter therefore explores three main areas of contention.

- First, digital sociology involves reframing the core technical features of contemporary technologies into sociological concerns. For example, as we shall go on to discuss, the idea of a "network" is usually seen in abstract, value-free terms – i.e. as the connecting of different nodes together. Yet, from a sociological point of view, the nature and significance of any network clearly alters when these nodes are people, institutions and machines.

- Second, digital sociology involves reusing and reconfiguring fundamental questions and concepts from the past 100 years of sociological thinking, as does any area of contemporary sociology. Digital sociologists are continuing an intellectual tradition that does not simply become irrelevant when confronted with a smartphone or an algorithm. Thus it is worth considering how digital researchers and writers are appropriating preceding sociological thinking and social theories and reassert them in powerful ways that address digital society.

- Third, digital sociology involves looking toward new forms of hybrid theory emerging from conflations of philosophy, computational sciences, design, politics, urban geography and other sources of critical thinking. While it rightly draws strength from its own disciplinary history, it also looks to get ideas from wherever it can. As we shall see, some of the most exciting and esoteric developments in digital critique originate a long way from traditional sources of sociological thinking.

So this is what digital sociology can do for us – pushing us outside of our comfort zones, prompting us to approach familiar aspects of the technological landscape in decidedly non-technical ways, and generally encouraging us to think in provocative, promiscuous and pragmatic ways. In this spirit, then, the first question that springs to mind is why we should cling on to the prefix of "digital" sociology? What is to be gained by distinguishing oneself as a *digital* sociologist?

Digital sociology as a "post-digital" take on "the digital"

As established in chapter 1, digital sociology approaches contemporary society as inherently digital and digitized. Of course, as we draw near to the 2020s, labeling something as "digital" or "non-digital" might come across as somewhat anachronistic – similar to how we now read 1990s talk of "cyberspace," "virtual communities" and "new media." We live in a world where digital technologies, systems and processes are barely noticeable and rarely seen as different. In many ways, "digital" now appears "a quintessentially twentieth – not twenty-first – century keyword" (Peters 2016: 93). Yet retaining the prefix of digital reflects a commitment to continuing to notice what has now largely become invisible. This is important if only because of the considerable disparities, differences and disjunctures that run throughout any digital society. Rather than being seamlessly woven into the fabric of everyday life, people's engagements with digital technologies vary dramatically around the world. As Sy Taffel (2016) points out, we are hardly living in a stable digital technoculture. As such, the label "digital sociology" reminds us that the digital is not simply now a case of "business as usual." This is not a topic that sociologists can afford to stop thinking critically about.

As such, one of the key ambitions of digital sociology is to make the digital visible, to highlight the flaws, glitches, gaps, seams and artifices. This chimes with the growing interest in "post-digital" perspectives – i.e. writing and research that looks beyond apparent technological progress and novelty and instead addresses a growing sense of "unease, fatigue, boredom and disillusionment" (Berry and Dieter 2015: 5) with contemporary technology-laden society. Thus, moving on from the initial rush of the digital, this requires scholarship where attention is focused on what is happening "after-the-digital" (Taffel 2016: 334).

Digital sociology, therefore, seeks to move beyond what Nathan Jurgenson (2012) calls the "digital dualism" of distinguishing between digital and analog, online and offline, real and virtual, and so on. Instead contemporary society is better understood as an entanglement of humanity, materiality and digitality. For example, it now makes increasing sense to describe urban environments as "code/spaces." Kitchin and Dodge (2011: 16) define this as where real-world spaces and software code "become mutually constituted, that is, produced through one another." Similarly, rather than being sometimes online and sometimes offline, most people are more accurately described as operating in a permanent state of "onlife" (Floridi 2014). As we shall discuss in chapter 3, a company such as Uber is simultaneously a technology platform, a transportation company *and* a labor organization. A "virtual community" is a blend of the physical and digital spaces, mediated sociability and in-personal social engagement (Maddox 2016). Digital sociology acknowledges and addresses the entangled nature of the material and the digital, people and machines.

Turning technical concepts into sociological concerns

Clearly, if Marx's writing about the handloom and steam engine is not directly transferable to making sense of Uber, then some new thinking is required. Against this background, one of the key thrusts of digital sociology is to (re)frame the technical characteristics of emerging digital technologies in sociological terms – i.e. cultural and social structures, social relationships and institutions, issues of power, conflict and control, political economy, and so on. In this respect, it is worth considering the ways in which digital sociologists have set about addressing the emerging technical concepts that underpin contemporary digital technologies, advancing the previous sociological theories of technology outlined in chapter 1 to highlight issues specific to contemporary digital technologies. Thus we can consider the following four key areas of writing in the recent digital sociology literature: (i) networks; (ii) platforms; (iii) data; and (iv) algorithms. Each of these examples illustrates the extension and recontextualization of previous sociological thinking for a digital age.

(i) Making sociological sense of "networks"

Networked computing – the connection of computers to permit the transfer of data – is a fundamental feature of digital technology. The idea of everything being connected to everything else in a flattened, non-hierarchical structure therefore drives commonsense understandings of digital technologies – for example, that the internet is inherently decentralized and democratic. As such, the notion of the social world being digitally networked has become "a way of life and a cultural norm" (Levina 2017: 127) that digital sociologists set out to problematize.

Of course, sociology has a long interest in the analysis of social networks, which was soon applied to emerging internet technologies during the 1990s. Most notable was Manuel Castells's (1996) description of the network society that he saw rising from the confluence of global capital and networked information technologies. Castells was particularly interested in the "networking logic" inherent in the reorganization of dominant societal functions and processes around networks rather than physical boundaries. He therefore developed a "network theory of power," describing how power in contemporary society is exercised through networks and how a reliance on dynamic networks was leading to the redefinition of time and space in everyday life.

Sociologists have subsequently extended and/or critiqued these ideas, all the time developing understandings of networked sociality. Alongside elaborations on network power are notions of network culture, network effects, network identity and network subjectivity. As Wendy Chun (2016) argues, the analytic appeal of networks lies in the promise to visualize otherwise incomprehensible complex flows of capital and power. In contrast to post-modernist celebrations of the unknownness of contemporary society, the idea of the network has become an increasingly popular "representational shorthand" (Jameson 1991: 36) for grasping otherwise unimaginable reconfigurations of society. Thus networks have quickly been established as a primary metaphor, method and theoretical tool of recent times.

Rather than taking networks at face value (for example, merely mapping online networks in terms of their size, shape and growth), digital sociology examines how networks "are being embedded into society and what conflicts this evokes" (Lovink 2011: 23). One key area of questioning is exploring how meanings are developed when the world is understood and arranged in terms of networks. For example, what are the social consequences of defining individuals on the basis of their interactions within networks? In what ways do networks "reassemble the social" (Chun 2015: 295) – for example, privileging the individual node while downplaying the role of community and wider society? What are the realities of network structures – where are inequalities, hierarchies, regulation and restrictions, and where are there disconnections, gaps, leaks and brokers (Cavanagh 2013)?

(ii) Making sociological sense of "platforms"

While today's technological infrastructure continues to compromise networks containing billions of devices, apps and software points, we are also seeing the increasing dominance of large "platforms" that are relatively centralized and closed. These platforms are often described as "intermediaries," bringing together customers, service providers, content producers and advertisers for social exchanges and economic interactions (Srnicek 2017). Such platforms infuse day-to-day digital practices and engagements. In much of the Western world, for example, dominant platforms include Google (search), Facebook (social networking) and Uber (taxi rides). Less obvious are cloud platforms renting out online storage space. All told, it is reckoned that most online traffic is concentrated on a dozen platforms and core servers owned by the likes of Microsoft, Google, Amazon and Apple (Scholz 2016).

Platforms constitute an arrangement of the digital ecosystem that differs substantially from the 1990s ideal of the open architecture worldwide web and therefore warrants close attention. Indeed, it is argued that we now live in a "platform society" where all areas of public and private life are permeated by platforms (van Dijck et al. 2018). One can certainly see a dominance of platforms in sectors of society such as news and journalism, retailing, hospitality and transportation. Van Dijck and his colleagues argue that these platforms have a profound impact on the way that social life is experienced and organized – from the changing neighborhood dynamics of Airbnb hotspots through to the (re)production and circulation of so-called fake news. In many ways, the largest platforms can be seen to "resemble states" in terms of their governance (Wark 2016).

The dominance of large-scale, monopolistic platforms is seen to derive from the "network effect" where "the more numerous the users who use a platform, the more valuable that platform becomes for everyone else" (Srnicek 2017: 45).

Thus users (and investors) are understandably attracted to the largest platforms. In turn, large numbers of users employ the data-driven business models of these platforms. Ostensibly "free" platforms such as Google and Facebook generate revenue by selling user data to advertisers. Similarly, "lean platforms" such as Uber and Airbnb are data-driven services that rent out assets that the company does not own. These economic characteristics are reflected in what has become termed "platform capitalism." Here, it is argued that these are not "tech" companies per se; rather, they are "businesses that increasingly rely on information technology, data, and the internet for their business models" (ibid.: 4). This means that a company such as Uber is a combination of a software platform, a business that seeks to extract and control data, a transportation company and a labor organization.

These latter characteristics raise a range of questions about the business practices of monopolistic platforms as well as the changing nature of work and labor that takes place around these platforms. Is a platform such as Uber promoting flexibility of work practices and increasing opportunities for previously underutilized/excluded elements of labor? Or is it reducing work stability and worker rights, as well as increasing discrimination through its reliance on data profiles, rating and reputation systems? As will be discussed in chapter 3, these questions are being addressed by growing numbers of digital sociologists around the world.

(iii) Making sociological sense of "data"

Running throughout these descriptions of networks and platforms is one of the key elements of contemporary digital society – "data." In a technical sense, digital data originates from a variety of different sources and takes a number of different forms. These include various forms of institutional monitoring and surveillance, data generated by routine operations of devices and software, and "user-generated" data volunteered by individuals while using digital technologies. The social significance of this lies in the computational "processing" work that predicts, models and distils data for human judgment. Once raw data begins to be processed it takes the form of more socially meaningful "data entities" – i.e. representations, models and calculations relating to "real-world things" such as people, places or products. In particular, the recent turn toward Big Data refers to these processes taking place on a mass, aggregated scale.

Recent work in digital sociology has therefore begun to challenge popular understandings of data as broadly neutral, objective and therefore non-problematic in nature. Instead, digital sociologists tend to approach data as political in nature – loaded with values, interests and assumptions that shape and limit what is done with it and by whom. As Gregg and Nafus (2017: 55) contend, "data play a major role in orchestrating contemporary power relations." In this sense, much of the sociological significance of digital data lies in its association with meaning-making – as Couldry and Hepp (2016: 213) put it, "what counts as social knowledge." This raises concerns over representation (with finite sets of characteristics being decided to "count" as a particular entity) alongside concerns over reductionism (with artificially neat boundaries and categories being drawn around data). As Halford et al. (2013: 180) conclude, "in short, the processes involved in naming, structuring and processing data ... are profoundly social with tremendous sociological implications."

Digital sociology also examines how digital data acts to define rather than simply describe social life. A key concept in this respect is the "social life" of digital data – i.e. the continual recirculation and reconstitution of data into different and new forms (Beer and Burrows 2013). This idea of a social life points to the fact that digital data is not used on a one-off basis. Instead, diverse sets of data are being continually combined and recombined, with different entities produced from varying iterations and calculations. As Andrew Webster (2013: 230) concludes, "data itself can take on its own life ... these data then travel, are transformed and are transcribed into novel 'derivative' forms."

(iv) Making sociological sense of "algorithms and automation"

The construction and use of algorithms has become a key way that digital data gets to shape everyday life. Whereas software engineers might see algorithms as a straightforward concept, from a social science perspective they are now a significant (albeit "invisible") concern (Mackenzie 2017). In a technical sense, an algorithm is simply a programmable series of logical steps that organize and act upon data to achieve specified outcomes, what is often described as a combination of "logic and control" (Kowalski 1979). First, a specific problem (and intended outcome) is formulated in computational terms (e.g. through the definition of variables, steps and indicators). This formulation is then "trained" on a body of existing data and its parameters adjusted and "tuned" to reach an accurate outcome more effectively. Eventually, the fully tuned algorithm will be incorporated into an application, giving it a capacity for automated reasoning and decision-making. This can be seen as an objective technical process, concerned with efficiency and elegance in reaching an outcome. Algorithms underpin most digital systems and practices that rely on decisions and predictions being made – from search engine results to credit scores, from driverless cars to economic forecasting. Algorithms, analytics and other forms of AI are all associated with the promise of bringing technical precision to what is an otherwise imprecise and unpredictable area of society, what Mattern (2016: 50) terms an allure of "instrumental rationality."

Of course, the sociological implications of algorithms are seen as far less straightforward, instead constituting "the insertion of procedure into human knowledge and social experience" (Gillespie 2016: 25). First, this has prompted much discussion among digital sociologists of the socially constructed nature of these processes, questioning how values are implicated in all stages of the algorithm design process. An obvious point to make from a sociological perspective, therefore, is that these processes of meaning-making are never wholly neutral, objective and "automated" but are fraught with problems and compromises, biases and omissions. There are clearly risks of reductionism in the disaggregation of complex social situations and contexts into neatly modeled and calculable problems that can be addressed through computational means (Mattern 2016). This is evident in the regular news media concerns over patterns of discrimination in algorithmic calculations and judgments – often resulting from biases in the assumptions of programmers and/or the data-sets that the algorithms are trained on. As such, many sociologists argue that discussion of "the algorithm" should not distract from the provider and designers. As Luciana Parisi (2013: 13) points out, the power that is now given up to algorithms throughout society belies their basis in "the indeterminacies of programming." For example, Google's much protected search algorithm is not an autonomous actor but actually the actions of Google (the company, its employees, its shareholders, and so on).

Second, digital sociologists are concerned with the implications and consequences of the insertion of algorithms throughout all areas of everyday life, leading to talk of algorithmic identity, algorithmic culture, algorithmic control and algorithmic governance. One key area of concern is how social actions and relations are conditioned by living in a world infused with algorithms. For example, as Frank Pasquale (2015) reasons, "we are increasingly pressured to adopt an algorithmic self, one conditioned to maximize exposure and approval." This leads to calls for increased transparency and "algorithmic accountability," thereby making algorithms more visible (and contestable) to the people on whom they impact.

Retaining and refining sociological questions and concerns

Running throughout these various discussions is a sense of holding up to sociological scrutiny "innovations" such as algorithms, data, platforms and networks. Digital sociology is not simply a matter of highlighting the social nature of these "new" things – rather, it is also concerned with unpacking the social issues and problems that are implicated in these digitizations. In this respect, digital sociology is driven by a number of familiar sociological questions and concerns. First, as reflected throughout chapter 1, is an interest in exploring the mutual shaping relationships between technology and society. This includes both what was referred to in chapter 1 as the social construction of technology and what Kennedy

(2017: 2) terms "the constitutive role of the digital." Wary of being branded technologically determinist, most sociologists remain keen to avoid any suggestion of the digital "impacting" directly on the social. Indeed, it can be rather comforting to suggest that digital society is largely a matter of "old wine in new bottles." Yet clearly the digital *does* impact on the social, albeit in inconsistent, unpredictable and compromised ways.

Making sense of "what is new here?" (as well as what remains the same) is something that digital sociologists therefore strive to "*make something of*, not shy away from" (Kennedy 2017, emphasis in original). This means that digital sociology pays close attention to the aspects of technology that people otherwise do not usually think about. In one sense, then, this involves a preoccupation with what might usually be considered the banal and mundane aspects of digital technology use. Distancing ourselves from everyday digital surroundings is notoriously difficult. Marshall McLuhan was fond of equating human awareness of media technologies to the way that a fish has no perception of the water in which it swims. In this sense, then, digital sociology follows C. Wright Mills's mantra to "make the familiar strange" and not to allow digital technology to recede into the background as something that is commonsense and unremarkable.

This said, digital sociologists also need to strive for the opposite effect – i.e. to make the strange familiar. Alongside the familiar devices and applications of our everyday lives, digital society involves highly complex systems and exotic digital practices. Here, digital sociologists have to come to terms quickly with unfamiliar new technologies and learn to engage with them as their expert users do. Bauman frames this as "familiarizing the unfamiliar" – i.e. "taming, domesticating, making manageable" (Bauman 2014: 98) what is otherwise well outside of our own experiences. Moving beyond the "shock of the new" is another important feature of digital sociology.

Of course, digital sociologists remain keen to address core disciplinary questions of social organization, social relations and social change. For example, digital sociology is intrinsically concerned with the politics and economics of digital society, not least the ways in which digital technologies play in complex, late modern social formations. Yet amid these macro level concerns it is important to remain mindful that digital technology is encountered and experienced along deeply personal, intimate, human lines. A concurrent concern therefore remains with what Lina Dencik (2017) describes as "approach[ing] the digital in relation to practices and experiences." Indeed, digital sociology reminds us that digital technology is something that is experienced within distinct human contexts and with distinct human consequences. Digital technology use is entwined with people's feelings and emotions, their (dis)pleasures and (in)sensitivities. People are not merely extraneous variables in any instance of digital technology use. In particular, when foregrounding the human experience of digital technology use, digital sociology plays a key role in pushing back against the hyper-individualized discourses that pervade discussion of digital technology in most areas of life. As with all other areas of the discipline, digital sociology is inherently interested in looking beyond the individual.

In this sense, digital sociology is also concerned implicitly with the social structures that shape and constrain human experience of the digital. This has been a central feature of sociological thinking since Karl Marx's description of "men making their own history, but not making it as they please." Over 150 years later, Zygmunt Bauman framed such issues in terms of "sociological hermeneutics" – i.e. "the interpretation of human choices as manifestations of strategies constructed in response to the challenges of the socially shaped situation and where one has been placed in it" (Bauman 2014: 50–1). This moves digital sociology beyond simply documenting the human thoughts and actions that coalesce around digital technology and compels us also to consider questions of how these thoughts and actions came to be – as Bauman puts it, "the socially shaped conditions of people whose thoughts or actions we intend to understand/explain" (ibid.: 52).

As such, making full sense of individuals' responses to digital technologies requires a good understanding of social context, what Dencik (2017) terms situating digital technology "in contexts of social structures and interests." In this sense, the social contexts of people's engagements with digital technology are varied. If we take the mundane example of how digital technologies are used by university students, then an obvious set of contextual influences relates to the organizational structures of higher education – from timetables and the curriculum to wider imperatives such as increasing student numbers through to meeting the skills needs of industry. Other broader contexts relate to social class, race, ethnicity and gender; the subtle ways that neighborhoods bump up against campuses; the philosophies that different universities adopt (e.g. being "Ivy League" or "community-focused"). All of these issues can transcend individual "choices" in how digital technologies are engaged with and how they are used.

Finally, digital sociology does not strive to provide definitive answers to technological issues (indeed, there are few areas of sociology that could be said to pose questions that are definitively answerable). At best, sociological inquiry seeks to produce detailed, deep, thick and rich description that addresses the central question of "how has this world come about?" (Bauman 2014: 122). Digital sociology therefore tasks itself with pointing to the complexity of things rather than reaching oversimplified answers and solutions. The sociologist is keenly aware that there is no one definitive explanation, only different perspectives and truths. Thus, given this recognition of alternatives, an important supplementary question of any sociological inquiry is always "how might things be otherwise?" If we are not happy with the digital conditions that currently dominate, then what *do* we want?

The (re)use of social theory in digital sociology

Running alongside these questions and concerns is the use of social theory – in terms both of adapting (and extending) existing theory and/or being involved in new theory-building. In both respects, digital technology can be a tricky topic to theorize. On the one hand, it is proving remarkably adept at making use of "old" social theory, reappropriating ideas for digital contexts that would have been unimaginable at the time these ideas were originally formulated. This use of theory is pragmatic rather than dogmatic, with many digital sociologists following Manuel Castells's (2000) recommendation of "disposable theory" – i.e. recognizing theory as an essential tool but also acknowledging it as something to be discarded once it has outlived its usefulness in illuminating the substantive world. In these terms, any analysis of the digital is best arranged around an assemblage of theoretical perspectives as and when they best fit. This pragmatic use of theory is reflected by Amin and Thrift (2005: 222) when arguing that

> Theory has taken on a different style which has a lighter touch than of old. For a start, few now believe that one theory can cover the world (or save the world, for that matter). No particular theoretical approach, even in combination with others, can be used to gain a total grip on what's going on. Theory-making is a hybrid assemblage of testable propositions and probable explanations derived from sensings of the world, the world's persistent ways of talking back, and the effort of abstraction.

So it is important to remain mindful that there is no one correct theoretical stance to adopt when looking at digital society. Different theories are suited to different forms of questioning and specific areas of investigation. Take, for instance, the following two examples of theory use that have become popular in digital sociology of late.

(i) From Marx to digital Marxist theory

The case for recognizing Karl Marx as an early sociologist of technology is certainly bolstered by the (re)appropriation of Marxian theory throughout digital sociology. This can be seen in the growing popularity of twenty-first-century Marxian accounts of the digitally shaped nature of economic production, exploitation and class struggle under post-industrial capitalism. For example, Jodi Dean's (2005) notion of "communicative capitalism" has been taken up by digital sociologists to explore the commodified nature of communicative exchanges through digital media. Dean contends that the circulation of communication is now a prime means of generating value for data collectors, brokers, and analysts – therefore creating an imperative that things are continually being said online regardless of their substance. Similarly, as outlined previously, Nick Srnicek's (2017) critique of "platform capitalism" is proving a useful means of problematizing the growing dominance of monopolistic businesses that profit from the extraction and circulation of data as their raw material. This mode of capitalism involves firms generating network effects to consolidate power, sustained through enclosed ecosystems that bound users within closed apps and proprietary operating systems.

The adaptation of these ideas imbues digital sociology with some familiar Marxist concepts and concerns. Notably, traditional Marxist interests in political economy are evident in digital sociology critiques of the IT industry-related constellations of power now operating on a transnational scale (such as the rise of Silicon Valley and "Big Tech" as a global economic force). Framing mega-corporations such as Facebook in this manner has pushed many digital sociologists to set their work against new forms of capitalist relations that underpin the digital economy. "User-driven" platforms such as Facebook and YouTube are cast in a different light when approached as arrangements where capital owns the means of production *and* consumption. Thus it has proved useful for sociologists to consider how companies such as Facebook are developing strategies to control and profit from forms of digital (rather than material) production. For example, this leads to complex questions of what it means to be a social media "user" amid emerging online business models that seek to control and profit from the collective intelligence and attention of online groups (Koloğlugil 2015).

Elsewhere, digital sociologists are extending Marxist understandings of labor relations to make sense of virtual (rather than physical) forms of work. As will be discussed in chapter 3, this is prompting a rich vein of sociological writing on the rise of online "microwork" and the fragmented labor conditions of the so-called gig economy. This is also raising concerns over the ways in which digital technology users act increasingly like laborers, producing value through their individual content production, networked communication and cooperation with other users (Greaves 2015). In making sense of such issues, some digital sociologists have found particular value in applying autonomist Marxist theories of "immaterial labor" (Hardt and Negri 2001) to various virtual settings – examining the different forms of exploitation, immiseration, domination and struggle implicated in these ostensibly new forms of labor (see Koloğlugil 2015).

All these reworkings of Marxist theory therefore lend digital sociologists sharpened insights into some of the key conflicts and dialectic tensions inherent in digital society. For example, Marxian theory offers a convincing explanation for the apparently contradictory promise of platforms such as Google and Facebook to provide commons-based services rooted in human cooperation while at the same time profiting from online surveillance and ongoing exploitation of users (Fuchs and Dyer-Witheford 2013). Elsewhere, writing from a Marxist feminist perspective, Kylie Jarrett (2015) has highlighted how prevalent forms of immaterial digital labor have close parallels with other forms of domestic and consumer labour – unpaid and largely unseen forms of work that are unquestionably exploitative but also socially meaningful and individually enriching. For some commentators, such antagonisms point to a foreclosure of digital technology as a site of exploitation and social control (e.g. Dean 2005). Others, however, retain hope for possible resistance – pointing to counter-examples of proletarian struggle through digital networks and the prospect of "the communist/commonist internet" (Greaves 2015: 204). Either way, reworkings of Marxist theory continue to be a useful means for digital sociology to make sense of the power dynamics underpinning contemporary digital infrastructure.

(ii) From Foucault to post-Foucauldian theory

Besides these Marxian approaches, post-structuralist accounts of power and control are proving to be another popular appropriation of social theory in digital sociology. This often takes one of two forms. First are various reworkings of Michel Foucault's work on governmentality and disciplinary power to explore the surveillant characteristics of digital technologies. Indeed, comparisons continue to be made between contemporary digital technologies and Foucault's accounts of disciplinary power exercised through "panoptic" modes of control implicit in nineteenth-century social institutions such as schools and prisons. Foucault described the Panopticon as disaggregating the crowd into a collection of "separated individualities," with individuals' lives carefully monitored, collated and categorized. The awareness that any individual might be watched continuously therefore underpinned a state of self-regulation and the "automatic functioning" of power. While not constrained by "literal readings of Foucault's panoptic prison" (Elmer 2003: 232), critical scholars over the past thirty years have contended that the surveillant characteristics of networked digital technologies constitute a continuation of the disciplinary patterns implicit in the Panopticon (e.g. Poster 1990).

This use of Foucault's work continues to inform sociological accounts of varied panoptic arrangements ranging from school internet use (Hope 2016) to the activities of online advertisers and state agencies (Lyon 2014). Such work provides important reminders of "the use of pervasive personal data systems to systematically monitor people and groups in order to regulate, govern, monitor and influence their behavior" (Coté et al. 2016: 8). Conversely, Foucault's work has also been used to explore individuals' agentic uses of digital technologies. For example, wearables such as Google Glass and Fit-Bit have been conceptualized in terms of Foucault's "techniques of the self" – i.e. ways in which individuals look after themselves and improve their "thoughts, conduct, and ways of being" (Petitfils 2014: 39). Indeed, there is increasing sociological interest in the growing attraction of using personal devices for self-tracking and "participatory surveillance" (Lupton 2016; Graham and Sauter 2013).

Of course, digital sociologists have been quick to point to limitations in applying Foucauldian thinking to contemporary digital contexts. In particular, it is reasoned that Foucault's "architectural" forms of surveillance are superseded in the digital age by "infrastructural" forms of surveillance. These are decentralized forms of surveillance that are networked and involve remote forms of watching over data entities rather than physical bodies (Galič et al. 2017). A second wave of digital sociological work therefore turns to the work of Gilles Deleuze, especially ideas of rhizomatic networks and "control societies." While Deleuze did not live long enough to witness the rise of Google and Facebook, his ideas derive (at least implicitly) from the emergence of the 1980s and 1990s computerized bureaucratic society.

Deleuze's writing certainly seem well suited to digital sociology. For example, his description of remote techniques of control superseding direct disciplinary techniques (Deleuze 1992) resonates with the rising significance of digital data throughout contemporary society. Deleuze described societies of control that were built around the monitoring of individuals' representations, what he termed the level of the "dividual." This is information that is deemed to represent an individual – what might be termed one's "data double" (Haggerty and Ericson 2000). These are not complete representations of an individual's physical self and their actions; instead they are composite representations and profiles of specific sets of technologically mediated behaviors (e.g. advertisers knowing someone only as a consumer with a history of online purchasing behaviors). Thus control in a Deleuzian society is exercised not by rendering people's "real" bodies docile but through attempts to monitor and control their data-bodies.

Approaching control and surveillance in these terms gives digital sociologists purchase on a range of prominent contemporary issues. Through Deleuze, for example, control can be seen as operating in an "ultrarapid" and "free-floating" manner across an assortment of networks that appear largely separate but ultimately connected (Galloway and Thacker 2007). Rather than being governed through a sense of being continually watched, individuals are subject to regular checks, permissions, the granting or denying of access, passwords and log-ins. Two important changes can be noted in comparison with the panoptic mode of control. First, it can be argued that the locus of power is relocated from immediate disciplinary institutions to remote databases, data profiles and data banks – what Latour (1987) termed "centers of calculation." Second, it can be argued that these forms of control become invisible and therefore imperceptible to most users.

These post-panoptic approaches have certainly pushed digital sociologists to address new assemblages of humans and technologies that now exercise forms of surveillance. Key areas of concern range from public awareness and critical

understandings of how individuals are constantly disas
sembled and recomposed into data doubles (Lupton 2016)
through to the inherent discrimination and inequalities inherent in data-based "sorting" (Leurs and Shepherd 2017). Post-
structuralist theory therefore prompts digital sociologists to
move away from descriptions of a ruthlessly efficient, all-
seeing "Big Brother" toward the rather more incomplete and
compromised realities of digital systems.

Moving beyond "pre-digital" theory

As these examples suggest, digital sociologists are making
insightful and eclectic use of established social theory. Besides
the work of Marx, Foucault and Deleuze, that of Erving
Goffman on the presentation of self in everyday life continues to be popular with analysts of social media and identity, with 1950s concepts such as "frontstage," "backstage"
and "facework" seen to translate neatly over to present-day
LinkedIn profiles and Facebook feeds (Belk 2013). As Greenfield (2017: 14) puts it, "try to imagine ... the presentation of
self without the selfie." Similarly, Pierre Bourdieu has found
a renewed audience among scholars of digital inequalities.
Here, the adaptation of concepts such as (online) "field"
and (digital) "capital" has prompted talk of a "Bourdieusian
digital sociology" (Ignatow and Robinson 2017: 956).

It is telling to consider why some "pre-digital" theorists
have been picked up by digital scholars while other "big
names" have not. It has been suggested that those theorists
whose popularity endures all share a fluid, network-like sensibility in their ideas, underpinned by relative loose ontological assumptions (Sterne 2003). For example, Ignatow and
Robinson (2017: 962) contend that "Bourdieu's ontological stance combining moderate realism and moderate social
constructionism has proven a solid foundation for empirical [digital] sociology." Yet, notwithstanding the popularity of such authors, it is increasingly recognized that digital
sociology should not be based wholly on the reappropriation of "pre-digital" theory. Indeed, it has been argued that
relying on the application of "respective *a priori* theoretical

commitments" leads only to limited understandings of digital technologies that are already socially ordered and organized by their producers and users (Brooker et al. 2017: 617). As Mackenzie Wark (2017 14) concludes, "perhaps it is no longer a time in which to use Foucault and Derrida to explain computing."

In another sense, then, digital sociology is proving to be a fertile site for the development of new theory – or at least a site where sociologists are exploring ways of making use of contemporary theories of digital society. Indeed, there is an array of recent theory that relates directly to the concerns and interests of digital sociology, albeit from writers who might not identify themselves as sociologists per se. This recent development of (post-)digital theoretical work has proven to be decidedly hybrid, collaborative and iterative in nature. Thus, rather than awaiting the emergence of a grand social theory for the digital age, digital sociologists are increasingly seeking out theoretical sustenance from across disciplinary boundaries. As Mackenzie Wark (2017 13) puts it, this is something that "general intellects might have to figure out together."

There are many writers and thinkers who fit this bill. For example, Wark highlights names such as Jodi Dean, Alexander Galloway and Wendy Chun as examples of such "general intellects" currently writing around the topics of digital media. Certainly, Galloway's work on interfaces, protocols and control deftly advances understandings of digital mediation and what the digital actually is. Similarly, Chun's historical expositions of the early internet have pushed understandings of online freedoms and constraints, as well the shifting nature of digital governance and organization. It is also well worth paying attention to the work of new media theorists such as Gert Lovink and Jussi Parikka in developing "network theories" and the notion of "media archaeology." Writers such as Ian Bogost and Lev Manovich have been working across areas such as computing, visual arts and design. Blending together philosophy, critical theory and media theory, Patricia Clough (2018) has also addressed extensively how digital technologies underpin an ever-altering sense of what it means to be human – especially in terms of the human body, subjectivity, affectivity and other "unconscious" processes. While these authors might not all be card-carrying sociologists, their work maps directly onto the concerns of digital sociology.

These theorists are notable for their broad terms of reference and knowledge bases, especially the ease with which they combine technical and philosophical concerns. Whereas social theory has always spanned disciplines such as philosophy, economics and sociology, the best digital theory-building of the past decade stems from social *and* computational origins. As such, it is increasingly apparent that digital sociologists need to develop a computational as well as a sociological imagination. This is not as daunting as it might sound. The computational and social sciences have a shared emphasis on analytical and logical thinking, as well as on developing deep theoretical understandings of complex systems. A field such as artificial intelligence draws as much on philosophy and linguistics as it does on mathematics and computer science. These are not areas of knowledge to which sociologists are wholly unsuited. Indeed, the most convincing current (post-)digital theorists are those who address digital philosophies and digital politics from the perspective of computational *and* human/social sciences. Writers such as Wark, Bogost and Lovink come from gamer, hacker and "hacktivist" backgrounds. Alexander Galloway is a philosopher with a long background in computer programing. Wendy Chun studied both systems design engineering and English literature – a mixture that she sees her work continuing to "combine and mutate" (Chun 2018). In short, the most insightful theoretical accounts of digital society seem to pay little regard to disciplinary boundaries.

The benefits of this approach are illustrated in Benjamin Bratton's (2016) recent account entitled *The Stack*. This ambitiously addresses the "planetary-scale computation" that has arisen over the past thirty years and the accompanying geopolitics that are now resulting. Bratton's thesis reflects his origins in sociology filtered through subsequent work in philosophy, design and computer sciences. This is theory-building that addresses the almost imperceptible machinations of global digital society. As such, it sets a high precedent for digital sociologists to follow. Tellingly Bratton's thesis is rooted in the computing metaphor of software "stacks," where layers of independent software components run on top of each other to form a complete platform. Approaching the digital world in these terms, Bratton outlines a complex multi-layered and modular "accidental megastructure" of computation, comprising six layers of the earth, cloud, city, address, interface and user.

There is much here that speaks directly to digital sociology. On a planetary level, for example, Bratton contrasts how the earth provides energetic and material sustenance for the technology of "The Stack" while also being increasingly diminished by the computational infrastructure that it sustains. In terms of the city layer, Bratton points to the reconstitution of urban spaces primarily to facilitate computationally driven consumption that is protected by computationally driven policing. In terms of users, Bratton reminds us of the growing dominance of non-human actors such as AI entities, bots, sensors, algorithms and animal users – all of which rely less on humans while humans rely increasingly on them. Yet, crucially, there is much in Bratton's thesis to challenge and unsettle digital sociologists, especially in terms of the computational elements of "The Stack." For example, he places great emphasis on the significance of software protocols and "deep" forms of mass digital address. Elsewhere, the significance of interfacial regimes reiterates the importance of interactions between humans and coded entities. These are all elements of the contemporary society on which it is less easy to gain sociological purchase.

These descriptions all convey a sense that governance and sovereignty are altering along lines that traditional sociological approaches are ill-equipped to accommodate. Bratton argues that, with the machine taking the place of familiar social structures such as the state, in short "we have no idea how to govern in this context" (2016: 213). This leads him to challenge the social sciences to jettison their "anthropocentric humanism" and "inadequate, immature" apprehensions over dehumanizing consequences of technology development and to suggest instead that the humanities and social sciences should focus attention on exploring opportunities to better integrate with the machine and design alternative components of this megastructure. As Bratton concludes, this requires directing efforts toward "not the Stack-we-have but the Stack-to-come."

Whether one agrees fully with this thesis or not, Bratton's provocations highlight the fact that sociology has a long way to go in making full sense of the digital. Of course, Bratton, Galloway, Chun et al. constitute an avant garde of digital theory-building which is already proving tremendously generative for digital sociologists to draw upon. Yet, while these new theoretical advances are clearly pertinent to the ongoing development of digital sociology, they also represent an implicit longer-term challenge to the relevance of a distinct digital sociology. These "computational philosophers" are amassing complex sets of ideas, all the time demonstrating that simply adding Foucault to Facebook is not a sufficient intellectual response to the complex machinations of the digital age. As such, there is a clear need for digital sociologists to strive to develop their *own* forms of powerful theorizing worthy of the computational twenty-first century.

Conclusions

At its heart, digital sociology marks a continuation of the sociological tradition. While the topics and subjects of inquiry might appear novel, digital sociologists are working in ways that are common to all areas of sociology. Digital sociology shares a commitment to asking difficult questions about issues such as structure and agency, power, domination, inequality and stratification. It is acutely aware of issues of political economy and cultural politics, and it is concerned with the privileging of individuals at the expense of the collective – the rise of private interests over public interests. These are concerns that persist across most aspects of sociology. As such, digital sociology can be seen as a space for sociologists of all different persuasions to come together.

Yet it important to see digital sociology as not merely a case of "more of the same." In many ways, it also marks a reconstitution of the sociological tradition. One of the core themes to emerge from this chapter is the need to combine sociological concerns with computational understandings. The lifeblood of digital sociology comes from a wide-ranging and fluid appropriation of ideas, theories and approaches.

This is an area of sociology that is eclectic, pragmatic and promiscuous in its reappropriation of theory (from all disciplines), while remaining rooted in the core sociological concerns that have developed since the 1900s. Digital sociologists should feel at ease in switching between continental *and* computational philosophy and in harboring interests in Marx *and* machine learning.

These past two chapters have concentrated on the precedents and foundations of digital sociology. It is now time to explore how these ideas are being put into practice. The next chapter therefore considers two important areas of empirical and theoretical scholarship of the digital by exploring recent sociological work in the areas of digital labor and digital race. What do all of the approaches discussed so far in this book look like when brought to bear on these two crucial areas of sociological inquiry – i.e. what it means to work and what it means to be black in contemporary society?

3
Digital Sociology in Action: Digital Labor and Digital Race

Introduction

Having explored the conceptual foundations of digital sociology, it is time to consider some practical examples of this scholarship of the digital. So what is the result of posing these questions, taking these theoretical approaches, and committing oneself to the critical scrutiny of digital technology? This chapter explores two illustrative examples of digital sociology inquiry – the areas of digital labor and digital race. Even for readers not usually drawn to the sociologies of work or race, these fast-growing areas of research and writing are useful ways to illustrate the practical application of concepts and approaches outlined in chapters 1 and 2.

Of course, there are many other topics of digital sociology inquiry that could be considered here. For example, there are strong bodies of research focusing on issues surrounding digital exclusion and the (non-)use of digital technologies among vulnerable and disadvantaged groups. There is growing interest in how engagements with digital technologies are stratified by social class, particularly those leading to unequal participation in domains such as health, education, social welfare and civic engagement. There is also a rich empirical literature around issues of gender and sexuality in the digital age, from moral panics over teenage "sexting" to online communities of relatively benign Furries and clearly less benign Incels. And there is an increasing number of empirical accounts of the digitization of various institutions across society, from families to schools, and from justice systems to religion. These include nuanced sociological investigations of the changing nature of digital parenting, the division of digital domestic labor, and the altered nature of online knowledge and authority.

All of these areas – and others – are worth exploring in order to get a full sense of digital sociology scholarship. For the time being, however, this chapter will focus specifically on how digital sociologists are making sense of two topics that are of long-standing sociological interest – (i) work and employment and (ii) race and ethnicity. Recent studies in each of these areas of inquiry show how researchers and writers are extending preceding "pre-digital" sociological literatures in these areas. In particular, the chapter will reflect on what these studies can tell us about the distinctly digital nature of these issues. In short, what is digital sociology adding to existing understandings of societal issues that are already widely discussed and known about?

Sociological studies of digital labor

We can first turn our attention to matters of work and employment. A popular expectation during the last few decades of the twentieth century was that new technologies would lessen the need for hard work and generally improve people's working lives. Indeed, technology marketing continues to promote a sense that new and exciting things simply get "done" through digital technologies without the need for work at all. As such, many people tend not to think about digital technology use specifically in terms of work and labor. Yet the ongoing digitization of contemporary society clearly involves substantial amounts of mental and manual labor alongside significant shifts in the coordination and distribution of work.

Despite this lack of popular consideration, the fast-changing nature of work in the digital age has emerged as a prominent interest within digital sociology, often in the guise of studies of "digital labor." This is research and writing that questions how digital technologies are altering work patterns in established jobs and professions, as well as how digital technologies underpin ostensibly new forms of distributed work. There is also considerable interest in the ways in which value is created from the unpaid actions of mass online audiences. Thus digital sociologists are keenly exploring questions of "what it means to 'labor' in the digital economy" (Kuehn and Corrigan 2013). Who is engaging in digital forms of work, under what conditions and with what outcomes? To what extent are workers being advantaged or exploited, empowered or alienated? How is such work experienced, and what inequalities are evident?

(i) The digitization of traditional work

First is the question of how digital technologies are altering traditional jobs and professions. Here, researchers have documented ways in which various existing jobs and professions are being reshaped by digital processes and practices. Take, for instance, what Nicole Cohen (2015a: 100) terms the "reformatting of journalism in a digital age" – i.e. how journalists' work is increasingly fragmented, automated and sped up by digital technologies. Cohen and others highlight a wide range of changes to consider. For example, news production has now reached a stage where reporting can be automated, with some sport, financial and weather bulletins now fully computer-generated. Other reporting is drawn from so-called content farms employing low-paid freelancers to quickly rewrite text drawn from data-mining and content aggregation. News outlets are also eager to rely on online audiences as a source of unpaid content – making increasing use of "citizen journalism" and invited bloggers as well as audience comments and feedback.

These developments all have considerable bearing on the nature of contemporary journalism. In particular, Cohen argues that journalistic output is now subject to continuous analytic scrutiny. This ranges from automated assessments of "newsworthiness" to real-time analysis of the audience "traffic" and "engagement." Cohen describes how journalists' writing decisions are disciplined by these meta data and analytics, and how they feel compelled to produce stories that reflect well in terms of "clicks" and "stickiness." As Cohen (2015a: 113) concludes, "digital production processes are undermining journalism as a creative endeavor, challenging independence and autonomy."

Similar issues and tensions are apparent across many other forms of professional work. For example, Selwyn et al. (2017) point to pervasive ways in which digital technologies are reshaping the work of schoolteachers. This includes the standardization of teaching activities and actions through the use of online "teacher-proof" pre-scripted lesson plans. Teachers are also increasingly working alongside content "recommender systems" and automated grading systems. Echoing the use of newsroom metrics, digital technologies further underpin a steady quantification and measurement of teachers' work – not least the growing use of "learning analytics" and other monitoring and feedback tools. Finally, Selwyn (2016: 21) notes that "perhaps the most significant trend is the digital expansion of schoolwork across space and time," with teachers increasingly expected to interact with students, parents and colleagues outside what were once considered "school hours."

Such uses of digital technology could be seen as bringing modern efficiencies to otherwise traditional work settings of the newsroom and classroom. Other research suggests that newsroom analytics can act as a source of motivation and reassurance for some journalists, with the nature of compliance varying considerably between different work contexts (Bunce 2018; Petre 2015). Yet digital sociology reminds us that there is also much to be wary of. For example, the developments detailed by Cohen and Selwyn mostly involve the fragmentation of professional work, leaving the conception of what should be complex and creative tasks increasingly separated from their execution. Enthusiasms for the capacity of digital technologies to "unbundle" work processes tend to gloss over the likelihood of deskilling highly trained professionals through persistent standardization and separation of work and the subversion of judgment and expertise. Cohen's and Selwyn's analyses quickly reach the conclusion that these are not technological changes that advantage the majority of journalists and teachers. Indeed, once tacit knowledge is devalued and tasks are standardized, they can be readily separated from specialized workers and then outsourced and/or automated.

These studies provide useful counterpoints to the hype of the twenty-first-century workplace. Indeed, many technological changes in contemporary workplaces could be said to be hastening the reconstitution of labor processes, from ones directed by workers to ones controlled by managers, administrators and commercial outside interests. Digital sociology therefore raises the suggestion that what appear to be technical efficiencies might actually act to increase alienation and disengagement of workers from their tasks. While not a root cause of these problems, digital technologies nevertheless amplify pressures of performativity, auditing, deskilling, life–work balance and the casualization of labor. As such, these are trends that digital sociology is proving well able to problematize.

(ii) New forms of distributed, discrete work

Alongside the digitization of "traditional" work, digital labor scholars are exploring new forms of distributed, automated and fragmented work – in particular the crowdsourcing of information-based "microwork" and digitally coordinated freelancing in the "gig economy." These "irregular forms of labor" (Sevignani 2013: 130) all reflect a growing trend for the distribution of work and the coordination of workers on a mass scale through networked technologies.

For example, the distribution and coordination of "microwork" involves small segments of much larger projects being contracted separately at low cost to dispersed individuals around the world (Walker 2012). Prominent microwork platforms with names such as Clickworker and Cloudfactory boast thousands of registered workers. The best known (and most widely researched) of these is Amazon's "Mechanical Turk" (AMT) platform. Established in 2005, AMT is marketed as offering "access [to] a global, on-demand, 24 × 7 workforce" estimated at over one million so-called Turkers whom any "Requester" can pre-test and then contract to carry out the task. Significantly, this model of online outsourcing derived initially from the IT industry's need to process large amounts of unstructured data. Indeed, microworkers continue to provide the bulk of "infrastructure labor" that sustains the running of the internet. These include low-paid evaluators who manually filter and moderate content, pretest algorithms and test code. Demand for cheap online data work has since expanded to many other information- and data-related domains, taking in academic researchers looking for cheap/plentiful sources of experimental subjects.

Another form of digital labor is the freelance gig economy, most familiar in the guise of popular ride sharing services (Uber, Lyft), delivery services (Deliveroo, Foodora), and services providing household work and chores (TaskRabbit). These platforms are touted as supporting the thriving "on-demand economy," recasting workers as "micro-entrepreneurs" who "are their own bosses, work flexible hours, and control nearly everything about the platform experience" (Schor and Attwood-Charles 2017). While the eventual tasks are usually physical in nature (e.g. driving cars, cycle couriering, cleaning houses), all exchanges take place through proprietary apps that link workers to specific tasks and assignments. As Malin and Chandler (2017: 382) describe the platform-based nature of Uber: "relying on mobile telephones' locative and messaging capacities, the entire exchange, including communications, payment, and post-drive ratings of both driver and passenger, takes place through these digital apps."

Looking beyond industry and investor enthusiasms for platforms such as Uber and AMT, an obvious sociological question is the extent to which these new forms of labor constitute the empowerment or the exploitation of workers. On the face of it, these are underpaid forms of employment with minimal worker protections and rights. Yet digital labor scholars are finding that, while microwork and gig work might appear low-skilled and exploitative, these are more complex forms of labor than might appear. For example, Irani (2017) reports that more than half of the "most active" Amazon Turkers have college degrees. As well as earning income, some workers value being able to make strategic use of platforms to supplement "downtime" in their primary careers and professions. Neither is this wholly unpleasurable work: studies suggest that microworkers experience intense "flow-like" experiences of absorption and enjoyment "lead[ing] to complete immersion in the tasks" (Bucher and Fieseler 2017: 1870) akin to playing computer games.

Empirical studies also give a sense of workers' tactical engagement with these labor conditions. Neha Gupta reports Indian Turkers setting up online forums to informally induct new members, set ethical norms, provide advice and social support, alert others to good jobs, review requesters and air grievances (Gupta et al. 2014). Similarly, Rosenblat and Stark (2016: 3759) found Uber drivers developing forums "to learn tricks and tips for success on Uber's platform; compare and share practices and screenshots; complain socially about passengers and the company; and debate Uber's practices, including discrepancies between the passenger and driver apps." Yet these instances of social capital building and sousveillance are limited. As Irani (2017: 3) concludes, "the dispersion of workers across geographies, however, may dampen workers' ability to identify with one another and take collective action."

Another recurring sociological concern is the technology-based control of these workers – i.e. "their increased subordination and dependence on the platforms to which they are tied" (Casilli 2017: 2068). For example, studies have explored how promises of increased freedom and flexibility for Uber and Lyft drivers are contradicted by "softer" and less visible forms of automated surveillance and algorithmic analysis (Shapiro 2018). Of particular significance are data-based forms of control, with platforms using information asymmetries to influence workers' decision-making. For example, Shapiro's research highlights how "remote company dispatchers maintain omniscient views of worker fleets on real-time digital maps," while providing drivers partial access to information as a means of "nudging" them toward accepting particular tasks that fulfil the platform's needs.

Another prominent finding is the differentiation of these workers along lines of class, race and geography. Such disparities are evident in a number of different forms. For example, studies of TaskRabbit use in Chicago found that "providers" were less likely to accept offers of work from consumers with addresses in low socioeconomic areas of the city. Moreover, the providers who did work in these areas tended to demand higher rates for their services (Thebault-Spieker et al. 2015). Elsewhere, Malin and Chandler (2017) suggest the increased likelihood of rides being cancelled on Uber after passengers see profiles of drivers of color. Similarly, the distribution of microwork opportunities is found to be tempered by what Mark Graham terms "the liability of foreignness" (Graham et al. 2017: 158). Analysis of microwork platforms set up in Hispanic, African and Asian regions notes consistent customer favoring of workers perceived as well-educated, first-language speakers. This contrasts with the negative stereotyping of workers from South Asia and Africa in terms of ethicized assumptions of work ethic and language skills (Graham et al. 2017; Galperin and Greppi 2017). As Irani (2013) concludes, these are "differences that build on old and gendered divisions of labor that, through infrastructure, can be reproduced at global scales."

(iii) Social media as sites of "free labor"

A third strand of digital labor literature relates to the ways in which value is created from the unpaid actions of online audiences. This is what Terranova (2000) describes as "free labor" – i.e. forms of online engagement "in which exploitation, pleasure, work and leisure become harder to distinguish" (Aroles 2014: 145). One prominent issue for digital labor scholars consists of the ways in which individuals' use of social media creates value that can be appropriated by other parties for profit generation (Bodle 2016). For example, the business model of Facebook relies on mining and selling data to third parties, both for targeted advertising on the platform and for detailed consumer profiling. In addition, content contributed to Facebook functions to create opinions, tastes, subjectivities and other cultural content that can be commercially profited from (Coté and Pybus 2011). As Fuchs and Sevignani (2013: 267) conclude, "Facebook labor creates commodities and profits. It is therefore productive work. It is however unpaid work."

Another form of free labor is the "co-creative labor" that users undertake in the course of their internet use (Banks and Deuze 2009). One example of this is the extensive amateur creation of online content by fans of popular cultural products such as films, comic books and sports teams. Online genres of fan fiction, fan art and fan "modding" have been noted as unofficial forms of publicity and marketing for the culture industries – adding "value to mass-produced commodities" in ways that are "worthy of compensation" (De Kosnik 2013: 110). Indeed, many firms now strive deliberately to have their brands and products featured in content being created and shared by social media users. Of course, for many users, social media activities might not seem like work. Indeed, this free labor is often celebrated as a voluntary, altruistic and empowering form of self-expression and creativity (see Lindgren 2017; Shullenberger 2014). Yet social media rely on users spending considerable amounts of time and effort to consume *and* produce content. Whether they see themselves as working or not, most social media users are therefore engaged in cognitive, communicative and cooperative activities that lead to the creation of new "immaterial" products.

Another type of free labor relates to activities that users pursue in the expectation of their subsequently leading to paid work. This has been described as "hope labor" – i.e. "un- or under-compensated work carried out in the present, often for experience or exposure, in the hope that future employment opportunities may follow" (Kuehn and Corrigan 2013). Examples here include individuals writing regular product reviews for sites such as Amazon or sports blogs for syndicated websites, submitting speculative designs to sites such as Threadless, and self-producing shows for video-sharing sites such as YouTube. All of these activities involve unpaid work undertaken "as a future-oriented investment" (ibid.) in the hope of being talent-spotted. These forms of "hope labor" mark a reframing of unpaid work as an expected (if not desirable) element of the digital economy.

Such aspirational activities are driven by the success of small numbers of social media users who have been able to monetize their content successfully. For example, many free-laborers aspire to the status of so-called influencers or micro-celebrities (Abidin 2017). These are individuals producing regular online content related particularly to their own personal lifestyles as well as particular topics such as fashion, beauty tips and gaming. Research into these forms of labor highlight the considerable demands of such work – not least the "contrived authenticity" and "calibrated amateurism" of maintaining an appearance of not being a paid professional (ibid.). For example, Duffy and Wissinger (2017) highlight stressful forms of "emotional labor, self-branding labor, and an always-on mode of entrepreneurial labor" implicit in in these forms of social media work. Elsewhere, Duffy (2017) notes recurring inequalities of gender, class and status evident in terms of which YouTubers and Instagrammers succeed in developing profitable careers. As with the microwork and gig work described earlier, while all internet users might have access to the same platforms, these forms of digital labor are certainly not equitable or democratic.

Digital labor – recurring themes and issues

One of the key themes in digital labor scholarship is a question that has recurred throughout our discussions – i.e. "what is new here?" To what extent does microwork, the gig economy, influencers and automated copy-editing represent "a reimagined capitalism" (Schor and Attwood-Charles 2017)? Conversely, in what ways are these merely continuations of long-standing economic and societal conditions? Digital labor scholars are quick to acknowledge that many of the tensions and dynamics associated with these forms of digital labor have existed for some time. For example, practices of freelancing, piecework, unpaid apprenticeships and creative workers not making money from their art are well established (Cohen 2015b). As the sociological literatures on prosumption (Ritzer 1993) and coproduction (Dujarier 2015) remind us, some of the most successful companies over the past fifty years (McDonald's, Ikea) have relied on putting consumers to work. There are clear similarities between unpaid domestic work and the ways in which digital capitalism is reliant on the capture and use of seemingly voluntary and unpaid activities undertaken by digital media users (Jarrett 2015). Thus while these instances of digital labor might involve altered configurations of the means of production, many of the unequal relations of production appear to remain intact (Schor and Attwood-Charles 2017).

Clearly, then, the rise of digital labor is entwined with wider general "reorganizations of work" implicit in post-industrial transitions (Flecker et al. 2017). The development of Facebook, Uber and AMT continue decades-old trends such as declining direct employment, the rise of "precarious" employment and casualized labor, and the diminishment of workers' rights. Similarly, the ways in which digital technologies are used in traditional workplaces such as newsrooms and schools reflect broader entrenchments across all employment sectors of strategies of efficiency, standardization, "new managerialism" and "corporate reform." In all these ways, then, our understandings of digital labor need to be contextualized in terms of these preceding economic and social logics.

In this sense, digital sociology is proving a useful means of moving debates over digital labor beyond simplistic questions of whether these forms of work are "good" or "bad." Any criticism is tempered by the fact that microworking, the gig economy, unpaid content creation and social media influencing appear to be practices in which some individuals engage by choice. Whether in terms of journalists' motivational use of metrics or social media users' creation of content, it could be argued that "control ultimately hinges on workers' willingness to conform to the calculative rationalities that companies project onto them" (Shapiro 2018). Rather than wholly dismissing this work as forms of servitude and exploitation, digital labor scholars are keen to reflect on why these practices are increasing in prominence. Thus much of the writing and research outlined above strives to deepen understandings of "the value that users might extract from their own labor" (Hughes 2014: 650). In this sense, these forms of work are clearly of personal benefit for many individuals that cannot be dismissed out of hand. There is a doubled-edged, contradictory nature to such work. It is socially meaningful but also economically vital, individually enriching but also individually exploitative (Jarrett 2015).

Yet, notwithstanding the need for a balanced perspective, digital sociology does raise a number of wider concerns over digital labor. First are the ways in which many of these digital settings obscure the labor that is being carried out – as Trebor Scholz (2013: 2) puts it, these are activities that do not "feel, look, or smell like labor at all." Social media, smartphones and other personal technologies are certainly effective means of lulling individuals into not feeling as if they are working, even when they plainly are. These are forms of technology use that are framed as a form of play rather than work (Scholz 2013) – for example, something that is "cool," "fun" and led by individual "passions" (Jarrett 2015).

These are also technologies that reframe labor in highly individualized, solitary and solipsistic terms. Many of the forms of digital labor just described place responsibility and risk firmly on individual workers rather than on employers (many of whom refuse to recognize themselves as employers at all). This leads to situations where individuals are alienated not only from productive processes and the products being created but also from other workers. Thus any sense of work being undertaken in collective or collegial ways is obscured, leading to a curtailed sense of workers' collective rights and protections as well as a diminished dignity of labor (Fish and Srinivasan 2012). In this sense, digital labor scholarship brings us back to many of the central concerns of digital sociology highlighted in chapters 1 and 2 – i.e. interplays between structure and agency, social relations and social change, and the importance of seeing digital technology in terms of human experiences.

Sociological studies of digital race

The digital labor literature certainly provides a critical rejoinder to the digital optimism of the 1990s and 2000s. In particular, these new forms of digital labor contradict the idea of digital technologies leading to fairer, more democratic and more just social processes. As Nakamura and Chow-White (2013: 7) put it, one of the enduring promises of the digital age has been "technology with a radical form of agency, endowed with the capacity ... to create an ideal 'information society' where everyone is radically equal." Yet, as the realities of working in digital "gigs" and "tasks" illustrate, this is clearly not turning out to be the case. The digital labor studies just reviewed point to a number of inequalities, not least issues of race. In times when African-American Uber drivers and Amazon Turkers from South Asia are negatively prejudged and profiled by their prospective customers, race clearly remains an issue that is interwoven throughout digital labor. Indeed, the topic of race offers a second important illustration of the breadth and depth of digital sociology.

Tellingly, academic discussions of digital technologies over much of the past thirty years have been notably non-racialized in nature. This stems partly from their coincidence with what has been termed the "post-racial" turn. This is the "commonplace yet hubristic ideological contention that contemporary liberal democracies have transcended the logics of race and racism" (Valluvan 2016: 2242). Thus social researchers became interested in digital technologies and the internet around the same time that many North American and European commentators were considering the possibilities of their countries moving "beyond race" and evolving into multicultural societies with "color-blind" institutions.

Until recently, the eagerness of academics to approach new digital technologies in a color-blind manner attracted little reflection or concern. After all, many researchers involved in social studies of digital media would consider themselves to be liberally inclined scholars hopeful about a racism-free future. It has been all too easy to presume that there is no racism to be found. However, this stance is now being challenged by sociologists attuned to the sharply racialized nature of contemporary digital life. These scholars are contributing to a critical literature on what might be termed "digital race" – i.e. considerations of how race is implicit in people's encounters and experiences of digital technology across various facets of everyday life. This is a particularly strident area of digital sociology, unafraid to call out the "color-blind racism" of other digital researchers willfully blind to racial dimensions of their chosen topics of study (Daniels 2015).

As such, digital race is proving a compelling example of digital sociology making a distinct and vital contribution to contemporary sociology.

(i) Moving beyond the "digital divide"

As just implied, the recent critical literature on digital race certainly marks a reaction to the weaknesses of preceding scholarship. In particular, digital race researchers are keen to distance themselves from the treatment of race developed in social research purporting to address the topics of digital inequalities and digital divides. Over the past thirty years digital divide studies have regularly pointed to race – alongside age, gender and social class – as a significant factor in the ongoing inequalities of opportunity and outcome associated with digital technology access and use. The digital divide literature since the 1990s has highlighted how people's engagements with digital technologies such as computers and the internet have remained patterned by race over time, even in high-tech regions of North America and Europe. In the US, for example, the authoritative Pew "Internet & American Life" program reports that "home broadband use" remains differentiated in favor of whites (78 percent of adults) as compared to black (65 percent) and Hispanic (58 percent) adults. So, while headline figures might appear to be improving, the race-related digital divide is acknowledged as far from being "bridged."

Such evidence continues to be used widely in policy and academic circles. Yet for many digital sociologists this research provides a dangerously restricted view of race and technology. A strong case can be made that people's encounters with digital media cannot be reduced simply to categories of being "users" or "non-users," digital "haves" or "have nots." For example, people's experiences of digital engagement and participation vary dramatically and do not result in consistent levels of power sharing or empowerment (Andrejevic 2007). Their interactions with what might appear to be the same digital technology will depend considerably on their circumstances, context and racialized agency. As Tressie McMillan Cottom (2016: 214) reasons, the idea of being on the right or wrong side of a "digital divide" does "not go far enough to capture the various intersections of privilege, access, and power that operate online and offline simultaneously and which can also be mutually constitutive."

Against this background, the argument is now being made that digital divide research is limited by its focus on correlations and individual attributions rather than on the more complex structural stratifications of people's digital choices and actions. Portraying groups of African Americans as stranded on the "wrong side" of a divide "leaves the way race is embedded in structures, industry, and the very idea of the internet largely unexamined" (Daniels 2015: 1377). In contrast to depicting race-related divides and digital inequalities, then, many digital sociologists position themselves as starting from the point that race is not a hard-and-fast variable but is socially constructed. As such, this is scholarship focused explicitly on the inherently racialized dimensions of digital culture, economics and politics and challenges the ways in which "whiteness" is continually affirmed as normative across the important features of digital society (Nakayama 2017). From these starting points, then, digital race research sets out to portray the dynamics of contemporary digital society in more nuanced and complex ways than has previously been the case.

(ii) Race and online interactions

The literature on digital race examines the racialized nature of digital media along a number of different lines. This includes work addressing the dynamics of online interactions. Early research in this area tended to focus on the visual (mis)representation of race in websites, videogames and user interfaces. However, this has shifted throughout the 2010s to addressing the actions and consequences of people's online interactions. As Nakamura and Chow-White (2013) reason, digital media are no longer texts that are consumed passively. Instead, their main social function is processual rather than visual, thereby demanding scrutiny of the racialized nature of what is being done to people through digital media, rather than what digital media show and represent.

These concerns have prompted various studies of how discrimination is enacted through digital media. For example, a series of studies from Harvard researchers detailed the systematic discrimination of African Americans on the Airbnb room-sharing platform. This found, for example, properties listed with pictures of black landlords receiving nightly rates that were 12 percent lower than those for proprietors depicted as not black (Edelman and Luca 2014). Similarly, guests with typically African-American names were 16 percent more likely to be rejected by hosts (Edelman et al. 2016). Other research reports that Airbnb hosts in areas with predominantly white populations receive better ratings and demand higher prices (Cansoy and Schor 2016). Crucially, the commodified market-like nature of exchanges means that such platforms do little to counter such differentiation. Indeed, as Niesen (2016: 173) concluded with regard to specified racial preferences on dating and hook-up sites such as Tinder, eHarmony and Grindr, "bigotry is generated through the labor of users themselves."

Alongside these forms of transactional discrimination, digital race research highlights various ways that digital media support direct harassment of people of color. This is explored in studies of online racialized harassment and hate speech, ranging from "cloaked" websites (Daniels 2009) to Twitter (Hardaker and McGlashan 2016). This research lends weight to Nakayama's (2017) contention that online communication tends to amplify harassment and vilification through a combination of anonymity, interactivity and access to a global audience. These shifts in social distance and scale mean that online environments can quickly become perceived by users as places where "expressing socially unacceptable views" can be "more socially acceptable" (Stein 2016: 29). Other studies find these traits evident in online gaming communities. For example, Kishonna Gray's (2016: 355) research on Twitch gaming communities describes in detail how gamers of color encounter sustained "racism and harassment by other gamers" alongside the regular performances of "hegemonic Whiteness and masculinity." Gray's work illustrates how these practices are quickly normalized, accepted as legitimate, and embedded in the continued cultural practices within online gaming.

One important theme throughout these studies is how such discriminations do not arise solely from the actions of individual users. Instead this research highlights ways in which applications and platforms are configured in ways that prompt and perpetuate racialized dynamics. For example, Matamoros-Fernández's (2017) description of "platformed racism" details how popular platforms such as Facebook are configured and implemented in ways that perpetuate whiteness. This ranges from their internal policies and external terms of service (which usually adhere to white and/or Western values and ethics) through to the commercially driven reuse of platform data. This latter point was illustrated by Facebook's development of an "ethnic affinity" indicator based on users' prior tracked engagement with specific pages and content. This data was sold to advertisers wanting to target their products only to particular ethnic groups. As Matamoros-Fernández (ibid.: 933) concluded, while Facebook acted on what was computationally possible, "the business orientation of this technical functionality overlooked its potentiality to be discriminatory."

Indeed, the racialized nature of computational processes and algorithmically determined encounters is a growing area of academic interest. Critical scholars have long noted racial differences in terms of "algorithmic visibility" (Introna and Nissenbaum 2000) and what Gandy (1993) terms the "panoptic sort" of online data. Here it is argued that data-based practices designed to classify, sort and evaluate populations inevitably reproduce existing racial inequalities, while then going on to generate new modes of racial discrimination through the cumulative recirculation and recombination of already racialized categories – what Gandy terms a "matrix of multiplication." In this vein, current scholars have begun to detail algorithmic racial exclusion on online dating sites (Robnett and Felliciano 2011), the biases inherent in biometrics and facial recognition software (Browne 2010), and the racist misrecognitions that are naturalized into the coding processes informing Google's search engine algorithms (Noble 2018). All these studies confirm the argument, as Gillborn et al. (2018: 158) observe, that computer-generated models and calculations are compromised by "hidden assumptions that frequently encode racist perspectives beneath the façade of supposed quantitative objectivity."

Some studies also examine the human basis of what might appear to be machine-led automated discrimination. For example, as was described earlier, much of the content moderation and filtering on platforms such as Facebook is carried out by microworkers rather than by automated systems. While platforms purport not to permit racist content, any actions to block or censor often depend on "complicated matters of judgment" on the part of these workers (Roberts 2016: 148). Studies of those involved in "commercial content moderation" point to the often racialized outcomes of these processes, as low-paid workers (often in located in low-income countries) are tasked with making rapid interpretations of their employers' internal policies and commercial imperatives. These are commercial environments where distasteful, sensationalist and disturbing content can be popular and profitable – as Roberts (ibid.: 151) notes bluntly, "racist content sells." As a result, these workers find themselves continually balancing their censorious role with their personal values and the underlying pressure of the profit motives of their employers.

(iii) Race and the digital formation of collective identity

Another strand of research examines the changing nature of collective identity formation and resistance through people's use of social media platforms. Whereas early internet research often focused on individuals' self-presentation and identity performance, these recent studies have shifted attention toward collective actions and the formation of social media publics. One much researched case considered the complex ways in which social media was used in the aftermath of the 2014 police killing of Michael Brown in the US town of Ferguson. As is now common in such events, digital media proved a significant conduit for the public exchange of information and commentary. Subsequent studies have therefore explored the roles that platforms such as Facebook, YouTube, Instagram, Tumblr, Vine and Twitter played in supporting collective reflection and commemorative "memory work" (Smit et al. 2017). In particular, this highlights how the operational logics and practices of platforms work to popularize particular narratives and representations over others. For example, Smit and his colleagues detail how collective memories of the Ferguson shooting were shaped by platform logics of privileging "sharable" iconic images, brief emotive slogans, simplified ideas and polarized arguments. As these researchers conclude, social media enabled the widespread co-construction of simplified discourses in lieu of "the complexities of the issues at hand" (ibid.: 19).

Another focus of this research is the collective use of hashtags to support awareness raising and protest – what has been termed "hash-tag publics" (Rambukkana 2015). This is most prevalent in the form of racially related hash-tags or "black tags" (Sharma 2013) such as #IfTheyGunnedMeDown, #HandsUpDontShoot and #BlackLivesMatter. The widespread use of such hash-tags has been explored in a number of studies. For example, Harlow and Benbrook's (2018) examination of the use of #BlackLivesMatter hash-tags from celebrity accounts detailed how these particular tweets were more likely to be used for community-building and identity-building rather than simply for marketing products or self-promotion. Thematic analysis of nearly 2.7 million posts identified a number of community-related intentions underpinning #BlackLivesMatter tweets, including what the researchers described as "speaking to whites" – i.e. messages intended to represent the black community to white Twitter audiences. Such uses of Twitter are also noted in "non-celebrity" use of the #BlackLivesMatter hash-tag, with ordinary people rationalizing their use of "black tags" as a means of making sense of discrimination experiences, identifying with their racial group, and contributing to the black community (Lee-Won et al. 2018).

Digital race research has also begun to document the broader phenomenon of "black Twitter" (Sharma 2013). This was initially noted in 2009 in terms of black users' propensity to contribute to "culturally relevant, humorous memes and chats" (Harlow and Benbrook 2018). Yet, in the wake of high-profile racial incidents such as Ferguson, research has increasingly explored the role of Twitter as a site of black activism to contest hegemony and create community.

Indeed, while often engaging in gossip about popular culture, black Twitter users remain more likely than other users to tweet on topics of social justice and politics (Williams 2016). In these ways, researchers have pointed to Twitter functioning as a "meaningful community" (ibid.), a "social public" (Brock 2012) and a "networked counterpublic" (Graham and Smith 2016) for African-American users.

Of course, the collective actions of black Twitter users are mirrored by groups with oppositional racial agendas. Digital race research also contrasts trends such as "black Twitter" with the online actions of pro-white and other racist groups. For example, Nadia Flores-Yeffal and her colleagues (2011, 2018) have addressed the role of the internet in sustaining public discourses in the US surrounding undocumented immigrants – what she terms the "Latino cyber-moral panic." This work explores how blogs, Facebook groups, Twitter and YouTube sustained the contestation of accurate information during the 2010s alongside a continuous circulation of specific phrases (e.g. "overhaul," "wake up," "secure our borders," "make America great again"). Flores-Yeffal argues that these views were then replicated in news media and representations of public opinion and subsequently became part of the dominant public discourse as a "problem" that needs to be solved.

As with all digital sociology research, Flores-Yeffal is careful to disentangle the social and technical dynamics at play in such developments. Drawing on Stanley Cohen's notion of "moral panic," Flores-Yeffal reasons that the internet did not cause people to express these views per se. However, online platforms undoubtedly "exacerbate people's framing of the issue in ways that are then amplified through other media sources" (Flores-Yeffal et al. 2018). Similar conclusions are drawn in Thomas Nakayama's account of the role of the internet in enabling the so-called Birther Movement to sustain the dispute of President Obama's legitimacy as US president on the fictitious grounds of being born in Kenya. As Nakayama (2017: 69) concluded, "despite the traditional mainstream media focus on the legal documents showing that the president was born in Hawaii, the internet enabled the Birther movement to empower its interpretation of President Obama's birthplace."

Digital race – recurring themes and Issues

This research and writing powerfully illustrates the racialized ways in which digital media are designed, configured and used, the racialized consequences of these shapings, and the role of digital media as an important "site of political struggle over racial meaning, knowledge and values" (Daniels 2013: 696). In part, this new wave of research is a matter of timing, emanating from a generation of researchers responding to issues that have come to prominence throughout the 2010s. Yet this research is also driven by what was identified in chapters 1 and 2 as the explicitly political focus of digital sociology and its underpinning interests in social relations, social conflict, power and control. In short, all digital researchers clearly need to consider the racialized dimensions of these issues if they want to claim relevance to contemporary digital society. As Jessie Daniels (2016: 337) reasons, "if digital sociology is to prove useful as a field, it must take seriously the ways that racialized and gendered bodies are attacked in and through digital media technologies."

As with this chapter's previous example of digital labor, the immediate question that the digital race literature raises is "what is new here?" Again these studies remind us that "what is new here?" is not a question with a clear-cut answer. This research and writing certainly portrays an increased messiness of racial dynamics in networked, software-based settings. Certainly these studies highlight the foregrounding of certain values and perspectives in the design and implementation of digital platforms and point to ways in which the configuration and governance of digital media continue to be built around an "assumed whiteness" (Kolko 2000: 225). Yet it could be argued that digital media do little more than mirror already established patterns of racial discrimination and oppression. In this respect, platforms such as Twitter, Facebook and Twitch could be seen as merely exposing well-established social relations and dynamics. Indeed, as Tressie Cottom (2016: 217) reasons, it is to be expected that "digitization ... should reproduce unequal social relations of the society that produces it."

Yet the emerging literature on digital race does point to some important differences in the ways that race is being played out through digital platforms, applications and systems. For example, one notable shift appears to be the constrained and disconnected nature of these interactions. The well-noted tendency of social media toward "filter bubbles" and "echo chambers" (Flaxman et al. 2016) means that the production and consumption of racial messages, ideas and understandings is more intense but perhaps not as expansive as they might previously have been. Thus the internet can easily accommodate millions of users vibrantly co-constructing the idea that "Black Lives Matter" while millions of other users blithely work to "Make America Great Again." The logics of digital media ensure that these ostensibly connected groups do not interact meaningfully with each other online, enter dialogue or refine their views.

Indeed, a notable change over the past ten years is the increasingly software-based, programmed constraint of people's interactions with ideas and knowledge. The logic of "platformed racism" certainly appears to be underpinning altered dynamics of racism. Many of these studies suggest that individuals' existing cultural values are directed and intensified in specific ways by the coded structures and politics of commercially produced platforms. Thus, it is not enough to say that online racism arises wholly from the intentions of racist individuals who happen to be using the internet. Instead, digital race research illustrates how structural oppression operates from within the IT industry that produces, provides and governs the digital media being used. Many of the studies just outlined highlight the complicity of platform providers in configuring their products in ways that often appear to exacerbate difference and reduce the possibilities for both nuanced conversation and respectful and open dialogue.

Indeed, much of the research just mentioned highlights the increasing influence of commercial IT industry actors in shaping the racialized dynamics of a nation such as the US. While Facebook, Twitter and Google espouse non-discriminatory values, their services clearly function in ways that reflect "bottom-line" economic imperatives. In this sense, movements such as #BlackLivesMatter can flourish on a platform like Twitter alongside counter-movements such as the pro-police #BlueLivesMatter and the tone-deaf #AllLivesMatter – each of which satisfies the economic imperative of the platform to increase users and volume of content production and circulation (Bock and Figueroa 2018). These are technologies that are shaped by concerns for what is "good for business" rather than any particular ideology or underlying intent. Much of what has just been described might therefore be seen as a consequence of the IT industry's libertarianism and willingness to "imagin[e] a world that's fundamentally without politics" (Turner 2017). Yet, instead of finding a utopian post-racial internet, the studies just outlined emphasize the color-blind racism that results from this approach. Rather than reflecting the actions of racist users, many of the concerns raised in digital race research could be seen as stemming from the position of white privilege and power that pervades the high-tech industry and the Silicon Valley culture.

Conclusions

While highlighting many salient issues specific to the areas of labor and race, these studies also point to a number of broader features of digital sociology as an approach to making sense of contemporary society. This includes a commitment to continually question the newness of "new" technologies. None of these studies conclude that digital technologies are somehow causing change or transforming social relations of their own accord; rather, they are more accurately understood as amplifying, exacerbating, extending and reconfiguring social issues. Crucially, many of these studies suggest that such exacerbations and reconfigurations often appear to take place through the lens of the IT industry and a profit-led technological solutionism which remains morally ambivalent to any imprecisions, inequalities and injustices that may result. Continuing a theme introduced in chapter 2, much of this research also points to the specifically "platformed" nature of contemporary experiences, engagements and encounters. In particular, many of the digital labor and digital race studies outlined in this chapter add to our understandings of the realities of "platform capitalism," especially for the marginalized individuals who work to produce excess value often for minimum reward.

Both these areas of research also illustrate the use of core concepts and social theory in digital sociology. For example, echoing themes from chapter 2, digital labor and digital race are topics that reflect the ambiguous outcomes of increasingly networked ways of being. Moreover, these are both areas of research that make good use of existing social theory, testing and extending ideas from labor process theory and critical race theory. These areas of research also illustrate the diversity of research methods that can be used in the study of digital society. While much can be identified from large-scale computational analyses of 2.7 million tweets, there is in addition much that can be learned from ethnographically "hanging around" with Uber drivers (both online and in their cars). There is also continued value in traditional empirical methods of face-to-face interviewing, observation and documentary analysis. These are research topics that benefit from researchers being as methodologically pluralistic and pragmatic as possible.

Finally, areas such as digital labor and digital race both speak to an underlying concern of digital sociology – i.e. how could things "be otherwise"? For example, in terms of digital labor research, a number of convincing arguments have emerged with regard to the need to reimagine and reconstitute the notion of organized labor and trade unionism for the digital age – what Walker (2012: 39) describes as "a high-tech labor movement." Elsewhere are suggestions for the establishment of alternative online platforms that function as worker cooperatives rather than as for-profit entities (Scholz 2016). Similarly, digital race research is proving a useful basis from which to imagine alternative forms of digital media and internet use. For example, in terms of education, Tanksley (2016) advances the idea of a "black feminist media literacy" that supports the development of skills to analyze media codes and speak back to or criticize dominant ideologies in digital media. Other suggestions include the development of alternative digital technologies – for example, interfaces, algorithms and other key mediating artifacts that are accommodating to (rather than dominating of) racial identities other than white (see Cheney-Lippold 2017).

All told, the burgeoning literatures around digital labor and digital race offer rich illustrations of digital sociology in practice. Extending this theme, the next two chapters reflect further on the practice of digital sociology research and scholarship. What are the methodological concerns that underpin studies such as those reviewed in this chapter? What do these researchers subsequently "do" with their writing and research in terms of making a contribution to the ongoing shaping of digital society? In the first instance, chapter 4 goes on to consider the methodology and methods of digital sociology research. Just how should we set about doing digital sociology research?

4
Digital Methods and Methodology

Introduction

The studies featured in chapter 3 illustrate an increasingly diverse use of research tools and techniques in digital sociology. Only a few years on from anticipation of a "new kind of social science" (Christakis 2012), digital sociologists are now engaged in all manner of innovative empirical methods and approaches. While remaining conscious of the limitations and compromises inherent in any empirical endeavor, digital sociologists are certainly thinking expansively and imaginatively about how they research, as well as about what they research.

The sense of methodological reinvention resonates with ongoing concerns across the discipline over the "fitness for purpose" of social research. Well before talk of a digital sociology, Savage and Burrows's (2007) "The coming crisis of empirical sociology" forewarned of the declining prominence and purpose of twentieth-century social sciences. Here it was contended that the authority of sociology, cultural studies and political sciences was fast fading in light of research innovations outside the academy that far exceeded the scale and scope of data generated through academic research. In particular, Burrows and Savage (2014) noted that corporations, government agencies and other "commercial sociology" actors are now utilizing digitally generated data with the promise of yielding comprehensive evidence of genuine actions.

Against this background, favored sociological methods such as the individual in-depth interview certainly appear rather paltry and under-powered in contrast to millions of users routinely reflecting their life-worlds and world-views through social media. "Big picture" data such as this, Savage and Burrows (2007: 885) reasoned, fundamentally undermines any claim that sociologists might have had previously to privileged or especially insightful "access to the social." Patricia Clough and her colleagues (2015: 147) have elsewhere referred to this as "the datalogical turn," where "large-scale databases and adaptive algorithms are calling forth a new onto-logic of sociality or the social itself." Mass quantities of digital data certainly constitute a significant challenge to sociology – offering a competing framework that promises to make sense of the social world on a far more expansive, comprehensive and rapid basis.

The empirical ambitions of digital sociology therefore fit alongside various like-minded attempts to rediscover the purpose and verve of sociological research. One such example is the manifesto for "live methods" of Les Back and his colleagues (Back 2012), which stresses the need for research infused with a spirit "alive to the processes by which society is made" (Michael 2012: 166). This description of live methods foregrounds inquiry that is in "real time" and constantly on the move with people and their practices. It suggests research approaches that are artful, creative, playful and deliberately provocative – pushing sociological researchers to develop empirical methods and "probes" that test and reinvent relations with social settings and environments. As the live methods movement reminds us, digital sociology is certainly not alone in looking to move beyond the traditional "qualitative vs. quantitative" concerns of the discipline.

Yet digital sociology has particular reason to look beyond the habitual use of social research methods past their prime. In short, digital sociologists are pursuing research interests that cannot be reflected or captured solely through interviews and sample surveys. As the past three chapters have established, digital sociology research addresses vast sociotechnical assemblages of human users and devices overlaid by all manner of software, data and algorithms. These are topics of research that demand methods that are "technology-centric," "data-centric" *and* "social-centric" (Marres 2017). As Marres continues, digital sociology research demands the combination of "external" approaches that address digital technology through the lens of sociality and society with "internal" approaches that address the social through the lens of digital architecture. As we shall now go on to discuss, current digital sociology research pursues this balance through a number of distinct methodological approaches.

Big Data and the computational social sciences

One key methodological concern for digital sociologists is so-called Big Data. While it is an overused term, Big Data signals an immensely expanded scale and scope of research, alongside heightened expectations of the social insights this can yield. In a basic sense, Big Data refers to computerized processing of massive sets of digital information. This takes place through automated archiving and tagging, linking and connecting, harvesting and mining of data through various computer-based processes. With the ever-increasing computational capacity of digital systems allowing such processes to take place on a mass aggregated scale, even modestly resourced individual researchers can now work with huge amounts of data to discover patterns that would otherwise be imperceptible (Boyd and Crawford 2012).

Big Data methods are well established throughout the natural sciences (e.g. genetics, environmental science and astronomy) as well as in business and government sectors. With increasing amounts of data relating to social domains being produced, sociological researchers have growing opportunities to follow suit. Indeed, massive quantities of social digital data now originate from a variety of different sources in a number of different forms. Large amounts of social data are generated deliberately. This includes the administrative measurement of people's interactions with government agencies and commercial interests, as well as more covert forms of institutional monitoring and evaluation of individuals. At the same time, vast quantities of data are generated through the operations of digital devices and systems. Moreover, people volunteer large volumes of data during the course of their use of digital technologies, in particular the curation of social media profiles and various other forms of user-generated content.

This all amounts to what has been described as an (over) abundance of "big and broad" social data (Housley et al. 2014) offering a ready means of addressing social science questions. The hype surrounding social uses of Big Data is considerable – often framed along lines of a "new way of knowing society" (Marres 2017: 17) that offers "to reveal the reality of human behavior at scale" (Carrigan 2015). The idea of Big Data certainly raises advantages in comparison to traditional sources of sociological data. Computational methods allow for considerably more data to be processed than would be possible manually, with "extended zoomability between micro and macro" (Evans and Rees 2012: 23). Most Big Data sets are updated regularly, thereby facilitating real-time (rather than snapshot) analysis over finite periods of weeks and months. This can support ongoing bottom-up inductions of social activity which reveal patterns and structures as they occur (rather than analyses based on *a priori* interests of the researcher).

The promise of Big Data certainly chimes with the interests of many sociologists. After all, detecting patterns among unstructured information is a central element of sociological research (Hannigan 2015). Of course, most sociologists are understandably circumspect about excessive claims of Big Data offering an all-seeing analytic eye. Yet, such hyperbole notwithstanding, Big Data has emboldened those sociologists who see themselves pursuing "analytic" work rather than "critique" (Williams et al. 2017). From this perspective, Big Data has been welcomed as a "watershed moment" (McFarland et al. 2016) that redresses the "imbalance of theory and data" hitherto characterizing many areas of sociology (Bail 2014: 476). Big Data might not "know everything," but there is growing belief that it dramatically increases researchers' insights into the social.

Interest in Big Data brings digital sociology into the realms of what has come to be known as the "computational social sciences." This "interdisciplinary renaissance" (Hannigan 2015: 5) sees social science questions being tackled through techniques developed within the data sciences. In an early call to arms, Lazer and his colleagues proposed that computational social science techniques could support ambitious sociological analyses, such as "what a 'macro' social network of society looks like" (Lazer et al. 2009: 722). Key techniques involve various means of data mining, modeling and mapping large-scale data-sets to support the simulation and analysis of social phenomena. In contrast to sociology's traditional preference for written text and (on occasion) numbers, computational social science approaches make extensive use of visual-based interpretations. All of this leaves Big Data methods appearing distinctly exotic in comparison to most other areas of sociological research.

Sociologists are making use of Big Data approaches in a number of ways. Alongside a resurgence of large-scale social network analysis, one particular area of interest is "topic modeling" from large corpora of textual data. As DiMaggio et al. (2013: 570) reason, the adoption of this approach from computer science and natural language processing addresses a long-standing methodological "puzzle" for sociologists faced with large quantities of textual data – i.e. "how can researchers ... capture the information we need, reduce its complexity, and provide interpretations that are substantively plausible and statistically validated?" Topic modeling does this by using algorithms to identify statistically proximate clusters of words (latent topics) that an analyst can then match to their knowledge of the field. By focusing on the co-occurrence of words, the technique offers a powerful means of highlighting contextual meanings, frames and symbolic boundaries of the patterns that are identified (Mützel 2015). Recent studies using this approach have explored everything from the prevalence of economic topics in the academic sociological literature to the public discourse surrounding Facebook's attempt to implement its "Free Basics" internet service in India (Shahin 2018). Big Data approaches allow these issues to be addressed at scale rather than on the basis of a few hundred texts. For example, Daoud and Kohl's (2016) study of economic sociology was based on analysis of 140,000 academic articles in 157 different journals between 1890 and 2014.

Perhaps the most popular forms of Big Data analyses involve examining outputs from Twitter, Instagram and other social media, which are appealing to sociologists for a number of reasons. These are mass archives of text, images and interactions between hundreds of millions of individuals. Moreover, these platforms are already configured to elicit sociological information from users – detailing networks of "friends," what people "like" and how they are feeling. Furthermore, from a technical point of view, platforms such as Twitter make data publicly available and provide APIs (application programming interfaces) that allow data to be easily extracted and reused. Academic journals now feature a growing number of social media Big Data studies which tend to analyze large corpora of posts by means of keyword tracking and sentiment analysis – examining how information is shared, alongside what emotions are expressed and opinions formed. The scale of these studies is often vast – for example, investigations of more than 60 million tweets relating to Occupy movements around the US (Agarwal et al. 2014) or nearly 4.6 billion tweets pertaining to public events over a 33-month period (Dodds et al. 2011). While many of these analyses are retrospective, some studies seek to analyze data on a real-time basis, supporting forms of "social listening" (Hollander and Hartt 2017) and even predictive forms of "social forecasting" and "social sensing" (Williams et al. 2017).

Notable early studies focused on social media activity that surrounded social movements such as Occupy, the Arab Spring and various instances of civil unrest and disorder around the world (see Bruns et al. 2013; Agarwal et al. 2014; Hoofd 2014). Other prominent areas of study include public discourse around national election campaigns and the sharing of images and videos in the aftermath of terror attacks in Europe (Williams and Burnap 2015; Bruns and Hanusch 2017). These latter studies seek to identify forms of "connective witnessing" and sense-making, exploring emotive as well as fact-sharing aspects of the responses. When replicated, such investigations allow for the tracking over time of significant societal shifts. As we saw in chapter 3, for example, studies of public reaction to repeated US race related incidents offer a powerful picture of the dynamics underpinning the still developing "national conversation on racism" (Houghton et al. 2018).

While such approaches have been well received and frequently cited, significant tensions have emerged between the promise and practicalities of Big Data analysis. These are incredibly complex procedures, and, while many sociologists remain wary of excessive claims of a new form of "forensic social science" (McFarland et al. 2016), it is easy to overlook the incomplete and inconsistent nature of such processes. Thus some observers are keen to stress that Big Data (and its analysis) needs to be seen as a contestable process, "often unreliable, prone to outages and losses" (Boyd and Crawford 2012: 668). Indeed, an obvious point to make from a sociological perspective is that these processes of meaning-making are never wholly neutral, objective and "automated" but are fraught with problems and compromises, biases and omissions. Thus, as with all forms of data generation, some of the key challenges to "big social data" relate to representation (with finite sets of characteristics being decided to "count" as a particular entity) and reductionism (with artificially neat boundaries and categories being drawn around data). These concerns extend into data analysis processes, with analysts invariably having to further clean up data-sets in order to render then "algorithm ready" (Mützel 2015), yet in the process inducing further omissions and simplifications. This also relates to concern over "machine bias" (Marres 2017: 120) and how analyses are shaped by the specific digital tools being used. For example, the predominance of studies favoring Twitter reflects the fact that Twitter makes data more readily available to researchers than platforms such as Facebook. Similarly, a researcher's choice of API to "scrape" data has been shown to generate substantially different results. Even before any interpretation takes place, it is important to acknowledge that these are not neutral data-sets and analytic tools which lead to objective results.

Perhaps the most serious limitation of Big Data is the issue of context. As Bail (2014: 477) concedes, "the most vexing problem is that Big Data often does not include information about the social context in which texts are produced." For example, while the large-scale Trisma data project involving 3.7 million Australian Twitter accounts was able to identify a "major spike" in Twitter signups coinciding with a devastating earthquake in Nepal, the researchers were forced to concede that "we've yet to determine why that event would lead to new Twitter accounts being created in Australia" (Bruns 2017). Concerns therefore remain over the descriptive nature of these analyses. As with all secondary data analysis, researchers inevitably suffer a "loss of control" over research design when using Big Data sets (Housley et al. 2014), limited in what can be achieved by the nature and form of the data at their disposal. Thus, it is increasingly suggested that this results in studies that offer little more than data exploration rather than data analysis. As Rieder and Röhle (2012: 70) put it, "while their results may be visually impressive and intuitively convincing, the methodological and epistemological status of their output seems unclear at best."

"Thick data" and the digital ethnographic turn

These latter concerns reflect a notable pushback against Big Data. While it would be misleading to talk of a methodological schism, growing numbers of digital sociologists are now questioning what is being lost in the turn toward the computational social sciences. Thus, while its stock might continue to rise in other disciplines, "the big data paradigm appears to have become somewhat becalmed" in terms of academic sociology (Halford and Savage 2017: 1139). Growing numbers of sociologists, it seems, have become suspicious of "the epistemological chutzpah of big data" (McFall and Deville 2017: 127).

In particular, while computational social science research can certainly lay claim to being "big," its application of "data" in a sociological sense is less convincing. As Venturini and Latour (2010) contend, the sociological idea of "data" infers some connection to context and setting, with sufficient meaning to allow the extraction of information. Instead Big Data – especially when derived from digital devices and platforms – is perhaps more accurately described as "traces." These traces are often linked to little more than an individual's "doings" (such as physical movements) and specific actions (such as transactions, choices, statements, interactions) (Ruppert et al. 2013). Thus the data that constitutes Big Data could reasonably be criticized as often "lacking in demographic detail" (Halford and Savage 2017) and other forms of sociologically "useful knowledge" (Venturini et al. 2017).

These suspicions are bolstered by growing acknowledgment of how the traces that constitute Big Data sets are shaped substantively by the digital devices and platforms by which they are produced. For example, a corpus of tweets represents a distinct form of communication – limited to 280 characters and shaped by protocols of hash-tags, sub-tweeting, "likes," and so on. In this sense, Twitter "conversations" are not natural speech acts but are structured and scripted by the platforms that facilitate their generation. Any conclusions drawn from a study of 4.6 billion tweets therefore carries the proviso that social media "perform and produce sociality as much as they describe it" (Burrows and Savage 2014: 5).

With these criticisms in mind, there is growing interest in contrasting the notion of "big and broad" social data with research that strives for specificity and granularity in the form of "small and deep" data. In particular, this has seen a notable resurgence of enthusiasm within digital sociology toward ethnographic sensibilities and approaches as a means of harnessing "the descriptive power of the social sciences" (Burrows and Savage 2014: 3). In contrast to Big Data, digitally related forms of ethnography suggest the use of a wide range of evidence sources to support the building of rich narrative and critical reflection. In this sense, it is reasoned that ethnographic studies of digital settings "can act as a contextual counter-balance" (Barrett and Maddox 2016: 703) to the computational social sciences through the generation of "thick data" with depth and meaning. As Tricia Wang (2013) describes, "Thick Data is data brought to light using qualitative, ethnographic research methods that uncover people's emotions, stories, and models of their world ... Thick Data can rescue Big Data from the context-loss that comes with the processes of making it usable."

One strand of this "thick" approach consists of so-called trace methods. These take inspiration from the STS notion of charting the journeys of objects, following how digital "things" move around and through coded architectures and networks. Such studies continue the tradition of "ethnography of infrastructure" (e.g. Star 1999), albeit with the distinction that these are investigations of coded rather than material structures. For example, "trace ethnography" of digital data (Geiger and Ribes 2011) focuses on the detailed traces generated and collated by online systems. These include transaction logs, version histories, institutional records, conversation transcripts and source code. Observation of how these various forms of data are (re)constituted and (re)circulated within digital systems can yield rich insights into online practices, collaborations and coordinations within the groups and organizations using them.

One example of this approach are trace studies of Wikipedia editing and administration, such as Geiger and Ribes's (2011) study of Wikipedia article deletion and Weltevrede and Borra's (2016) tracing of "processes of dispute" within Wikipedia's edit history and talk page functions. As Geiger and Ribes (2011: 1) observe:

> Analysis of these detailed and heterogeneous data ... can provide rich qualitative insight into the interactions of users, allowing us to retroactively reconstruct specific actions at a fine level of granularity. Once decoded, sets of such documentary traces can then be assembled into rich narratives of interaction, allowing researchers to carefully follow coordination practices, information flows, situated routines, and other social and organizational phenomena across a variety of scales.

This emphasis on software-based inquiry is also reflected in the continuing production of ethnographies of online communities situated wholly "in the network" (Lane 2016: 47). One of the best known of these studies is Tom Boellstorff's (2008) ethnography of the popular 2000s virtual world "Second Life." This study took place wholly online, reflecting Boellstorff's (2008: 60) commitment to researching online settings "in their own terms." Approaching Second Life in this manner led to detailed descriptions of inhabitants' enactment of online forms of intimacy and community alongside the development of shared understandings of place, time and "virtual personhood." The study also produced rich descriptions of the dominant forms of governance, surveillance and resistance within the virtual world. All told, Boellstorff produced accounts of Second Life that were as detailed as he might have produced of any face-to-face community or locality. Such studies therefore shine a valuable light on logics and practices of digital culture that other approaches underrepresent or overlook altogether. This is evident, for example, in recent ethnographic studies of the "dark web" (Gehl 2016) and communities of drug users using anonymous dark-web "cyptomarkets" (Barratt and Maddox 2016). It is hard to imagine how else these significant (albeit unfamiliar and under-reported) aspects of digital culture might otherwise be studied.

Alongside these fully "online" ethnographies are studies that combine digitally mediated descriptions with data generated through face-to-face encounters. The past ten years have seen a proliferation of such ethnographies, covering topics such as teenagers' everyday uses of digital media (Takahashi 2014), the working practices of software developers (Seaver 2017), and the establishment of community wireless networks in rapidly gentrifying urban areas (Cardullio 2017). While many of these studies are focused primarily on digital issues and topics, this growth also reflects acknowledgment among traditional on-the-ground ethnographers of the need to delve into the digital. For example, Jeffrey Lane's ethnographic study of street life in a Harlem neighborhood illustrates the ways in which the researcher quickly realized that "social life on the street unfolds in person and through social media" (Lane 2016: 43). As Lane continues, "my observations on the sidewalk were insufficient without the relevant digital data. The digital data alone would also have been inadequate … street life is characterized by its flow online and offline. As ethnographers, we have to keep up" (ibid.: 44)

Running throughout these studies is an interest in people's lived experiences of the digital. This is research that seeks to explore the multiple ways that the digital is encountered, the emergence of digital practices, and the cultural logics and shared understandings that develop around digital forms. One particular strength of this research is developing understandings of how people come into contact with the digital.

As noted in chapter 2, approaching the digital in terms of human experience is a key concern of digital sociology, yet this is an understandably tricky aspect to research. As Sarah Pink and her colleagues (2016: 16) reason, "experience is ultimately unique to individuals. We cannot actually access other people's experiences in any direct way." Thus while still relying on classic ethnographic methods of being-in-place, observing, talking, and generally hanging around, digital ethnography is increasingly exploring the empirical study of the sensually rich and varied nature of technology use. For example, using digital video, geolocation data and touch-responsive technologies, ethnographers are exploring how digital media are experienced through all senses. This therefore encompasses the bodily movements that take place around digital technologies, the three-dimensional shaping and textures of digital devices, the beeps, clicks, whirrs and other noises of technology, and even the heat and smells generated by devices.

All of the studies just outlined illustrate the value of ethnographic approaches in accounting for the digital. Most of these studies retain a fundamental essence of traditional ethnographic work, describing digital technology use as messy, performed, taking symbolic and material forms, and being locally enacted. In continuing these long-standing points of concern, digital ethnography offers a useful way "to understand the digital as part of something wider, rather than situating it at the center of our work" (Pink et al. 2016: 11). That said, all these studies involve the modification and refinement of traditional ethnographic practices. As Hine (2015: 6) puts it, this is "ethnography adapted for the circumstances that the contemporary internet provides." Hine distinguishes this as developing an ethnography "for" the internet, in contrast to ethnography "of" or "through" the internet.

Coding, programming and software development

Alongside Big Data and digital ethnographies is a burgeoning trend of research based around the design, development and implementation of software and coded artifacts. This approach chimes with a number of methodological ideas, not least Richard Rogers's notion of "natively digital" research, where he argues for repurposing the techniques and protocols of digital objects in the service of social research. As Rogers (2013: 1) puts it, this involves "thinking along with" (rather than thinking against) the digital devices and digital objects being studied. This can involve either repurposing digital media in ways that make them productive sources of social research data or even creating new code and software from scratch.

Such research also echoes Noortje Marres's notion of "approaching the digital *from the inside out*" – i.e. making use of methods that are "embedded in digital infrastructures and practices" (Marres 2017: 84, emphasis in original). However, some of the most generative examples of this approach occur when researchers are responsible themselves for embedding these methods into digital media. In this sense, clear parallels can be drawn with the idea of live methods, in particular the notion of playful and sometimes obtuse ways of doing research through the creation of artifacts and objects. All told, then, this is research that responds directly to the challenge that, "in relation to digital devices ..., we need to get our hands dirty" (Ruppert et al. 2013: 32).

There are a number of studies that reflect these aspirations. First is what Benjamin Haber (2016: 153) describes as code-based "active experimentation with the forms and formulas of digital media." Such an approach fits with recent thinking elsewhere in sociology and beyond. For example, there has of late been an uptake of experimental and interventionist research designs across many areas of sociology, as well as a rise of programming-based interventions in the humanities areas of "critical code studies" and "software studies" (e.g. Fuller 2008). In common with these areas, the driving impetus for digital sociology is to engage in design and implementation of software that is likely to push boundaries and test the limits of coded environments.

Interesting applications of this "build it yourself" approach include Birkbak and Carlsen's (2016) experimental analyses of the algorithms deployed by platforms such as Facebook,

Twitter and Google. Elsewhere, cultural geographers in the niche area of "drone methods" have been involved in piloting drones into unauthorized areas to test the material and coded parameters of data-based "geo-fencing" (Fish et al. 2017). Also of note is the use by Murthy and his colleagues (2016) of Twitter "bots" to explore the nature of public discourse during the 2015 UK general election. This latter study saw the researchers developing a series of "social bots" – algorithmically controlled Twitter accounts that are programmed to attempt to appear human. Social bots can either directly control their own accounts and create new content autonomously or else relay and repurpose messages from other pre-existing accounts. The researchers asked human volunteers to tweet using hash-tags from purpose-made Twitter accounts during key televised events in the election process. Bots were linked to the accounts of some participants, while other accounts remained untouched. This allowed the researchers to monitor how online political communication was influenced by autonomous as well as human interactions. These activities produced a series of temporal network graphs showing the development and diversification of the "bot-influenced" and "bot-free" online discussions.

Another strand of work has emerged from research in the emerging area of "critical data studies." One line of inquiry here is to explore processes of making "personal data" and the machinations of the commercial data-brokering industry more accessible to ordinary users (Kennedy and Moss 2015). Research by Skeggs and Yuill (2016) pursued this by combining information gleaned from Facebook's own official API with their own bespoke developed plug-in tool that was designed to extract data relating to participants' Facebook activity that was otherwise not available from the API. This plug-in revealed the advertising shown to users on Facebook, as well as indicating how Facebook was tracking users as they browsed elsewhere. This information was then used by participants to reflect on their engagements with Facebook – allowing the researchers to "open up the black box" of the platform, if only temporarily.

Other studies have worked with young social media users to co-create software tools to gain a similar sense of their personal data generation and its reuse by third parties such as advertisers and data brokers. Pybus et al. (2015) augmented the development of their "MobileMiner" plug-in with a series of hackathons to support participants' understandings of the personal data that was being generated and reused. Similarly, Selwyn and Pangrazio's (2018) "PDQ" smartphone app was co-created with young people to give participants insight into how their personal data was processed by industry-standard data analytics and profiling tools (in the form of three commercial APIs concerned with facial recognition, sentiment analysis and geolocation data). The focus of both these projects on repurposing APIs was deliberate. As Pybus et al. (2015: 4) reasoned, "if a user does not understand how they can leverage their API, nor understand its technical constraints, then they are unable to effectively interact with the platform."

Another strand of this approach is perhaps more obtrusive and bordering on absurdist. This work follows the live methods ethos of developing and letting loose "cultural probes" that test and reinvent relations with social settings and environments. Particularly noteworthy is Mike Michael's (2012) encouragement of "idiotic" methods, such as the "speculative design" of provocative objects and probes that might disrupt or misbehave in social settings. Indeed, Michael has pursued this approach in research involving the programming of nonsensical automated Twitter bots. In one study, researchers sought to explore the dynamics of Twitter-based discussions of energy reduction (Wilkie et al. 2015), testing the limits of what might be constitute acceptable actors, communities and practices. They developed and implemented three distinct social bots designed to respond earnestly, unpredictably or nonsensically to other users' messages that they calculated to be related to energy reduction topics. These coded incursions provoked many Twitter users to engage with the bots and therefore expose and test the constitution and dynamics of the community of Twitter accounts engaged in the area. As the researchers put it, this study used these coded interventions to "make visible the emergent actors, collectives and communities" on Twitter (ibid.: 90).

A similar approach was taken by Bayne (2015) in her development of a deliberately "dumb" teaching Twitter bot for a university online master's course with over 12,000 students. This coded experiment was intended to probe pedagogically generative instances where students encountered what they presumed to be a knowledgeable tutor, but soon realized this was not the case. Instead, the bot was programmed to return a series of pre-prepared statements, questions and provocations which were triggered by particular keywords as they appeared in students' course-related tweets. These researchers were interested in exploring the micro-level interactional implications of education delivered along AI-based, "post-human" lines. The study's use of what many students quickly came to befriend as "Botty" provided a speculative means of addressing these issues.

These latter provocative and contrary research approaches certainly offer an alternative to the grand, authoritative sensibility of the computational social sciences. These are interventions that are intrusive, annoying and antagonistic, yet serve an important purpose in unpacking the human/code entanglements that constitute all digital practices and environments. It could be argued that such "device-driven" (rather than "data-driven") perspectives on digital research direct attention toward "the operational capacities of digital media" (Weltevrede 2016: 2). Certainly, many of the examples just mentioned act to repurpose digital tools away from (and even against) commercial logics and imperatives of dominant platforms. Indeed, it is reasoned that these approaches are valuable in generating what has been termed thick data (as opposed to Big Data) that "trace the articulations of technical, corporate and media logics" (Langlois and Elmer 2013: 2). As Skeggs and Yuill (2016: 1368) concluded of their critical incursions into Facebook:

> We did "get inside" one example of capital's new lines of flight. Our understandings of lifeness and rhythms, via software and methods that visualized networks, interfaces, entanglements, algorithms, encounters, person/a/s, conductivity, platformativity, time, tone, transduction and lifeness, hopefully open out ways of understanding some of the ways by which Facebook works. ... It is a small sample of big data, designed not to just describe patterns and networks, but also temporal rhythms, attention and activity beyond and through the interface.

Looking to the future of digital sociological methods

Rather than facing a methodological crisis, it could be contended that digital sociology is emerging during a time of methodological opportunity. As this chapter has illustrated, digital sociologists have license to be flexible and eclectic in their appropriation of methods. If there is a common methodological approach to digital sociology, then it might perhaps best be described as a broad spirit of adventure rather than as a narrowly prescriptive set of rules and tools. In particular, digital sociologists are becoming increasingly confident in appropriating the digital aspects of what is being researched as potential tools (as well as objects) of study. As Ruppert (2013: 273) puts it, this is an area of sociology that demands the use of methods that are "more in and of" digital worlds – "not standing outside and detached from them as objects or subjects of inquiry."

As the examples in this chapter suggest, this involves being mindful of the forms of inquiry that might be inscribed within the devices, platforms and systems that we are researching – taking advantage of what Marres (2017: 103) terms "the methods of the medium" to engage in "a critique from within" (Ruppert 2013: 273). Sometimes this might call for being creative, playful and pragmatic, as can be seen in the act of repurposing (or even mis-purposing) digital media for social research purposes (Rogers 2013). Yet, for every instance of letting a few "idiotic" social bots loose on Twitter and seeing what happens, digital sociology is also home to studies that engage carefully and sensitively with collections of 4.6 million tweets. Digital sociology research can be broad and diverse in its approaches.

Indeed, alongside these developments it is important to recognize the importance of retaining and revitalizing traditional methods of research. As Marres (2017: 38) reflects, "we must not fall into the trap of "overstat[ing] the newness of digital sociology." Many digital sociology studies continue to make good use of interviews, observations, visual methods and documentary approaches in researching digital contexts. Much can continue to be gained from working with older sociological methods and methodological traditions, particularly as a respite from the relentless churn of digital systems and real-time data streams. Indeed, an undoubted benefit of "old-fashioned" interviews, observations and sample surveys is their capacity to force even the most hurried researcher or participant to slow down, take stock and pause for thought. Simply sitting down with interviewees face to face while "scrolling back" through their Facebook timelines can be a surprisingly effective method of inquiry (Robards and Lincoln 2017). However lively in intent, social research always benefits from taking one's time and thinking carefully.

Thus most digital sociologists remain open to using any type of method that offers them insights into the digital. Rather than sticking blindly to a limited and approved repertoire, digital sociologists are in the enviable position of being encouraged (if not expected) to take methods from software studies, computer sciences and data sciences and "adjust them to serve sociological purposes" (Marres 2017: 81). This does not mean grabbing hold of novel methods and techniques "simply because they are easy to use" (ibid.: 112). Instead, it means making appropriate use of the insights offered by "technology-centric," "data-centric" and "social-centric" approaches.

Of course, this entails a range of skills and competencies that might well lie outside the "comfort zone" of many sociologists (Zook et al. 2017: 1). Thus it is important that they gain a good grasp of the technological underpinnings of the new methods they are deploying. Anyone looking to enter digital sociology would do well to develop a working knowledge of data structures and algorithms, alongside skills in coding, programming and statistics. Digital sociologists also need to be skilled in terms of data visualization. This is not to say that we should all enroll for computer science degrees. Yet it is helpful at least to be able to have informed conversations about these tools we are "using" (or, more accurately, that are being "used" in our research). Another key area of development relates to ethical understandings of these methods. Having access to swathes of Big Data does not absolve researchers from the usual ethical standards expected from academic research – after all, it needs to be remembered that most Big Data "represent or impact people" (Zook et al. 2017).

Similarly, being "playful" does not diminish researchers' ethical responsibilities. Many sociologists were quick to condemn Facebook's "emotional contagion" experiments (conducted with psychologists from Princeton) that altered the newsfeeds of 689,000 Facebook users (Kramer et al. 2014). Yet how does this compare with the research ethics of introducing disruptive social bots into Twitter conversations and communities? The ethics of digital research are increasingly complex and contentious.

As these latter points imply, such methods do not require that digital sociologists simply develop technical skills. More important, perhaps, is developing understandings of these methods and "tuning in" to the sensibilities of these approaches and what they can do. This includes the ability to anticipate issues that are capable of being raised by the data being generated and therefore formulating appropriate questions. In terms of Big Data, for example, this is seen to involve viewing the social world on a considerably different scale from that which sociologists might otherwise be accustomed (Mann 2012). Thus, perhaps the biggest challenges raised by these methods are ontological. As Burrows and Savage (2014: 3) put it, the scope and scale of what these digital methods can tell us about social life "might demand nothing less than a fundamental re-description of what it is that needs to be explained and understood by the social sciences."

So to what extent does capacity exist within the sociological workforce to rise to these challenges? If capacity is lacking, then to what extent are these methods inherently interdisciplinary and demanding that sociologists collaborate with computational disciplines? For sure, the skilled labor of programming APIs, scraping data-sets and developing apps calls for expertise in the computer sciences and data sciences. What was referred to earlier as "build it yourself" is usually more practically a case of "get it built by somebody else." Even developing a simple app or plug-in is a complex, elongated technical process. Ideally, then, digital sociology is not something that can be conducted by lone sociologists. At the moment these are methods that are most successfully deployed through combinations of "computationally literate social scientists and socially literate computer scientists" (Lazer et al. 2009: 722).

The interesting question raised here, then, is whether such work might best be conducted by a new breed of trans-disciplinary "computational social scientists" – i.e. newly formed experts in the combination of both approaches. There are certainly moves afoot in many universities to train and nurture students along these lines. Yet the experiences of those already involved in interdisciplinary teams suggest that perhaps the most fruitful approach might remain collabora-tions between expert sociologists working alongside expert computer scientists. As Venturini et al. (2017: 3) reflected after ten years working in the "médialab" at Sciences Po in Paris, "engineers, computer scientists, developers and data geeks know how to nurture this kind of data in ways that social scientists still have to learn."

Thus, perhaps digital sociologists are best advised to get involved enthusiastically in these methodological advances while also retaining a detached critical sociological eye over proceedings. While developments such as Big Data certainly "challenge the praxis of doing sociology" (Mützel 2015: 3), this does not mean that sociologists need feel that they are placed on the back foot. Instead, digital sociology is already playing an important role in pushing back – questioning, challenging and subverting these methods in ways that best fit the interests and purposes of the discipline. All told, digital sociology can play a leading role in developing a compelling case for the need for sociological research in a digital age – as Burrows and Savage (2014: 3) put it, "to reinvigorate a sociological imagination ... in ways that could claim back a distinctive jurisdiction over the study of the social."

Conclusions

In times when sociological research faces a number of challenges (if perhaps not full-blown crises), digital sociol-ogy certainly offers an intriguing set of possibilities. This chapter has outlined a number of ways that digital sociology allows researchers to move beyond the usual social methods "toolbox." There is plenty of scope for the imaginative and ambitious use of Big Data, digital ethnography, and critical coding approaches. Yet, while these methods provide a useful space for sociologists to establish interdisciplinary approaches and collaborations with computational disciplines, we should not lose sight of the need to adopt and adapt such approaches in an appropriately sociological manner. Digital sociology is not simply a call for sociological researchers to reorientate themselves unthinkingly as data scientists, computer programmers and developers.

Indeed, digital sociology should perhaps be seen as a prompt for sociologists to augment and broaden their skills and competencies rather than narrow and displace them. In this spirit, we can now move on to the final chapter. This addresses the most practical of the four strands of the digital sociology project – i.e. implications of the digital for how we "do" sociology. This relates to the ways in which digital technologies and digital sensibilities are implicated in an expanded notion of sociological craft, scholarship and practice. So, what is the impact of digital technologies on the ways that sociologists are now able to work – particularly in terms of sharing content and engaging with others in more open and collaborative ways? What does it mean to be a digital sociologist in an age of online engagement and "impact"? How can we become genuine "digital scholars" while still remaining scholarly in what we do?

5
Being a Digital Sociologist

Introduction

For many readers, perhaps the most familiar aspect of digital sociology will be its implications for how sociology is "done." This final chapter reflects on the craft, scholarship and practice of digital sociology. In particular, it considers the close alignment between digital sociology and what has been described as "digital scholarship" (Weller 2011) and "networked participatory scholarship" (Veletsianos and Kimmons 2012). These labels convey the idea that academics now operate as "digitized knowledge workers" (Lupton 2014: 66) – i.e. working in ways that are inherently social, accelerated and openly connected with others.

Martin Weller (2011) – an early proponent of digital scholarship – points to three distinct shifts in digital practice that he sees as reshaping contemporary academic work. This entails (i) the diverse nature of the digital content that scholars now find themselves producing and consuming, (ii) the growing significance of social networks in academic work, and (iii) the "open" models of interaction and access inherent in working online. These characteristics differ significantly from twentieth-century scholarly practices, which were shaped by the analogue systems within which they took place. Weller contends that academic libraries, print-based publishing, face-to-face conferences, seminars and courses are all systems built upon the premise of maintaining high thresholds to accessing knowledge. In contrast, networked digital technologies can now support scholarly practices that are far less bounded. Key here are practices of "openness" and "sharing," which Weller (2011: 7) sees as technical features of new digital technologies as well as a "state of mind" for the people who are using them. So, if we accept that these shifts are now prevalent in academic practice, what does this mean for sociologists? Most importantly, in what ways is digital sociology entwined with these forms of scholarship?

The diverse nature of digital sociology practitioners

There is certainly an openness regarding who is engaged in digital sociology. As evident throughout this book, digital sociology involves scholars from a broad range of backgrounds. For example, as highlighted in chapter 4, digital sociology is an increasingly collaborative, interdisciplinary venture between social sciences, humanities, and computational and data sciences. Tellingly, many of the social scientists whose research comes under the aegis of digital sociology would consider themselves working firmly outside of "sociology." As was noted in chapter 2, some of the most sophisticated sociological questions of technology are being asked by academics who would describe themselves as urban geographers, critical data scholars, social media researchers, and so on. Digital sociology is not a field that fits easily into traditional notions of what "sociology" is.

This cross-disciplinary nature reflects the status of digital sociology as a "born digital" field of study. People are finding digital sociology to be an appealing base from which to work because of its development primarily in online environments rather than physical university departments. Regardless of an individual's immediate circumstances and contacts, the #DigitalSociology hash-tag and similar ports of call provide an invaluable "virtual staffroom" and supporting "collegial solidarity" for anyone interested in these issues (Lupton et al. 2017: 12). Unlike their colleagues in some other areas of sociology, digital sociologists are less concerned with your sociological clique or the institution where you happen to be employed.

This characteristic of digital sociology as a free floating field has proven especially significant for those researchers and writers employed in precarious quasi-academic jobs – what has become termed the "alt-ac" (alternative academic) workforce. Perhaps more than most other areas of the social sciences, digital sociology is home to a preponderance of individuals in non-research jobs within university administrations, as well as in roles such as librarian, museum curator and the catch-all category of "independent scholar." Indeed, digital sociology emerges during a time when it is increasingly difficult to secure employment as a university academic in any discipline at all. What Weller describes as lower "thresholds to access" therefore means that digital technologies are supporting the intellectual activities of early career, untenured and/or adjunct sociologists, all of whom are pursuing their intellectual passions without the safety net of full-time tenured academic employment. Digital sociology could therefore be seen as an inclusive field of study that operates around (and in between) traditional academic structures and boundaries. This stems directly from the acceptance of digital practices as a primary means of "doing" digital sociology.

The distinct nature of digital sociology practices

Digital sociology is an area driven by distinct ways of engaging with sociological work through digital means. These practices could all be seen to reflect what Weller described earlier as an embrace of networked ways of interacting and are illustrated in four broad areas of activity – i.e. communicating and interacting, writing and publishing, teaching and pedagogy, and engaging with publics beyond academia.

(i) Interactions between digital sociologists

One of the most notable shifts in academic practice over the past twenty years has been the rise of digital communication

and interaction between academics around the world. Unsur-
prisingly, then, digital media is a *de facto* means of how
digital sociologists become more knowledgeable, find things
out, and communicate information. This is especially the case
with social media, where questions are posed, information is
passed on, and references and links to work are shared. Social
media is also a valuable means of keeping "in the loop" –
from announcing calls for papers and funding opportunities
through to job offers and irrelevant gossip. In this sense, the
idea of "digital sociology" has been formed and sustained
largely through social media platforms and practices.

For many digital sociologists, this interactive engagement
is most frequently experienced through so-called academic
Twitter. While other social media are used by academics, this
particular platform has developed into a distinctive space for
scholarly interactions. Weller talks in enthusiastic terms of his
own personal networks of thousands of different contacts,
arguing that Twitter provides him with "an interdisciplinary network" par excellence. Certainly, the notion of digital
sociology continues to be explored and expanded through the
judicious use of hash-tags such as #DigitalLabor, #Sociology
and, of course, #DigitalSociology. The influence of Twitter
on academic practice is reflected in the changing nature of
the traditionally stuffy and staid academic conference cycle.
Now academic conferences are notable for high numbers of
people participating remotely, the backchannel of conversation that takes place on platforms such as Twitter, alternative
session formats (such as "un-conferences," "teach-meets,"
and so on), and offline social events where already digitally
connected collegial groups gather to meet on a rare face-
to-face basis. Small-scale digital sociology conferences and
symposia are followed online by many more people than
those attending in person, and a few events now take place
wholly online.

As might be expected, Twitter is better suited to some
forms of academic exchange than others. Academics soon
have to get used to operating in a different register – as
Stewart (2016) puts it, "navigat[ing] the cognitive dissonance
between orality-based expectations of sociality and print-
based interpretations of speech." One of the appealing features of a tweet – limited to messages of 280 characters – is

the lack of verbose academic discourse and waffle. Twitter is great for "Did you see?" or "Isn't this interesting?" type of interactions, hence the popularity of posts beginning with acronyms such as ICYMI ("in case you missed it"). Twitter also favors bold visualizations and snappy data presentations. Kieran Healy (2017: 778) praises the reach of "a simple graphic summarizing a bus-ride's worth of data analysis." On the other hand, reasoned discussions often tend to progress less successfully. Any interaction that might benefit from elaboration or clarification either migrates quickly to a different medium or else abruptly ceases. As Healy (ibid.: 776) concludes, academic Twitter is marked by "the tendency toward low engagement and rapid bouncing around."

Such uses of digital media therefore make digital sociology practices more immediate but not necessarily more straightforward. Through digital technology, the research community is no longer confined to the institution in which one works and the conferences that one can attend. From a positive point of view, it is argued that the dictum of "publish or perish" might be now reinterpreted as "platform and flourish" (Frost 2017), since some emerging digital sociologists amass considerable online academic reputations well before being awarded a tenured post. Yet digital communication is fraught with issues of public presentation of self. Social media have certainly emerged as an integral element "of constructing and performing the professional self for many workers in higher education" (Lupton 2014: 66). Thus there are obvious rewards and risks associated with being "seen" as a social media academic and the vulnerabilities of sharing one's "private deliberations in a public space" (Rainford 2016: 102).

(ii) Digital sociology writing

Of course, the thoughts of digital sociologists are not expressed exclusively through social media sass and snark – a large part of sociological scholarship remains "academic writing." Here, too, digital technology has impacted significantly on the ways in which sociologists write and how this writing is then seen. Digital sociologists are involved in a variety of different forms of academic writing, all of which are increasingly entwined and iterative in nature. For example, rather than devoting months to crafting a solitary 8,000-word journal article in the hope of its eventually becoming recognized as a magnum opus, many digital sociologists are happy to spend time riffing ideas on Twitter and later rounding these up to a few "blog-worthy" paragraphs. This might then morph into slightly longer and more polished pieces for outlets such as Medium, The Conversation or Huffington Post. Subsequent longer articles might then be directed toward various options – from open-access online titles such as *Sociological Research Online* through to one of the "print" journal titles. In these latter cases, "pre-publication" versions of the article might be posted to paywall-free sites such as Academia.edu, SocArXiv or university open repositories.

These varied forms of output also have a significant influence on the rhythm of academic writing. Many academic authors now engage in what might be termed serial "bricolage," writing in short bursts and garnering public responses to segments of material that might later be reworked and reconstituted in parts of a journal article or even a whole book. Thus, as Deborah Lupton (2014: 79) observes, "there is no longer an end-point to a publication, as its online form can be continually reworked, revised, mashed-up and otherwise transformed continually. This brings up the idea of the circulation of digital material on the internet and how such material may be constantly reinvented." For this reason, in contrast to its declining popularity elsewhere, blogging continues to find favor with academic audiences. Melissa Gregg (2006) praises academic blogging as a valuable form of "conversational scholarship," with many academics welcoming the opportunity for "slow thinking" and the iterative generation of ideas and knowledge sharing (Mewburn and Thomson 2017). Indeed, digital technologies also support collective forms of writing such as the movement of #ShutUpAndWrite groups coordinated through Twitter. There have even been a few instances of crowdsourced co-authoring of whole journal articles through collaborative tools such as Google Docs or Wikispaces (e.g. Al Lily 2016).

Many of the options listed above reflect growing motivations for academics to share access to their written output on a free-of-charge basis. This support for "the academic gift economy" (Lupton 2014: 77) in part reflects a belief in scholarship as a social good, as well as self-interest in getting one's work read as widely as possible. While most academics still shy away from self-publishing, there has been a recent resurgence of academic presses producing books that are distributed online free of charge and sold only in physical form. This has seen calls from some commentators for universities to embrace fully a "pirate philosophy" where academic writing is freely copied and redistributed (Hall 2016).

Of course, despite these good intentions, most digital sociologists still aspire to publish in the high-status outlets operated by commercial academic publishers. Thus the process of writing journal articles, book chapters and academic monographs continues to involve scholars engaging with a digitally driven academic publishing industry that is almost unrecognizable from academic publishing twenty years ago. For example, the dominance of online rather than physical distribution has led to a number of changes in the form and nature of academic publishing. A full-length monograph is now required to be planned and written in an "unbundled" form – i.e. with each chapter appearing in a standalone format with separate abstracts, keywords, and lack of cross-referencing. The old standard monograph of 80,000 words is being replaced by the "rapid" response "pivot" format of 20,000 to 40,000 words. Some texts are sold only in e-book format, with print-on-demand options for the occasional customer wanting a paper version. Similarly, while most of the prestigious academic journals operate behind expensive paywalls priced for institutional "block" subscriptions, an individual article can be designated "open access" at a cost to the author of around $2,000 to $3,000. Article titles, abstracts and keywords are now expected to be crafted with a primary emphasis on "search engine optimization." This means, for example, that article titles are now brief and to the point – with no puns or clever allusions and limited to a length of no more than seventy characters (after which Google will truncate them with ellipses). All told, writing for academic publication is a much altered proposition from what it was even ten years ago.

(iii) Digital sociology pedagogy

Another important aspect of digital sociology is teaching. On the one hand, this relates to opportunities to teach sociology using digital approaches – particularly on a "public pedagogy" basis where education is supported outside of institutionalized educational settings (Giroux 2003). These efforts often seek to make use of technology-based open approaches such as "open education resources" and the much hyped "massive open online courses" of a few years ago. These approaches seek to capitalize on what Weller (2011: 85) terms a "pedagogy of abundance." Weller reasons that digital technology has turned many of the traditional assumptions of teaching on their head – i.e. that teaching talent is scarce, that locating good teaching talent is difficult, that content must be physical, that content is manufactured to demand, and that access to content is scarce (ibid.). Many digital scholars see these developments as supporting the reimagining of education provision in subjects such as sociology. The argument is made that education can be provided in qualitatively and quantitatively different ways, with content and expert knowledge made freely available to be accessed and shared by mass numbers of learners. Teaching is no longer a case of expert-led instruction; rather, it is supporting individuals to learn how to make connections, develop the capacity to know more, nurture and maintain connections to support continual learning, and be able to choose what is best to learn at any particular time.

Second – and perhaps of more significance for digital sociology – are new opportunities to teach about digital topics and issues along sociological lines. As might be expected, digital sociology researchers are also beginning to develop and deliver courses around their topics of expertise. There are burgeoning graduate and post-graduate programs in "digital sociology," "digital society" and "digital media and society." There is also growing interest in developing teaching provision that harnesses the interdisciplinary nature of digital sociology. This relates to the teaching of technology and computational subjects to social science students, as well as the reciprocal teaching of social science subjects to technology and computer-related students. This has seen the growth of courses being taught to sociology majors on topics such as R, Python and "data carpentry." Conversely, there are efforts to teach issues surrounding morals, ethics and society to engineering and computer science students.

In addition, there is the development of "critical digital literacy" courses and provision. These are avowedly political reflections on digital technology and society – seeking to support what Emejulu and McGregor (2018) describe as "radical digital citizenship," and focus on critically analyzing the social, political, economic and environmental consequences of technologies in everyday life. Critical digital literacy courses often seek to support students to "collectively deliberate and take action to build alternative and emancipatory technologies and technological practices" (ibid.). In this sense, digital sociology offers an alternative to the apolitical, skills-based teaching of "digital literacy" that has developed in many levels of school and university education.

Third, there are clear implications for the orientation, training and preparation of professional sociologists at all stages of their careers. For example, meaningful engagement with the research methods outlined in chapter 3 requires various practical skills in interrogating software and code and in handling digital data alongside expanding people's "methodological imagination" in terms of the epistemological possibilities of digital techniques and tools (Marres 2017). Similarly, the various facets of "digital scholarship" just outlined in this chapter demand considerable amounts of practice. Of course, much of this knowledge can be developed through sustained personal engagement with the digital. In many instances, the most straightforward way of learning to be a digital sociologist is simply "doing" digital sociology – experimenting with digital tools and techniques and developing through experiential learning. While it is not necessary to reach the status of a fully expert user, it certainly helps if digital sociologists are adept and flexible. There is much to be said for being able quickly to get to grips with the various devices, systems and software that we encounter in our studies.

Yet, while much can be "learned on the job," some aspects of digital sociology undoubtedly require more structured approaches to development. Thus a major challenge is rethinking what "professional development" might now entail for sociologists. Here, a number of leads can be taken from developments in the digital humanities and allied subjects. For example, efforts to develop the technical skills of scholars working in the digital humanities suggest a need to look beyond "Coding 101" courses that provide a knowledge of programming languages and programming concepts. As Peirson et al. (2016) note, while some degree of technical competency is welcome, the ability to engage broadly with technical processes is more desirable than any specific ability to lead or conduct complex technological work.

Thus, instead of being trained to be data scientists or computer programmers per se, sociologists might more usefully be trained as "mediators" between sociological and computational communities. This suggests the development of "hybrid expertise" – i.e. skills and competencies to communicate and cooperate effectively with software engineers. Peirson et al. (2016) suggest that these "soft" skills can be developed by non-expert scholars being embedded within software engineering projects through work-based placements and internships. These secondments can position social scientists as participant observers who engage in "candid interactions" with software engineers and become adept at translating sociological concerns into a computational framework. Such knowledge can also be developed by sociologists being supported to "build their own" software. Regardless of the quality of any final products, the main benefit here is learning about software development processes and cultures. Peirson suggests that involvement in open source communities might be one low-stakes way of participating in software development.

All these latter suggestions involve professional sociologists reaching out to other disciplines. Many of the professional learning activities just described are best conducted in collaboration with computer scientists, data scientists and information specialists – all of whom stand to benefit equally from working alongside sociologists. While digital sociologists have already proven to be remarkably adept at self-organizing such activities along informal lines, clearly universities and faculties can begin to take more responsibility for providing such training. There is also scope for scholarly societies and professional associations to take a broader role in developing the digital capacities of their members. Indeed, the initial growth of digital sociology throughout the 2010s benefited from support from organizations such as the British Sociological Association and the Eastern Sociological Society. While to date it has developed largely *outside* of formal university bureaucracy, if digital sociology is to become an embedded, integral element of the discipline, there is an increasing requirement for institutional support.

iv) Public digital sociology

All these previous examples of digital sociology practice relate mainly to what can be done for groups of academics and students. In contrast, another important strand of digital sociology relates to what is described as "public sociology." Following Michael Burawoy's calls in the 2000s for sociologists to work toward the challenge "to engage multiple publics in multiple ways" (Burawoy 2005: 4), the imperative to engage in public sociology has been widely recognized. While some other areas of sociological inquiry might not have a ready public component, the topics and tools of digital sociology certainly take sociologists well beyond the academy.

In one sense, it is tempting to imagine that any instance of working online is a form of public accessibility and engagement. Healy (2017: 771) describes social media facilitating "a distinctive field of public conversation, exchange, and engagement" between academics and academic publics. Social media certainly make it easier for sociologists "to be seen" and, it follows, make it easier to "see" sociology in action. However, doubts remain over how engaging these public actions actually are. For example, after analyzing 153,000 tweets from 130 sociologists, Schneider and Simonetto (2017: 243) concluded that most were using Twitter primarily to generate information and "publish academic materials in publicly accessible spaces" with little sustained follow-up engagement with publics. Most often, Twitter was being used to "selectively engag[e] with colleagues about research matters" ibid.).

Thus simply working online seems, at best, to meet Burawoy's criteria for "traditional public sociology" – i.e. the online equivalent of writing opinion pieces for print media and offering comments on "matters of public importance." While this work is useful, it hardly fulfills the idea of "organic" public engagement – what Burawoy (2005: 8) describes as sociologists engaging in dialogue with members of the public in "a process of mutual education." In contrast, then, some digital sociologists are also exploring how meaningful forms of public sociology can be supported through more elaborate uses of digital technology.

For example, promising examples of this type of engagement have made use of digital technology to engage large numbers of public collaborators in what might be termed "citizen social science." As with the "citizen science" movement in environmental sciences, these activities support mass participation in research activities, thereby engaging the public in all stages of the research process. Mike Savage's "Great British Class Survey" (Savage et al. 2013) was one such example – using digital tools (notably a web-based "class calculator") and various forms of online dissemination and discussion to engage over 9 million people across the UK to explore the changing dimensions of social class. The project data-sets from the survey sample of 325,000 respondents were made publicly available through the UK Data Service, and public discussions were sustained through activities brokered through the BBC, newspapers and other forums. This is seen as a largely successful attempt to initiate a national conversation about social class underpinned by the use of simple but accessible digital tools.

The Great British Class Survey reflects growing interest in using digital media to make social data available for public analysis and consumption. In the UK, Cardiff University's "COSMOS" platform was developed as a publicly accessible digital observatory, offering various computational tools for harvesting, analyzing and visualizing social media data streams. Yet, such efforts to stimulate online public sociology are not as straightforward as they might appear. While it reached an agreement with Twitter in 2010 to archive every tweet ever posted in the US, the Library of Congress has still to work out how to make this vast, expanding archive accessible to the public, and recently it scaled back its initial ambitions. As Michael Zimmer reflected, "this is a warning as we start dealing with Big Data – we have to be careful what we sign up for" (cited in Daley 2017).

Finally, alongside these consensus-related forms of public engagement are more radical, politically driven approaches toward public sociology based around online forms of activism, advocacy and agitating for rights. For example, research around critical data studies is directed toward enhancing public understandings of data privacy and dataveillance, as well as alternative actions that advantage citizens rather than corporations. These include the co-constructed personal data projects outlined in chapter 4, alongside events such as Alison Powell's "Data Walking" initiative, where researchers lead community explorations of local data industry infrastructure – all efforts to support greater public understanding of contemporary data-intensive digital culture. Kennedy and Moss (2015) describe such activities as working toward the cultivation of "knowing publics" – i.e. publics who are knowledgeable about their engagements with digital technology, therefore increasing the potential for digital societies to know better themselves.

Other forms of public engagement with digital politics include more direct interventions. One high-profile example is the ongoing work of Trebor Scholz, a scholar-activist who has done much to define the field of "digital labor" outlined in chapter 3, while also advocating and agitating toward the establishment of platform cooperativism. This has seen Scholz and his colleagues work with local groups, lawyers and developers in order to establish cooperative platforms around the world to support the ethical "gig" employment of workers. Successful examples range from platforms brokering the services of refugee software programmers in Berlin to house cleaners in New York City. Scholz's form of scholar-activism demonstrates the possibility of working toward the practical addressing of issues raised by academic digital sociology. From this perspective, to paraphrase Karl Marx, the point of digital sociology is not only to interpret the digital world but also to change it.

Critical perspectives on "digital scholarship"

Whether striving to redefine the platform economy or simply share tips on Twitter about how best to teach introductory Durkheim, digital sociologists are clearly working in markedly different ways than might have been the case a few years previously. In fact, it could be argued that contemporary sociologists are compelled to engage in many of these practices. It is increasingly impossible for academics to avoid communicating with other academics online, teaching students online and/or engaging with the digital publishing industry. Whether they are aware of it or not, it could be said that all sociologists now engage in "latently public, ambiently visible" work (Healy 2017: 780).

Yet these new forms of digital sociology practice – and the work that is involved – require close attention (Allmer and Bulut 2018). If digital sociology takes pride in its capacity to remain circumspect about digital promises and technological solutions, then any excitement over the digital scholar needs to be approached with similar scrutiny. While there is much to admire in the enthusiasm of the "digital scholar" turn, it sometimes seems that these messages are tone-deaf to the politics of contemporary academic work. It could be argued that any embrace of digital scholarship ignores the problematic issues of digital labor politics, performativity and affect which need to be thought through more thoroughly (Woodcock 2018). These are all issues that digital sociologists are well used to discussing with regard to other people's digital media use. Amid the general enthusiasm for digital scholarship, there is growing need for some sociological critique and pushback.

First, if we see digital scholarship as a form of digital work, then it takes on a less empowering tone. It is important to acknowledge that digital sociology emerges at a time when academic sociologists are increasingly struggling to engage in sociological research. These are times of reduced funding for social science research, justified on the grounds of austerity and a steady shift away from funding the social sciences and humanities in preference to "proper" science. Put bluntly, sociological research is no longer deemed as fashionable or necessary as it once was. As such, the "agile," "innovative" and "guerrilla" practices outlined above all work in the favor of institutions and governments looking to divest disciplines such as sociology. Innovative practices such as "open access" resources, "crowdfunding" research projects, and so on, can be seen as low-cost alternatives to the proper funding and resourcing of sociology.

Moreover, it is important not to see the activities and practices described earlier as frictionless and effort-free. Many of these practices and approaches constitute additional (and potentially exploitative) work for academics and others around them. For example, maintaining a regular scholarly presence on channels such as Twitter or Academia.edu involves a considerable amount of unpaid academic labor. Similarly, the "rock star" lecturer broadcasting their wisdom to masses of students through a MOOC relies on the support of a range of labor from others behind the scenes. Most forms of online education rely on the casual labor of teaching assistants, e-learning support staff and other low-paid colleagues (Freund et al. 2017). Similarly, freely accessible outlets such as The Conversation and SocArXiv are reliant on considerable behind-the-scenes (often voluntary) labor. None of these innovations happen of their own accord.

Similarly, the capacity of digital sociology to accommodate sociologists working outside of the university system can be seen as problematic. Digital sociology emerges at a time when a majority of people pursing doctorates in academic sociology research will not end up working in full-time academic positions. Most young academics can expect to move job types and sectors during their working lives (Locke et al. 2016). While some are able to make a living as freelancers, increasing numbers of sociology PhDs are compelled to work outside the academy. Again, digital sociology could be seen as an enabler for institutions and funders looking to reduce costs and overheads associated with fully staffed, fully funded academic disciplines. There is a danger that digital sociology becomes the preserve of independently resourced part-time practitioners – a field reliant on people engaging in sociological work in their own (free) time and at their own expense.

Second, then, is the growing co-opting of these forms of digital scholarship into forms of performativity, accountability and measurement-based management that now pervade contemporary academia. This is sometimes presented in empowering terms. For example, it is argued that sociologists have all manner of indicators they can now draw upon in order to gain a sense of their online impact – from the number of followers and likes, through to who is downloading one's writing and from which part of the world. These measures combine to form "the academic quantified self" (Honan et al. 2015: 44). As our previous critiques of digital data suggest, such forms of feedback do not function solely in the interests of individual academics. This is particularly the case with metrics pertaining to reflect the "value" of academic writing and, it is extrapolated, the value of academics as writers. As Roger Burrows (2012) puts it, all academics are now "living with the H-index" – i.e. subject to various forms of "quantified control," accountability and auditing that stem in no small part from many of the digitized writing, publishing and dissemination practices described earlier.

Indeed, a profitable bibliometrics and citations industry has emerged to sell tools and analytics to universities eager to gauge the value of the academics that they employ. This includes various permeations of data related to official citations, which allow authors' success to be calculated in terms of an H-index, i10-index or mquotient. This logic is extended to other possible indicators of impact and engagement. For example, publishers and university authorities are making increasing use of so-called alt-metric measures – pertaining to reflect the social media impact of any article or book. Successful writing is now equated with maximizing one's number of clicks, views, downloads, recommends, shares, tweets and retweets. As Duffy (2017: 1) argues, the influence of "social media logic" is far removed from what academics might consider "the university's knowledge-making ideals."

The heightened accountability of online academic work clearly contributes to the fraught working conditions of contemporary academia. As Healy (2017: 771) reasons, the "attention economy" of academic work online creates "conditions for a new wave of administrative and market elaboration in the field of public conversation ... encourage[ing] new methods of monitoring, and new systems of punishment and reward for participation." The enhanced significance of online attention and "status" could be argued to be commodifying academics' actions in divisive ways. For example, universities now are keen to publicize academics whom they consider to be social media "stars," while at the same time censuring those whose social media activities do not chime with the institutional "brand." Social media are no longer something that an academic engages with on a personal basis.

Indeed, the work of most academics is becoming shaped by these prevailing conditions of metricization and the diminishment of writers to the status of content provider. Some individuals are adept at working in ways that "game" these systems – writing in a manner that mimics the popular online vernacular of clickbait content. Even if they are not engaging in such nefarious practices, the need to write in a manner that results in online impact is influencing what academics do. For example, being restricted to title lengths of seventy characters which feature keywords best suited to Google's search algorithm might seem like a minor inconvenience but marks a significant imposition on the freedom of academics to create knowledge. Crucially, as Burrows (2012: 368) contends, any academic who engages in online publishing and working through social media platforms is therefore "fully implicated" in the enactment of these forms of measurement and metricized scholarship: "we are all involved in the co-construction of statistics and organizational life."

Questions also need to be raised about the affective risks and conflicts inherent in digital scholarship work. Online academic communities reflect the best and worst characteristics of online communities in general. Digital sociologists are not immune to online acts of self-promotion, self-aggrandizement, over-sharing and passive-aggressive interaction. Indeed, it could be argued that digital sociologists can sometimes lapse into behaviors and practices that they might demean in others but of which they are less aware in their own online conduct. In many ways, social media amplify some of the less edifying aspects of academic life. For example, the emergence of online micro-celebrities in digital sociology replicates the hierarchizing of academic disciplines by "big names" and "celebrity dons." Similarly, despite talk of collaboration and interdisciplinary work, academia continues to operate along competitive lines. Grants, paper acceptances and job promotions are all finite resources being competed for by ever-growing numbers of scholars. At best, then, many academics could be said to engage in forms of selective – if not strategic – sharing. One can see how not every sociologist might experience digital scholarship as a completely collegial practice.

Indeed, there are aspects of digital scholarship that might be termed challenging. By working with online publics, sociologists are inviting multiple publics to contest their work. These include interest groups with particular ideological perspectives to promote, as well as trolls and other online abusers. As Lareau and Muñoz (2017: 19) put it diplomatically, sociologists who work online are exposing themselves to "audiences who do not have a neutral, dispassionate approach. And audiences may not always welcome the sociological analysis or research." Jessie Daniels (2017) argues that this is especially the case for sociologists who are female, queer and/or of color. Even if they are not subjected to personal abuse, then there is a strong chance that "these conflicts can create a turbulent environment where sociologists can lose control of their message" (Lareau and Muñoz 2017: 19). The internet is not the most welcoming place for *all* sociologists to present their work.

Finally, concerns can be raised over the potentially exclusionary nature of digital scholarship. As with any area of academia, digital sociology is not a totally "open" space or a wholly level playing field. Despite being well aware of the phenomenon, digital sociologists are not immune to the social media phenomenon of "filter bubbles." Depending on whom one follows, academic Twitter can come across as a supportive community or a self-congratulatory, smug clique. This sense of a homogeneous digital scholarship is certainly evident in the reproduction of academic hierarchies on platforms such as Twitter. While social media have promoted the careers of a few social media-savvy early career researchers, such success stories are not typical. Instead, established professors will often tend to attract more followers (and engage in fewer "follow-backs"), while established institutional "brands" often continue to carry more credibility in the sharing of content (see, for example, Jäschke et al. 2017).

Other forms of digital scholarship are also structured by the "network effects" that are exploited so effectively by companies such as Uber and Amazon. For example, there has been much recent excitement over the possibility of academics raising crowdfunding for their research through platforms such as Experiment.com. Yet the academics who are most successful in raising money in this way are those with expansive social networks, most notably their respective "reach" through online social media (Palmer and Verhoeven 2016). Given the trend for established professorial "names" to attract the largest social media following, there is a danger that trends such as crowdfunding increase the privilege of high-status academics rather than representing an alternative way of working around the system.

Conclusions: so what is digital sociology?

As these latter points illustrate, it is important that sociologists maintain critical distance from their own digital practices and passions. Developments such as "academic Twitter" and online publishing are no less problematic than any other aspect of digital society. Enthusiasms for digital scholarship should be tempered by concerns over unpaid labor, inequalities of participation, discrimination, and the like. Digital sociologists need to be as questioning and skeptical of their own digital practices as they are of the practices of others. Yet, beyond the need to be self-aware and reflexive, what else can be concluded about the question of "What is digital sociology?"? We therefore conclude the book with a set of final reflections on the benefits of taking digital sociology seriously.

The work reviewed over the course of this book certainly offers a critical perspective on what might otherwise appear to be relentless and unfathomable social change. In particular, digital sociology provides rich insights into the ways in which social life increasingly revolves around entanglements of code and physical space, human and non-human actors, and the automated generation and processing of data. While such shifts are being explored across many disciplines, digital sociology seems particularly adept at pointing to associated changes in social relations, social structure and social processes. For example, it is well placed to explore what it means to live in conditions where power and control is exercised though digital profiles, permissions and protocols. Digital sociology helps us understand the growing dominance of reconstituted and intensified forms of technology-based capital accumulation. And it challenges the idea that these changes can be governed only along profit-hungry lines of transnational tech-industry interests.

As has been argued throughout this book, digital sociology is able to make good sense of such shifts through the appropriation of interdisciplinary theory and methods and new modes of scholarly work. Crucially, this involves subjecting "sociology" to a number of necessary relocations. This chapter has considered, for example, how various forms of digital sociology work take place in predominantly online spaces. Elsewhere, we have discussed how digital sociology routinely looks beyond established disciplinary boundaries of "sociology," and often outside the academy altogether. All told, digital sociology is pushing the discipline in a number of new directions and dispositions.

Yet, it would be misleading to reach a set of conclusions about digital sociology that are too neat and tidy. It is important to acknowledge that there is not a unified approach to digital sociology with one consistent narrative. As with all areas of sociology, there will always be disagreement and contention over what digital sociology is and what it is not. People will continue to hold different views of what methods are most insightful and which theories are most perceptive and probing. In this sense, asking ten different authors to write a book such as this would undoubtedly result in ten significantly different lines of argument. Crucially, though, digital sociology thrives on its capacity to accommodate difference. This is an open field rather than a closed shop, and it has already proven a welcoming home for diverse perspectives, interests and convictions about the digital. Most importantly, coming together under the aegis of digital sociology offers a way of bringing these different approaches into dialogue (and hopefully collaboration) with each other.

One important theme that has emerged throughout this book is the ways in which digital sociology is intrinsically rooted in — rather than fundamentally opposed to — a long history of sociological work that precedes it. Digital sociology poses questions about technology that have long been asked within the discipline. Theoretically, then, much digital sociology work is grounded within traditions stemming back through the twentieth century. For example, methodological debates over the value of Big Data in comparison to "small data" and "thick data" could be seen as continuations of long-standing methodological "paradigm wars" and tussles over "mathematical sociology." Even the ostensibly novel aspects of open, networked digital scholarship map onto broader ongoing debates over how social scientists might best work in public and for the public good. In short, digital sociology is part of an ongoing evolution of the discipline – revitalizing classic sociological concerns while introducing novel (or at least substantially altered) points of contention and curiosity.

Hopefully, then, this book dispels any misconception of digital sociology being a new, superior or radically different form of sociology. It does not look to usurp or demean other areas of sociological work but, instead, is a means of augmenting and expanding sociological inquiry. This contrasts with the recent pushback against developments in the digital humanities, where critics have objected to a "destructiveness toward whatever is considered 'non-digital' among digital partisans" (Golumbia 2017). In contrast, digital sociologists have no interest in being disparaging or dismissive of what has come before. To date, there has been little hubris over the perceived merits of digital sociology in comparison to what might be seen as out-of-date, old-fashioned or "dead" forms of sociology. Sociology is not a competition, and digital sociology should not be placed in opposition to any other part of the discipline.

Returning to a theme raised at the beginning of chapter 2, it could be reasoned that describing the work outlined in this book in specific terms of "sociology" is not particularly helpful. Much of this text has considered critical digital research and writing conducted by scholars who might be sociological in their approach but would not limit themselves to being classified as "sociologists." Indeed, much of the best digital sociology work is being conducted at the interfaces of cultural and media studies, communication and information studies, anthropology, urban geography, and similar outposts of the social sciences and humanities. Tellingly, the journals where such ideas are being explored most vigorously are located beyond traditional catalogues of "sociology" literature. For example, *Big Data & Society*, *Social Media + Society*, *New Media & Society* and *Information, Communication & Society* feature a range of insightful digital sociological work alongside research and writing that is definitely non-sociological in approach. In this sense, a narrowly bounded idea of sociology fails to capture fully the sociologically complex work that is being conducted on digital issues and topics.

Nevertheless, continuing to stress the idea of a digital *sociology* remains a useful way of foregrounding long-standing sociological concerns in areas where discussions can otherwise slip quickly into the realms of the superficial and "pop." While there is always room for playful, provocative and creatively subversive approaches, digital sociology is also well placed to reflect our current post-Snowden, post-digital times of dissatisfaction and suspicion of the technologies that we have built for ourselves (or, more accurately, that have been built for us). In this sense, then, digital sociology offers a timely corrective to hitherto optimistic and individually focused accounts of digital society. Locating these discussions specifically in terms of sociology reminds us that this is a time for problematizing rather than celebrating digital technology. Whereas the early 2010s might have seemed an appropriate time for playful, cutesy and optimistic scholarship, the years leading up to the 2020s demand more critically aware and antagonistic approaches toward the technologies that are now dominating society. Sociology pushes us to ask questions of what we are *not* happy with (i.e. what we see as inappropriate and/or unacceptable), what we are going to do about it, and what we might want as an alternative.

Of course, developing a clear sense of the question "What is digital sociology?" now leaves us facing the practical task of making things happen. There is a host of hard work implicit in the development of any academic field. This includes the establishment of spaces that can support and sustain dialogue, such us conferences, journals and graduate courses. There is also considerable intellectual work that remains to be done, such as the various forms of theory-building, co-construction of knowledge, and testing of ideas and approaches outlined in this book. All told, there is plenty of work outstanding for digital sociology to be established as a sustained academic presence. In this sense, digital sociology is perhaps most usefully understood as a "moment" rather than a "movement." Digital sociology is not a unified set of principles to be followed dogmatically. Rather, it is a deliberate refocusing of attention, effort and thinking. Twenty years from now there may well not be a digital sociology per se ... but it is highly probable that all elements of sociology will be digital. Forward!

References

Abidin, C. (2017) #familygoals: family influencers, calibrated amateurism, and justifying young digital labor, *Social Media + Society* 3(2), https://doi.org/10.1177/2056305117707191.

Agarwal, S., Bennett, W., Johnson, C., and Walker, S. (2014) A model of crowd enabled organization, *International Journal of Communication* 8: 646–72.

Al Lily, A. (2016) A crowd-authoring project on the scholarship of educational technology, *Information Development* 32(5): 1707–17.

Allmer, T., and Bulut, E. (2018) Academic labour, digital media and capitalism, *tripleC* 16(1): 44–8.

Amin, A., and Thrift, N. (2005) What's left? Just the future, *Antipode* 37(2): 220–38.

Andrejevic, M. (2007) *iSpy: Surveillance and Power in the Interactive Era*. Lawrence: University Press of Kansas.

Aroles, J. (2014) Book review: Trebor Scholtz (ed.), *Digital Labor: The Internet as Playground and Factory, Work, Employment and Society* 28(1): 144–5.

Back, L. (2012) Live sociology: social research and its futures, *Sociological Review* 60(S1): 18–39.

Bail, C. (2014) The cultural environment: measuring culture with Big Data, *Theory and Society* 43(3/4): 465–82.

Banks, J., and Deuze, M. (2009) Co-creative labour, *International Journal of Cultural Studies* 12(5): 419–31.

Barratt, M., and Maddox, A. (2016) Active engagement with stigmatised communities through digital ethnography, *Qualitative Research* 16(6): 701–19.

Bauman, Z. (2014) *What Use is Sociology?* Cambridge: Polity [interviews with M. Jacobsen and K. Tester].

Bayne, S. (2015) Teacherbot: interventions in automated teaching, *Teaching in Higher Education* 20(4): 455–67.

Beer, D. (2014) *Punk Sociology*. Basingstoke: Palgrave Macmillan.

Beer, D., and Burrows, R. (2013) Popular culture, digital archives and the new social life of data, *Theory, Culture and Society* 30(4): 47–71.

Belk, R. (2013) Extended self in a digital world, *Journal of Consumer Research* 40(3): 477–500.

Bell, D. ([1973] 1999) *The Coming of Post-Industrial Society*. New York: Basic Books.

Berry, D., and Dieter, M. (2015) *Postdigital Aesthetics: Art, Computation and Design*. Basingstoke: Palgrave Macmillan.

Birkbak, A., and Carlsen, H. (2016) The public and its algorithms: comparing and experimenting with calculated publics, in Amoore, L., and Piotukh, V. (eds), *Algorithmic Life*. Abingdon: Routledge (pp. 21–34).

Bock, M., and Figueroa, E. (2018) Faith and reason: an analysis of the homologies of Black and Blue Lives Facebook pages, *New Media & Society*, https://doi.org/10.1177/1461444817740822.

Bodle, R. (2016) A critical theory of advertising as surveillance, in Hamilton, J., Bodle, R., and Korin, E. (eds), *Explorations in Critical Studies of Advertising*. Abingdon: Routledge (pp. 138–52).

Boellstorff, T. (2008) *Coming of Age in Second Life*. Princeton, NJ: Princeton University Press.

Boyd, D., and Crawford, K. (2012) Critical questions for Big Data, *Information, Communication & Society* 15(5): 662–79.

Bratton, B. (2016) *The Stack*. Cambridge, MA: MIT Press.

Brock, A. (2012) From the blackhand side: Twitter as a cultural conversation, *Journal of Broadcasting and Electronic Media* 56(4): 529–49.

Brooker, P., Dutton, W., and Greiffenhagen, C. (2017) What would Wittgenstein say about social media? *Qualitative Research* 17(6): 610–26.

Browne, S. (2010) Digital epidermalization: race, identity and biometrics, *Critical Sociology* 36(1): 131–50.

Bruns, A. (2017) Australian Twitter is more diverse than you think, *The Conversation*, May 3, http://theconversation.com/australian-twitter-is-more-diverse-than-you-think-76864.

Bruns, A., and Hanusch, F. (2017) Conflict imagery in a connective environment, *Media, Culture and Society* 39(8): 1122–41.

Bruns, A., Highfield, T., and Burgess, J. (2013) The Arab Spring and social media audiences, *American Behavioral Scientist* 57(7): 871–98.

Bucher, E., and Fieseler, C. (2017) The flow of digital labor, *New Media & Society* 19(11): 1868–86.

Bunce, M. (2018) Management and resistance in the digital newsroom, *Journalism*, https://doi.org/10.1177/1464884916688963.

Burawoy, M. (2005) For public sociology: 2004 presidential address, *American Sociological Review* 70(1): 4–28.

Burrows, R. (2012) Living with the h-index? Metric assemblages in the contemporary academy, *Sociological Review* 60(2): 355–72.

Burrows, R., and Savage, M. (2014) After the crisis? Big data and the methodological challenges of empirical sociology, *Big Data & Society* 1(1), https://doi.org/10.1177/2053951714540280.

Cansoy, M., and Schor, J. (2016) Who gets to share in the "sharing economy": understanding the patterns of participation and exchange in Airbnb, Unpubd paper, Boston College, www.bc.edu/content/dam/files/schools/cas_sites/sociology/pdf/SharingEconomy.pdf.

Cardullo, P. (2017) Gentrification in the mesh? An ethnography of Open Wireless Network (OWN) in Deptford, *City* 21(3–4): 405–19.

Carrigan, M. (2015) Towards a meta-critique of data science, October 13, https://markcarrigan.net/2015/10/13/towards-a-meta-critique-of-data-science/.

Casilli, A. (2017) Venture labor: how venture labor sheds light on the digital platform economy, *International Journal of Communication* 11(4): 2067–70.

Castells, M. (1996–8) *The Information Age: Economy, Society and Culture*, Vol. 1: *The Rise of the Network Society*; Vol. 2: *The Power of Identity*; Vol. 3: *End of Millennium*. Oxford: Blackwell.

Castells, M. (2000) Materials for an exploratory theory of the network society, *British Journal of Sociology* 51(1): 5–24.

Cavanagh, A. (2013) Imagining networks: the sociology of connection in the digital age, in Orton-Johnson, K., and Prior. N. (eds), *Digital Sociology*. Basingstoke: Palgrave Macmillan (pp. 169–85).

Cheney-Lippold, J. (2017) *We Are Data: Algorithms and the Making of our Digital Selves*. New York: New York University Press.

Christakis, N. (2012) A new kind of social science for the 21st century, *The Edge*, August 21, www.edge.org/conversation/nicholas_a_christakis-a-new-kind-of-social-science-for-the-21st-century.

Chun, W. (2015) Networks NOW: belated too early, in Berry, D., and Dieter, M. (eds), *Postdigital Aesthetics: Art, Computation and Design*. Basingstoke: Palgrave Macmillan (pp. 289–315).

Chun, W. (2016) Updating to Remain the Same: *Habitual New Media*. Cambridge, MA: MIT Press.

Chun, W. (2018) Faculty profile, Brown University, https://vivo.brown.edu/display/wchun.

Clough, P. (2018) *The User Unconscious: On Affect, Media, and Measure*. Minneapolis: Minnesota University Press.

Clough, P., Gregory, K., Haber, B., and Scannell, J. (2015) The datalogical turn, in Vannini, P. (ed.), *Non-Representational Methodologies*. Abingdon: Routledge (pp. 146–64).

Cockburn, C. (1992) The circuit of technology: gender, identity and power, in Hirsch, E., and Silverstone, R. (eds), *Consuming Technologies: Media and Information in Domestic Spaces*. London: Routledge (pp. 32–42).

Cohen, N. (2015a) From pink slips to pink slime: transforming media labor in a digital age, *Communication Review* 18(2): 98–122.

Cohen, N. (2015b) Cultural work as a site of struggle: freelancers and exploitation, in Fuchs, C., and Mosco, V. (eds), *Marx and the Political Economy of the Media*. Boston: Brill (pp. 36–64).

Coté, M., and Pybus, J. (2011) Learning to immaterial labor 2.0: Facebook and social networks, in Peters, M., and Bulut, E. (eds), *Cognitive Capitalism, Education and Digital Labour*. New York: Peter Lang (pp. 169–94).

Coté, M., Gerbaudo, P., and Pybus, J. (2016) Introduction: politics of Big Data, *Digital Culture and Society* 2(2): 5–16.

Cottom, T. (2016) Black cyberfeminism: ways forward for classification situations, intersectionality and digital sociology, in Daniels, J., Cottom, T., and Gregory, K. (eds), *Digital Sociologies*. Bristol: Policy Press (pp. 211–30).

Couldry, N., and Hepp, A. (2016) *The Mediated Construction of Reality*. Cambridge: Polity.

Daley, J. (2017) The Library of Congress will stop archiving Twitter, December 27, www.smithsonianmag.com/smart-news/library-congress-will-stop-archiving-twitter-180967651/#1xrrFrfTYRcsX hfa.99.

Daniels, J. (2009) Cloaked websites: propaganda, cyber-racism and epistemology in the digital era, *New Media & Society* 11(5): 659–83.

Daniels, J. (2013) Race and racism in Internet studies: a review and critique, *New Media & Society* 15(5): 695–719.

Daniels, J. (2015) "My brain database doesn't see skin color": colorblind racism in the technology industry and in theorizing the Web, *American Behavioral Scientist* 59(11): 1377–93.

Daniels, J. (2016) Bodies in code, in Daniels, J., Cottom, T., and Gregory, K. (eds), *Digital Sociologies*. Bristol: Policy Press (pp. 335–8).

Daniels, J. (2017) Interview with Inger Mewburn, in Lupton, D., Mewburn, I., and Thomson P. (eds), *The Digital Academic: Critical Perspectives on Digital Technologies in Higher Education*. Abingdon: Routledge (pp. 162–7).

Daoud, A., and Kohl, S. (2016) *How Much Do Sociologists Write about Economic Topics? Using Big Data to Test Some Conventional Views in Economic Sociology*, 1890 to 2014, Discussion Paper 16/7. Cologne: Max Planck Institut für Gesellschaftsforschung.

De Kosnik, A. (2013) Fandom as free labor, in Scholz, T. (ed.), *Digital Labor: The Internet as Playground and Factory*. New York: Routledge (pp. 98–111).

Dean, J. (2005) Communicative capitalism: circulation and the foreclosure of politics, *Cultural Politics* 1(1): 51–74.

Deleuze, G. (1992) Postscript on the societies of control, *October* 59: 3–7.

Dencik, L. (2017) Paper given at the ECREA Symposium, "Digital Democracy: Critical Perspectives in the Age of Big Data," Stockholm, November 10–11.

DiMaggio, P., Nag, M., and Blei, D. (2013) Exploiting affinities between topic modelling and the sociological perspective on culture, *Poetics* 41(6): 570–606.

Dodds, P., Harris, K., Kloumann, I., Bliss, C., and Danforth, C. (2011) Temporal patterns of happiness and information in a global social network: hedonometrics and Twitter, *PloS one* 6(12): e26752.

Duffy, B. (2017) *(Not) Getting Paid to Do What You Love: Gender, Social Media, and Aspirational Work*. New Haven, CT: Yale University Press.

Duffy, B., and Wissinger, E. (2017) Mythologies of creative work in the social media age: fun, free, and "just being me," *International Journal of Communication* 11: 4652–71.

Dujarier, M. (2015) The activity of the consumer: strengthening, transforming, or contesting capitalism?, *Sociological Quarterly* 56(3): 460–71.

Dutton, W. (2013) Internet studies: the foundations of a transformative field, in Dutton, W. (ed.), *Oxford Handbook of Internet Studies*. Oxford: Oxford University Press (pp. 1–23).

Edelman, B., and Luca, M. (2014) *Digital Discrimination: The Case of Airbnb*, Working Paper 14-054, Harvard Business School, www.hbs.edu/faculty/Publication Files/Airbnb_92dd6086-6e46-4eaf-9cea-60fe5ba3c596.pdf.

Edelman, B., Luca, M., and Svirsky, D. (2016) Racial Discrimination in the Sharing Economy: Evidence from a Field Experiment, Working Paper 16-069, Harvard Business School, www.hbs.edu/faculty/Publication Files/16-069_5c3b2b36-d9f8-4b38-9639-2175aaf9ebc9.pdf.

Ellul, J. (1964) *The Technological Society*. New York: Knopf.

Ellul, J. (1990) *The Technological Bluff* (trans. Bromley, G.). Grand Rapids, MI: Eerdmans.

Elmer, G. (2003) A diagram of panoptic surveillance, *New Media & Society* 5(2): 231–47.

Emejulu, A., and McGregor, C. (2018) Towards a radical digital citizenship in digital education, *Critical Studies in Education*, https://doi.org/10.1080/17508487.2016.1234494.

Evans, L., and Rees, S. (2012) An interpretation of digital humanities, in Berry, D. (ed.), *Understanding Digital Humanities*. Basingstoke: Palgrave Macmillan (pp. 21–41).

Feenberg, A. (1995) *Alternative Modernity: The Technical Turn in Philosophy and Social Theory*. Berkeley: University of California Press.

Fish, A., and Srinivasan, R. (2012) Digital labor is the new killer app, *New Media & Society* 14(1): 137–52.

120   References

Fish, A., Garrett, B., and Case, O. (2017) Drones caught in the net, *Imaginations: Journal of Cross-Cultural Image Studies* 8(2), http://imaginations.glendon.yorku.ca/?p=9961.

Flaxman, S., Goel, S., and Rao, J. (2016) Filter bubbles, echo chambers, and online news consumption, *Public Opinion Quarterly* 80(1): 298–320.

Flecker, J., Fibich, T., and Kraemer, K. (2017) Socio-economic changes and the reorganization of work, in Korunka, C., and Kubicek, B. (eds), *Job Demands in a Changing World of Work*. Rotterdam: Springer (pp. 7–24).

Flores-Yeffal, N., Vidales, G., and Martinez, G. (2018). #WakeUp America, #IllegalsAreCriminals: the role of the cyber public sphere in the perpetuation of the Latino cyber-moral panic in the US, *Information, Communication & Society*, https://doi.org/10.1080/1369118X.2017.1388428.

Flores-Yeffal, N., Vidales, G., and Plemons, A. (2011) The Latino cyber-moral panic process in the United States, *Information, Communication & Society* 14(4): 568–89.

Floridi, L. (2014) *The Fourth Revolution: How the Infosphere is Reshaping Human Reality*. Oxford: Oxford University Press.

Freund, K., Kizimchuk, S., Zapasnik, J., Esteves, K., and Mewburn, I. (2017) A labour of love: a critical examination of the "labour icebergs" of massive open online courses, in Lupton, D., Mewburn, I. and Thomson P. (eds), *The Digital Academic: Critical Perspectives on Digital Technologies in Higher Education*. Abingdon: Routledge (pp. 122–39).

Frost, C. (2017) Going from PhD to platform, in Lupton, D., Mewburn, I., and Thomson, P. (eds), *The Digital Academic: Critical Perspectives on Digital Technologies in Higher Education*. Abingdon: Routledge (pp. 36–46).

Fuchs, C., and Dyer-Witheford, N. (2013) Karl Marx @ internet studies, *New Media & Society* 15(5): 782–96.

Fuchs, C., and Sevignani, S. (2013) What is digital labour? What is digital work? What's their difference? And why do these questions matter for understanding social media? *tripleC* 11(2): 237–93.

Fuller, M. (2008) *Software Studies: A Lexicon*. Cambridge, MA: MIT Press.

Galič, M., Timan, T., and Koops, B. (2017) Bentham, Deleuze and beyond: an overview of surveillance theories from the Panopticon to participation, *Philosophy of Technology* 30: 9–37.

Galloway, A., and Thacker, E. (2007) *The Exploit: A Theory of Networks*. Minneapolis: University of Minnesota Press.

Galperin, H., and Greppi, C. (2017) *Geographical Discrimination in the Gig Economy*, Social Science Research Network, https://ssrn.com/abstract=2922874.

Gandy, O. (1993) *The Panoptic Sort*. Boulder, CO: Westview Press.

Garrison, K. (2010) Perpetuating the technological ideology, *Bulletin of Science, Technology and Society* 30(3): 195–204.

Gehl, R. (2016) Power/freedom on the dark web: a digital ethnography of the Dark Web Social Network, *New Media & Society* 18(7): 1219–35.

Geiger, R., and Ribes, D. (2011) Trace ethnography, in *Proceedings of the 44th Annual Hawai'i International Conference on System Sciences*. Los Alamitos, CA: IEEE (pp. 1–10).

Gillborn, D., Warmington, P., and Demack, S. (2018) QuantCrit: education, policy, "Big Data" and principles for a critical race theory of statistics, *Race Ethnicity and Education* 21(2): 158–79.

Gillespie, T. (2016) Algorithm, in Peters, B. (ed.), *Digital Keywords: A Vocabulary of Information Society and Culture*. Princeton, NJ: Princeton University Press (pp. 18–30).

Giroux, H. (2003) Public pedagogy and the politics of resistance: notes on a critical theory of educational struggle, *Educational Philosophy and Theory* 35(1): 5–16.

Golumbia, D. (2017) *The Destructiveness of the Digital Humanities*, June 5, www.uncomputing.org/?p=1868.

Graham, M., Hjorth, I., and Lehdonvirta, V. (2017) Digital labour and development: impacts of global digital labour platforms and the gig economy on worker livelihoods, *Transfer: European Review of Labour and Research* 23(2): 135–62.

Graham, R., and Smith, S. (2016) The content of our #characters: Black Twitter as counterpublic, *Sociology of Race and Ethnicity* 2(4): 433–49.

Graham, T., and Sauter, T. (2013) Google Glass as a technique of self and the revitalisation of the monad, in Osbaldiston, N., Strong, C., and Forbes-Mewett, H. (eds), *TASA 2013: Reflections, Intersections and Aspirations: Proceedings of the Australian Sociological Association 2013 Conference*, Caulfield, VIC, 25–8 November (pp. 1–13).

Gray, K. (2016) "They're just too urban": black gamers streaming on Twitch, in Daniels, J., Cottom, T., and Gregory, K. (eds), *Digital Sociologies*. Bristol: Policy Press (pp. 355–68).

Greaves, M. (2015) The rethinking of technology in class struggle: communicative affirmation and foreclosure politics, *Rethinking Marxism* 27(2): 195–211.

Greenfield, A. (2017) *Radical Technologies*. London: Verso.

Gregg, M. (2006) Feeling ordinary: blogging as conversational scholarship, *Continuum* 20(2): 147–60.

Gregg, M., and Nafus, D. (2017) Data, in Ouellette, L., and Gray, J. (eds), *Keywords for Media Studies*. New York: New York University Press (pp. 55–8).

Gunderson, R. (2016) The sociology of technology before the turn to technology, *Technology in Society* 47: 40–8.

Gupta, N., Crabtree, A., Rodden, T., Martin, D., and O'Neill, J. (2014) Understanding Indian crowdworkers, in *Proceedings of the 17th Conference on Computer Supported Cooperative Work*. New York: ACM (pp. 1–5).

Haber, B. (2016) The queer ontology of digital method, *Women's Studies Quarterly* 44(3/4): 150–69.

Haggerty, K., and Ericson, R. (2000) The surveillant assemblage, *British Journal of Sociology* 51(4): 605–22.

Halford, S., and Savage, M. (2017) Speaking sociologically with Big Data: symphonic social science and the future for Big Data research, *Sociology* 51(6): 1132–48.

Halford, S., Pope, C., and Weal, M. (2013) Digital futures? Sociological challenges and opportunities in the emergent semantic web, *Sociology* 47(1): 173–89.

Hall, G. (2016) *Pirate Philosophy*. Cambridge, MA: MIT Press.

Hannigan, T. (2015) Close encounters of the conceptual kind: disambiguating social structure from text, *Big Data & Society* 2(2), https://doi.org/10.1177/2053951715608655.

Haraway, D. (1985) *A Manifesto for Cyborgs: Science, Technology, and Socialist Feminism in the 1980s*. San Francisco: Center for Social Research and Education.

Hardaker, C., and McGlashan, M. (2016) Real men don't hate women: Twitter rape threats and group identity, *Journal of Pragmatics* 91: 80–93.

Hardt, M., and Negri, A. (2001) *Empire*. Cambridge, MA: Harvard University Press.

Harlow, S., and Benbrook, A. (2018) How #Blacklivesmatter: exploring the role of hip-hop celebrities in constructing racial identity on Black Twitter, *Information, Communication & Society*, https://doi.org/10.1080/1369118X.2017.1386705.

Healy, K. (2017) Public sociology in the age of social media, *Perspectives on Politics* 15: 771–80.

Hine, C. (2015) *Ethnography for the Internet*. London: Bloomsbury.

Hollander, J., and Hartt, M. (2017) Big data and shrinking cities, in Schintler, L., and Chen, Z. (eds), *Big Data for Regional Science*. Abingdon: Routledge (pp. 265–74).

Honan, E., Henderson, L., and Loch, S. (2015) Producing moments of pleasure within the confines of an academic quantified self, *Creative Approaches to Research* 8(3): 44–62.

Hoofd, M. (2014) The London riots and the simulation of sociality in social media research, *Journal of Critical Globalisation Studies* 7: 122–42.

Hope, A. (2016) Biopower and school surveillance technologies 2.0, *British Journal of Sociology of Education* 37(7): 885–904.

Houghton, J., Siegel, M., Madnick, S., Tounaka, N., Nakamura, K., Sugiyama, T., and Shirnen, B. (2018) Beyond keywords: tracking the evolution of conversational clusters in social media, *Sociological Methods & Research* [forthcoming].

Housley, W., Procter, R., Edwards, A., Burnap, P., Williams, M., Sloan, L., Farooq, O., Voss, A., and Greenhill, A. (2014) Big and broad social data and the sociological imagination, *Big Data & Society* 1(2), https://doi.org/10.1177/2053951714545135.

Hughes, K. (2014) "Work/place" media: locating laboring audiences, *Media, Culture and Society* 36(5): 644–60.

Hughes, T. (1983) *Networks of Power: Electrification in Western Society, 1880–1930*. Baltimore: Johns Hopkins University Press.

Ignatow, G., and Robinson, L. (2017) Pierre Bourdieu: theorizing the digital, *Information, Communication & Society* 20(7): 950–66.

Introna, L., and Nissenbaum, H. (2000) Shaping the web: why the politics of search engines matters, *Information Society* 16(3): 169–85.

Irani, L. (2013) The cultural work of microwork infrastructures: hacking Amazon Mechanical Turk, *Selected Papers of Internet Research 14.0*. Denver Association of Internet Researchers, https://spir.aoir.org/index.php/spir/article/viewFile/870/447.

Irani, L. (2017) Mechanical Turk, *Blackwell Encyclopedia of Sociology*. 2nd edn, New York: Wiley-Blackwell (pp. 1–3).

ITU (2017) *Measuring the Information Society Report*. Geneva: International Telecommunication Union.

Jackson, K. (2011) The drive-in culture of contemporary America, in LeGates, R., and Stout, F. (eds), *The City Reader*. 5th edn, London: Routledge (pp. 65–74).

Jameson, F. (1991) *Postmodernism, or, The Cultural Logic of Late Capitalism*. Durham, NC: Duke University Press.

Jarrett, K. (2015) *Feminism, Labour and Digital Media*. Abingdon: Routledge.

Jäschke, R., Linek, S., and Hoffmann, C. (2017) New media, familiar dynamics: academic hierarchies influence academics' following behaviour on Twitter, *LSE Impact Blog*, October 3, http://blogs.lse.ac.uk/impactofsocialsciences/2017/10/03/new-media-familiar-dynamics-academic-hierarchies-influence-academics-following-behaviour-on-twitter/.

Jurgenson, N. (2012) When atoms meet bits: social media, the mobile web and augmented revolution, *Future Internet* 4(1): 83–91, doi:10.3390/fi4010083.

Kennedy, H. (2017) Book review: Noortje Marres, *Digital Sociology: The Re-Invention of Social Research*, *Sociology*, https://doi.org/10.1177/0038038517732257.

Kennedy, H., and Moss, G. (2015) Known or knowing publics? *Big Data & Society* 2(2), https://doi.org/10.1177/2053951715611145.

Kitchin, R., and Dodge, M. (2011) *Code/Space: Software and Everyday Life*. Cambridge, MA: MIT Press.

Kolko, B. (2000) Erasing @race: going white in the (inter)face, in Kolko, B., Nakamura, L., and Rodman, G. (eds), *Race in Cyberspace*. New York: Routledge (pp. 213–32).

Kologlugil, S. (2015) Digitizing Karl Marx: the new political economy of general intellect and immaterial labor, *Rethinking Marxism* 27(1): 123–37.

Kowalski, R. (1979) Algorithm = logic + control, *Communications of the ACM* 22(7): 424–36.

Kramer, A., Guillory, J., and Hancock, J. (2014) Experimental evidence of massive-scale emotional contagion through social networks, *Proceedings of the National Academy of Sciences* 111(24): 8788–90.

Kuehn, K., and Corrigan, T. (2013) Hope labor: the role of employment prospects in online social production, *Political Economy of Communication* 1(1), www.polecom.org/index.php/polecom/article/view/9/64.

Lane, L. (2016) The digital street: an ethnographic study of networked street life in Harlem, *American Behavioral Scientist* 60(1): 43–58.

Langlois, G., and Elmer, G. (2013) The research politics of social media platforms, *Culture Machine* 14: 1–17.

Lareau, A., and Muñoz, V. (2017) Conflict in public sociology, *Sociological Quarterly* 58(1): 19–23.

Latour, B. (1987) *Science in Action*. Cambridge, MA: Harvard University Press.

Lazer, D., Pentland, A., Adamic, L., Aral, S., Barabasi, A., Brewer, D., and Jebara, T. (2009) Life in the network: the coming age of computational social science, *Science* 323(5915): 721–3.

Lee-Won, R., White, T., and Potocki, B. (2018) The black catalyst to tweet, *Information, Communication & Society* 21(8): 1097–115.

Leurs, K., and Shepherd, T. (2017) Datafication and discrimination, in Schäfer, M., and van Es, K. (eds), *The Datafied Society: Studying Culture through Data*. Amsterdam: Amsterdam University Press (pp. 211–34).

Levina, M. (2017) Network, in Ouellette, L., and Gray, J. (eds), *Keywords for Media Studies*. New York: New York University Press (pp. 127–9).

Lindgren, S. (2017) *Digital Media and Society*. London: Sage.

Locke, W., Whitchurch, C., Smith, H., and Mazenod, A. (2016) *Shifting Landscapes: Meeting the Staff Development Needs of the Changing Academic Workforce*. York: Higher Education Academy.

Lovink, G. (2011) *Networks without a Cause: A Critique of Social Media*. Cambridge: Polity.

Lupton, D. (2014) *Digital Sociology*. Abingdon: Routledge.

Lupton, D. (2016) The diverse domains of quantified selves: self-tracking modes and dataveillance, *Economy and Society* 45(1): 101–22.

Lupton, D., Mewburn, I., and Thomson P. (2017) The digital academic: identities, contexts and politics, in Lupton, D., Mewburn, I., and Thomson P. (eds), *The Digital Academic: Critical Perspectives* on *Digital Technologies in Higher Education*. Abingdon: Routledge (pp. 1–19).

Lyon, D. (2014) Surveillance, Snowden, and Big Data: capacities, consequences, critique, *Big Data & Society* 1(2), https://doi.org/10.1177/2053951714541861.

Mackenzie, A. (2017) *Machine Learners: Archaeology of a Data Practice*. Cambridge, MA: MIT Press.

Maddox, A. (2016) Beyond digital dualism, in Daniels, J., Cottom, T., and Gregory, K. (eds), *Digital Sociologies*. Bristol: Policy Press (pp. 9–26).

Maley, T. (2004) Max Weber and the iron cage of technology, *Bulletin of Science, Technology and Society* 24(1): 69–86.

Malin, B., and Chandler, C. (2017) Free to work anxiously: splintering precarity among drivers for Uber and Lyft, *Communication, Culture and Critique* 10(2): 382–400.

Mann, R. (2012) Five minutes with Prabhakar Raghavan: Big Data and social science at Google, *Impact of Social Sciences*, http://blogs.lse.ac.uk/impactofsocialsciences/2012/09/19/five-minutes-with-prabhakar-raghavan.

Marcuse, H. ([1964] 1991) *One-Dimensional Man*. 2nd edn, London: Routledge.

Marres, N. (2017) *Digital Sociology: The Reinvention of Social Research*. Cambridge: Polity.

Matamoros-Fernández, A. (2017) Platformed racism: the mediation and circulation of an Australian race-based controversy on Twitter, Facebook and YouTube, *Information, Communication & Society* 20(6): 930–46.

Mattern, S. (2016) Interfacing urban intelligence, in Kitchin, R., and Perng, S. (eds), *Code and the City*. New York: Routledge (pp. 49–60).

Matthewman, S. (2011) *Technology and Social Theory*. Basingstoke: Palgrave Macmillan.

McFall, E., and Deville, J. (2017) The market will have you, in Cochoy, F., Deville, J., and McFall, E. (eds), *Markets and the Arts of Attachment*. Abingdon: Routledge (pp. 108–31).

McFarland, D., Lewis, K., and Goldberg, A. (2016) Sociology in the era of Big Data: the ascent of forensic social science, *American Sociologist* 47(1): 12–35.

Mewburn, I., and Thomson, P. (2017) Towards an academic self: blogging during the doctorate, in Lupton, D., Mewburn, I., and Thomson P. (eds), *The Digital Academic: Critical Perspectives on Digital Technologies in Higher Education*. Abingdon: Routledge (pp. 20–35).

Michael, M. (2012) De-signing the object of sociology: toward an 'idiotic' methodology, *Sociological Review* 60(1): 166–83.

Morozov, E. (2011) e-Salvation, *The New Republic*, March 3, https://newrepublic.com/article/84525/morozov-kelly-technology-book-wired.

Mumford, L. ([1934] 2010) *Technics and Civilization*. Chicago: University of Chicago Press.

Mumford, L. (1970) *The Pentagon of Power*. San Diego: Harcourt Brace Jovanovich.

Murthy, D., Powell, A., Tinati, R., Anstead, N., Carr, L., Halford, S., and Weal, M. (2016) Bots and political influence: a sociotechnical investigation of social network capital, *International Journal of Communication* 10: 4952–71.

Mützel, S. (2015) Facing Big Data: making sociology relevant, *Big Data & Society* 1(1), https://doi.org/10.1177/2053951715599179.

Nakamura, L., and Chow-White, P. (2013) *Race after the Internet*. Abingdon: Routledge.

Nakayama, T. (2017) What's next for whiteness and the internet? *Critical Studies in Media Communication* 34(1): 68–72.

Neate, R. (2018) Apple leads race to become world's first $1tn company, *The Guardian*, January 3, www.theguardian.com/business/2018/jan/03/apple-leads-race-to-become-world-first-1tn-dollar-company.

Niesen, M. (2016) Love Inc., in Noble, S., and Tynes, B. (eds), *The Intersectional Internet*. New York: Peter Lang (pp. 161–78).

Noble, S. (2018) *Algorithms of Oppression*. New York: New York University Press.

Norris, P. (2001) *Digital Divide: Civic Engagement, Information Poverty, and the Internet Worldwide*. Cambridge: Cambridge University Press.

Ogburn, W. (1936) Technology and governmental change, *Journal of Business of the University of Chicago* 9(1): 1–13.

Ogburn, W., and Thomas, D. (1937) Are inventions inevitable? *Political Science Quarterly* 37(1): 83–98.

Orton-Johnson, K., and Prior, N. (2013) *Digital Sociology: Critical Perspectives*. Basingstoke: Palgrave Macmillan.

Palmer, S., and Verhoeven, D. (2016) Crowdfunding academic researchers: the importance of academic social media profiles, in *ECSM 2016: Proceedings of the 3rd European Conference on Social Media*. Sonning Common, Oxon.: Academic Conferences and Publishing International (pp. 291–9), http://dro.deakin.edu.au/eserv/DU:30084895/palmer-crowdfunding-2016.pdf.

Parisi, L. (2013) *Contagious Architecture: Computation, Aesthetics, and Space*. Cambridge, MA: MIT Press.

Pasquale, F. (2015) The algorithmic self, *Hedgehog Review* 17(1), www.iasc-culture.org/THR/THR_article_2015_Spring_Pasquale.php.

Peirson, B., Damerow, J., and Laubichler, M. (2016) Software development and trans-disciplinary training at the interface of digital humanities and computer science, *Digital Studies/Le champ numérique*, www.digitalstudies.org//article/10.16995/dscn.17/.

Peters, B. (2016) *Digital Keywords: A Vocabulary of Information Society and Culture*. Princeton, NJ: Princeton University Press.

Petitfils, B. (2014) Researching the posthuman paradigm, in Snaza, N., and Weaver, J. (eds), *Posthumanism and Educational Research*. Abingdon, Routledge (pp. 30–42).

Petre, C. (2015) *The Traffic Factories: Metrics at Chartbeat, Gawker Media, and the New York Times*. New York: Tow Center for Digital Journalism.

Pinch, T. (1998) Theoretical approaches to science, technology and social change: recent developments, *Southeast Asian Journal of Social Science* 26(1): 7–16.

Pink, S., Horst, H., Postill, J., Hjorth, L., Lewis, T., and Tacchi, J. (2016) *Digital Ethnography: Principles and Practice*. London: Sage.

Plant, S. (1996) *Zeroes + Ones: Digital Women and the New Technoculture*. New York: Doubleday.

Poster, M. (1990) *The Mode of Information: Poststructuralism and Social Context*. Chicago: University of Chicago Press.

Pybus, J., Coté, M., and Blanke, T. (2015) Hacking the social life of Big Data, *Big Data & Society* 1(1), https://doi.org/10.1177/2053951715616649.

Quill, L. (2016) Technological conspiracies: Comte, technology, and spiritual despotism, *Critical Review* 28(1): 89–111.

Rainford, J. (2016) Becoming a doctoral researcher in a digital world: reflections on the role of Twitter for reflexivity and the internal conversation, *E-Learning and Digital Media* 13(1–2): 99–105.

Rambukkana, N. (2015) *Hashtag Publics: The Power and Politics of Discursive Networks*. New York: Peter Lang.

Rheingold, H. (2000) *The Virtual Community: Homesteading on the Electronic Frontier*. Cambridge, MA: MIT Press.

Rieder, B., and Röhle, T. (2012) Digital methods: five challenges, in Berry, D. (ed.), *Understanding Digital Humanities*. Basingstoke: Palgrave Macmillan (pp. 67–84).

Ritzer, G. (1993) *The McDonaldization of Society: An Investigation into the Changing Character of Contemporary Social Life*. Newbury Park, CA: Pine Forge Press.

Ritzer, G. (2013) The technological society: social theory, McDonaldization and the prosumer, in Jerónimo, H., Garcia, J., and Mitcham, C. (eds), *Jacques Ellul and the Technological Society in the 21st Century*. Rotterdam: Springer (pp. 35–47).

Robards, B., and Lincoln, S. (2017) Uncovering longitudinal life narratives: scrolling back on Facebook, *Qualitative Research* 17(6): 715–30.

Roberts, S. (2016) Commercial content moderation, in Noble, S., and Tynes, B. (eds), *The Intersectional Internet*. New York: Peter Lang (pp. 147–59).

Robnett, B., and Feliciano, C. (2011) Patterns of racial-ethnic exclusion by internet daters, *Social Forces* 89(3): 807–28.

Rogers, R. (2013) *Digital Methods*. Cambridge, MA: MIT Press.

Rosenblat, A., and Stark, L. (2016) Algorithmic labor and information asymmetries: a case study of Uber's drivers, *International Journal of Communication* 10(27): 3758–84.

Roth, R. (2010) Marx on technical change in the critical edition, *European Journal of Economic Thought* 17(5): 1223–51.

Ruppert, E. (2013) Rethinking empirical social sciences, *Dialogues in Human Geography* 3(3): 268–73.

Ruppert, E., Law, J., and Savage, M. (2013) Reassembling social science methods: the challenge of digital devices, *Theory, Culture and Society* 30(4): 22–46.

Savage, M., and Burrows, R. (2007) The coming crisis of empirical sociology, *Sociology* 41(5): 885–99.

Savage, M., Devine, F., Cunningham, N., Taylor, M., Li, Y., Hjellbrekke, J., ... and Miles, A. (2013) A new model of social class? Findings from the BBC's Great British Class Survey experiment, *Sociology* 47(2): 219–50.

Schneider, C., and Simonetto, D. (2017) Public sociology on Twitter: a space for public pedagogy? *American Sociologist* 48(2): 233–45.

Scholz, T. (2013) Why does digital labor matter now?, in Scholz, T. (ed.), *Digital Labor: The Internet as Playground and Factory*. New York: Routledge (pp. 1–9).

Scholz, T. (2016) *Platform Cooperativism: Challenging the Corporate Sharing Economy*. New York: Rosa Luxemburg Stiftung.

Schor, J., and Attwood-Charles, W. (2017) The "sharing" economy: labor, inequality and sociability on for-profit platforms, *Sociology Compass* 11(8): e12493.

Seaver, N. (2017) Algorithms as culture: some tactics for the ethnography of algorithmic systems, *Big Data & Society* 4(2), http://journals.sagepub.com/doi/pdf/10.1177/2053951717738104.

Selwyn, N. (2016) Teachers vs. technology: rethinking the digitisation of teachers' work, *Professional Voice* 11(2): 18–24.

Selwyn, N., and Pangrazio, L. (2018) Doing data differently? Developing personal data strategies and tactics amongst young social media users, *Big Data & Society* 5(1), https://doi.org/10.1177/2053951718765021.

Selwyn, N., Nemorin, S., and Johnson, N. (2017) High-tech, hard work: an investigation of teachers' work in the digital age, *Learning, Media and Technology* 42(4): 390–405.

Sevignani, S. (2013) *Review of Digital Labor: The Internet as Playground and Factory, tripleC* 11(1): 127–35.

Shahin, S. (2018) Facing up to Facebook, *Information, Communication & Society*, https://doi.org/10.1080/1369118X.2017.1340494.

Shapiro, A. (2018) Between autonomy and control: strategies of arbitrage in the "on-demand" economy, *New Media & Society*, https://doi.org/10.1177/1461444817738236.

Sharma, S. (2013) Black Twitter? Racial hashtags, networks and contagion, *New Formations* 78: 46–64.

Shullenberger, G. (2014) The rise of the voluntariat, *Jacobin*, May 15, www.jacobinmag.com/2014/05/the-rise-of-the-voluntariat/.

Skeggs, B., and Yuill, S. (2016) The methodology of a multi-model project examining how Facebook infrastructures social relations, *Information, Communication & Society* 19(10): 1356–72.

Smit, R., Ansgard, H., and Broersma, M. (2017) Activating the past in the Ferguson protests: memory work, digital activism and the politics of platforms, *New Media & Society*, https://doi.org/10.1177/1461444817741849.

Srnicek, N. (2017) *Platform Capitalism*. Cambridge: Polity.

Stanworth, M. (1987) *Reproductive Technologies: Gender, Motherhood and Medicine*. Minneapolis: University of Minnesota Press.

Star, S. (1999) The ethnography of infrastructure, *American Behavioral Scientist* 43(3): 377–91.

Statistica (2018) Most popular social networks worldwide as of April 2018, ranked by number of active users, www.statista.com/statistics/272014/global-social-networks-ranked-by-number-of-users/.

Stein, J. (2016) Tyranny of the mob, *Time* 188(8): 26–32.

Sterne, J. (2003) Bourdieu, technique and technology, *Cultural Studies* 17(3/4): 367–89.

Stewart, B. (2016) Collapsed publics: orality, literacy, and vulnerability in academic Twitter, *Journal of Applied Social Theory* 1(1), http://socialtheoryapplied.com/journal/jast/article/view/33/9.

Taffel, S. (2016) Perspectives on the postdigital, *Convergence* 22(3): 324–38.

Takahashi, T. (2014) Youth, social media and connectivity in Japan, in Seargeant, P., and Tagg, C. (eds), *The Language of Social Media*. Basingstoke: Palgrave Macmillan (pp. 186–207).

Tanksley, T. (2016) Education, representation and resistance, in Noble, S., and Tynes, B. (eds), *The Intersectional Internet*. New York: Peter Lang (pp. 243–59).

Terranova, T. (2000) Free labor: producing culture for the digital economy, *Social Text* 18(2): 33–58.

Thebault-Spieker, J., Terveen, L., and Hecht, B. (2015) Avoiding the south side and the suburbs: the geography of mobile crowdsourcing markets, in *Proceedings of the 18th ACM Conference on Computer Supported Cooperative Work and Social Computing*. New York: ACM (pp. 265–75).

Turkle, S. (1995) *Life on the Screen: Identity in the Age of the Internet*. New York: Simon & Schuster.

Turner, F. (2017) Don't be evil: Fred Turner on utopias, frontiers, and brogrammers, *Logic* no. 3, https://logicmag.io/03-dont-be-evil/.

Valluvan, S. (2016) What is "post-race" and what does it reveal about contemporary racisms? *Ethnic and Racial Studies* 39(13): 2241–51.

van Dijck, J., Poell, T., and de Waal, M. (2018) *The Platform Society: Public Values for a Connective World / De platformsamenleving:*

strijd om publieke waarden in een online wereld. Oxford: Oxford University Press.

van Zoonen, L. (1992) Feminist theory and information technology, *Media, Culture and Society* 14(1): 9–29.

Veblen, T. (1904) *The Theory of Business Enterprise.* New Brunswick, NJ: Transaction Books.

Veletsianos, G., and Kimmons, R. (2012) Assumptions and challenges of open scholarship, *International Review of Research in Open and Distributed Learning* 13(4): 166–89.

Venturini, T., and Latour, B. (2010) The social fabric: digital traces and quali-quantitative methods, *Proceedings of Futur en Seine 2009: The Digital Future of the City.* Paris: Cap Digital (pp. 87–101).

Venturini, T., Jacomy, M., Meunier, A., and Latour, B. (2017) An unexpected journey: a few lessons from sciences Po médialab's experience, *Big Data & Society* 4(2), https://doi.org/10.1177/2053951717720949.

Volti, R. (2004) William F. Ogburn, social change with respect to culture and original nature, *Technology and Culture* 45: 396–405.

Wajcman, J. (2009) Feminist theories of technology, *Cambridge Journal of Economics* 34(1): 143–52.

Walker, A. (2012) Labor of recombination, *Subjectivity: International Journal of Critical Psychology* 5(1): 36–53.

Wang, T. (2013) Why Big Data needs thick data, *Ethnography Matters*, May 13, https://medium.com/ethnography-matters/why-big-data-needs-thick-data-b4b3e75e3d7.

Wark, M. (2016) The stack to come, *Public Seminar*, December 28, www.publicseminar.org/2016/12/stack/.

Wark, M. (2017) *General Intellects: Twenty-Five Thinkers for the Twenty-First Century.* London: Verso.

Webster, A. (2013) Afterword: digital technology and social windows, in Orton-Johnson, K., and Prior, N. (ed.), *Digital Sociology: Critical Perspectives.* Basingstoke: Palgrave Macmillan (pp. 227–33).

Weinstein, J. (1982) *Sociology/Technology.* New Brunswick, NJ: Transaction Books.

Weller, M. (2011) *The Digital Scholar: How Technology is Transforming Scholarly Practice.* London: Continuum.

Wellman, B. (2004) The three ages of internet studies: ten, five and zero years ago, *New Media Society* 6: 123–9.

Weltevrede, E. J. T. (2016) *Repurposing Digital Methods: The Research Affordances of Platforms and Engines.* Doctoral dissertation, University of Amsterdam, http://dare.uva.nl/document/2/168511.

Weltevrede, E., and Borra, E. (2016) Platform affordances and data practices: the value of dispute on Wikipedia, *Big Data & Society* 3(1), https://doi.org/10.1177/2053951716653418.

Wilkie, A., Michael, M., and Plummer-Fernandez, M. (2015) Speculative method and Twitter: bots, energy and three conceptual characters, *Sociological Review* 63(1): 79–101.

Williams, A. (2016) On Thursdays we watch *Scandal*: communal viewing and Black Twitter, in Daniels, J., Cottom, T., and Gregory, K. (eds), *Digital Sociologies*. Bristol: Policy Press (pp. 273–91).

Williams, M., and Burnap, P. (2015) Cyberhate on social media in the aftermath of Woolwich: a case study in computational criminology and Big Data, *British Journal of Criminology* 56(2): 211–38.

Williams, M., Burnap, P., and Sloan, L. (2017) Crime sensing with Big Data: the affordances and limitations of using open-source communications to estimate crime patterns, *British Journal of Criminology* 57(2): 320–40.

Willis, E. (1996) *The Sociological Quest: An Introduction to the Study of Social Life*. New Brunswick, NJ: Rutgers University Press.

Winner, L. (1986) Do artefacts have politics?, in Winner, *The Whale and the Reactor*. Chicago: University of Chicago Press (pp. 19–39).

Winner, L. (1993) Upon opening the black box and finding it empty: social constructivism and the philosophy of technology, *Science, Technology and Human Values* 18(3): 362–78.

Woodcock, J. (2018) Digital labour in the university: understanding the transformations of academic work in the UK, *tripleC* 16(1): 114–28.

Woolgar, S. (1991) The turn to technology in social studies of science, *Science, Technology and Human Values* 16(1): 20–50.

Zook, M., Barocas, S., Boyd, D., Crawford, K., Keller, E., and Gangadharan, S. (2017) Ten simple rules for responsible Big Data research, *PLoS Computational Biology* 13(3):e1005399.

Index

The Gig Economy

The Gig Economy

A Critical Introduction

Jamie Woodcock
Mark Graham

polity

First published in 2020 by Polity Press

Polity Press
65 Bridge Street
Cambridge CB2 1UR, UK

Polity Press
101 Station Landing
Suite 300
Medford, MA 02155, USA

ISBN-13: 978-1-5095-3635-1
ISBN-13: 978-1-5095-3636-8 (pb)

A catalogue record for this book is available from the British Library.

Typeset in 11 on 13 pt Monotype Bembo by Servis Filmsetting Ltd, Stockport, Cheshire
Printed and bound in the UK by CPI Group (UK) Ltd, Croydon

The publisher has used its best endeavours to ensure that the URLs for external websites referred to in this book are correct and active at the time of going to press. However, the publisher has no responsibility for the websites and can make no guarantee that a site will remain live or that the content is or will remain appropriate.

Every effort has been made to trace all copyright holders, but if any have been overlooked the publisher will be pleased to include any necessary credits in any subsequent reprint or edition.

For further information on Polity, visit our website: politybooks.com

Contents

Figures and tables

Figures

Table

Acknowledgements

We would first like to thank George Owers for commissioning and then supporting the book throughout the whole process, as well as Julia Davies and the rest of the team at Polity. We would also like to thank our three anonymous reviewers for their critical and constructive feedback. We are very grateful to Adam Badger who worked with us to source background material for the book and provided many insights and suggestions along the way. Adam is a wonderful colleague to work with on this sort of project. Thanks as well to David Sutcliffe for his extensive editorial support and always sharp suggestions, and to Ian Tuttle for his careful copyediting.

Giorgio Marani patiently worked with us on many drafts to get figure 1 just right, and we appreciate his skill and attention to detail in the final product. The fantastic illustrations in the final chapter were made by John Philip Sage. Thank you for visualizing the futures we hope to travel towards.

We owe an important thanks to the German Federal Ministry for Economic Cooperation and Development (BMZ) and the Deutsche Gesellschaft für Internationale Zusammenarbeit (GIZ), as well as the ESRC (ES/S00081X/1) for supporting our research in this area. We would like to acknowledge also the Leverhulme

Prize (PLP-2016-155), the European Research Council (ERC-2013-StG335716-GeoNet), and The Alan Turing Institute (EPSRC grant EP/N510129/1) for their ongoing support.

The book has drawn on previous and ongoing research projects at the Oxford Internet Institute. We are particularly thankful to the Fairwork team, including Sandy Fredman, Paul Mungai, Richard Heeks, Darcy du Toit, Jean-Paul van Belle and Abigail Osiki on the South African project; Balaji Parthasarathy, Mounika Neerukonda and Pradyumna Taduri in India; Sai Englert, Adam Badger and Fabian Ferrari in the UK; as well as Noopur Raval, Srujana Katta, Alison Gillwald, Anri van der Spuy, Trebor Scholz, Niels van Doorn, Anna Thomas and Janine Berg – many of whom also discussed the ideas and offered feedback on the manuscript. We also owe a debt of gratitude to our brilliant colleagues at the Oxford Internet Institute who apply a critical lens to digital work and the gig economy. We especially wish to thank Amir Anwar and Alex Wood for the many collaborations and conversations that have shaped our thinking on this topic. But we also acknowledge the rest of our research cluster for collectively building a research environment so conducive to critical, innovative and engaged research into the digital economy. Thank you to Sanna Ojanperä, Michel Wahome, Sai Englert, Adam Badger, Martin Dittus, Joe Shaw, Margie Cheesman, Marie-Therese Png, Fabian Braesemann, Chris Foster, Stefano de Sabbata and Ralph Straumann.

In addition, we would like to thank Phil Jennings, Abigail Hunt, Sanna Ojanperä, Nick Srnicek, Alessandro Gandini, Callum Cant, Wendy Liu, Robert Ovetz, Darcy du Toit, Sandy Fredman, Marc Thompson and Jason Moyer-Lee for taking the time to read an earlier draft of this book and for offering their incredibly valuable insights and feedback on the manuscript. Any faults or omissions are of course only our own. We are grateful to the role played by Antonio Casilli and ENDL in building a community of scholars focused on digital labour: a community that provided a fertile group for discussions that shaped this book. We would also both like to acknowledge Six Silberman and Christina Colclough for their support and friendship over the last few years. It has inspired and shaped much of the work we do.

Jamie would like to thank Lydia for her continuing and invaluable support, both in general and with more book writing projects. He would also like to thank the editors of Notes from Below who offered feedback as well as ongoing theoretical and practical inspiration. Callum Cant's *Riding for Deliveroo* (which is due to be published at the same time as this book) has been an important influence on making sense of the gig economy from the perspective of workers. Mark would like to thank his family. Jean Graham for raising a family whilst working in the gig economy. Thanks for your endless support to all of us despite all the challenges you have encountered as a precarious worker. And thanks to Kat: for always being a steady source of wisdom, advice and good humour – no matter how difficult a day of work has become.

Finally, we would like to thank all of the workers we have spoken to and whose voices we have tried to feature within the book. Ultimately, this is a book about hope for fairer futures of work. As such, we dedicate it to the workers whose stories are not already written.

Introduction

Everybody is talking about the gig economy. From newscasters to taxi drivers to pizza deliverers to the unemployed, we are all aware of the changes to our jobs, our professions, our economies and our everyday lives wrought by the gig economy. There are now an estimated 1.1 million people in the UK working in the gig economy, delivering food, driving taxis and offering other services – this is as many people as work for the National Health Service (Balaram et al., 2017). Eleven per cent of workers in the UK have earned income from working on digital labour platforms (Huws and Joyce, 2016), while 8 per cent of Americans worked on a 'gig' platform in 2016, rising to 16 per cent for the 18–29 age bracket (Smith, 2016). An increasingly common feature of the gig economy is the use of digital labour platforms – tools that allow employers to access a pool of on-demand workers. It is predicted that by 2025, one-third of all labour transactions will be mediated by digital platforms (Standing, 2016). Around the world, the number of people who have found work via platforms is estimated to be over 70 million (Heeks, 2017). Even more headline-grabbing are the numbers released in a 2015 study by McKinsey:

Up to 540 million people could benefit from online talent platforms by 2025. As many as 230 million could find new jobs more quickly, reducing the duration of unemployment, while 200 million who are inactive or employed part time could gain additional hours through freelance platforms. As many as 60 million people could find work that more closely suits their skills or preferences, while an additional 50 million could shift from informal to formal employment. (Manyika et al., 2015)

We have written this book as a critical introduction for those who want to find out more about how work is changing today. Throughout the book we draw on examples from our own research, stories from workers themselves, and the key debates in the field. Work is not just an interesting concept or debating point, but also something that most of us have to do. The conditions under which we find and undertake work can therefore tell us much about society around us – including issues of power, technology and who benefits in the economy. We wrote this book as engaged researchers, not only to document the rise of the gig economy, but also to critically explore how it is being changed right now by both workers and platforms, as well as how it could be transformed in future.

The focus of this book is on the precarious and fractured forms of work that have become known as 'gigs' (that is casual, piecemeal work) within the so-called 'gig economy'. These include things like delivery, taxis and domestic work. We also focus specifically on platform work, in which gigs are mediated digitally via platforms like Uber and Deliveroo. While 'gigs' have always existed across many sectors of the economy, the gig economy enabled by digital platforms is growing rapidly, and increasingly replacing non-platform gig work. By focusing on the platform, we can begin to understand how other kinds of precarious work are being reshaped, but also how this has already begun to affect the rest of the economy. In other words, we are in an important historical moment: one in which we are witnessing an unprecedented normalization of the platform-based labour model. It is therefore crucial to not just describe it, but also to shape it so that it can become more just and fair.

What do we mean by the gig economy?

The 'gig' in the term 'gig economy' refers back to the short-term arrangements typical of a musical event. An aspiring musician might celebrate getting a gig, or tell a friend that they have got a gig in the back room of a pub or other venue. This is of course no guarantee that they will get to perform regularly. There might be the chance of a repeat performance if they play particularly well, or are particularly popular – or it may just be a one-off. They might get paid – either a fixed fee, a share of the ticket price, or payment in kind (some free drinks perhaps). Their expenses might get covered. But also, they might not.

There are clearly some parallels here with the work we have already discussed. The tasks that underpin the gig economy are also typically short, temporary, precarious and unpredictable, and gaining access to more of them depends on good performance and reputation. However, work in the gig economy, as we will show, is very different to musical gigs. With much gig work, there is little possibility of career advancement – particularly if you are stuck doing endless tasks rather than 'a job'. What the term 'gig economy' captures is an economic transformation in which work in many sectors is becoming temporary, unstable and patchworked. It entails workers spending less time at one job, a risk of time spent without income, workers undertaking more jobs (possibly at the same time), and unpaid time spent searching for tasks or gigs.

In this book, we use the term 'gig economy' to refer to labour markets that are characterized by independent contracting that happens through, via, and on digital platforms. The kind of work that is offered is contingent: casual and non-permanent work. It may have variable hours and little job security, involve payment on a piece-work basis, and lack any options for career development. This relationship is sometimes termed 'independent contracting', 'freelancing' or 'temporary work' ('temp' for short). While the term has traditionally been used to refer to a broader range of activities that happen in both digitally mediated and non-mediated ways (such as bike messengers and cab drivers), we focus in this book on digital platforms because of the scale they involve. The platform is the digital base upon which the gig firm is built. It provides 'tools to bring together the supply of, and demand for, labour' (Graham and Woodcock, 2018: 242), including the app, digital infrastructure and algorithms for managing the work. As Nick Srnicek (2017: 48) has argued:

> Platforms, in sum, are a new type of firm; they are characterized by providing the infrastructure to intermediate between different user groups, by displaying monopoly tendencies driven by network effects, by employing cross-subsidization to draw in different user groups, and by having designed a core architecture that governs the interaction possibilities.

Platforms have become central to our social activities. They bring together users, capture and monetize data, as well as needing to scale to be effective. Indeed, they are now starting to mediate just about every imaginable economic activity, and they tend to do so through gig economy models. Many digital platforms have a low entry requirement and deliberately recruit as many workers as possible, often to create an oversupply of labour power, and therefore guarantee a steady supply of workers on demand to those who need them. In a world where people are talking about 'Uber' as a verb: 'the Uber for dog walking', 'the Uber for doctors', and even 'the Uber for drugs', it is important to understand both the histories and futures of this emerging – and increasingly normalized – model of work. The gig economy naturally has immediate effects on gig workers, but as it develops it will affect work more broadly in profound ways.

The rise of the 'gig economy' has become symbolic of the way that work is changing. The term refers to the increase in short-term contracts rather than permanent or stable jobs. It has been touted by many as offering much greater flexibility for workers, employers and customers, rather than the stifling nature of some traditional employment contracts. Employers can choose when and how they want to hire workers. And clients and customers can reap the benefits of this flexibility: getting food delivered quickly, hiring a web developer and ordering a taxi on demand has never been easier. Workers can supposedly choose what to do, how, when, where and for whom. Many are able to find jobs and income previously hard to obtain.

The gig economy, however, also has a dark side. Emerging evidence is pointing towards a range of negative outcomes for workers: low pay, precarity, stressful and dangerous working conditions, one-sided contracts and a lack of employment protection (Wood et al., 2019b). This can result in 'a raw deal' for workers, which in the US context can also be seen as an attempt to 'replace the New Deal' (Hill, 2017: 4). Some platforms have replaced previous kinds of work – for example, minicabs being replaced by Uber – whereas others are creating new kinds of jobs – the training of machine learning systems by image tagging and data entry, for instance. In all cases, existing working practices are being transformed. The so-called 'standard employment relationship' is being undermined through fragmented work and increased casualization. Activities that were previously considered to be a formal or standard job can be mediated through platforms to try and bypass rules, standards and traditions that have protected working standards. One example of this is the new platform being proposed for the UK's National Health Service that would have nurses bid for shifts under the guise of offering flexibility rather than being provided with more stable contracts.[1]

We focus on two kinds of work in this book. The first is what we refer to as 'geographically tethered work'. You may have used an app to order takeaway food, a taxi, or even someone to clean your house. This kind of work existed before digital platforms, and requires a worker to be in a particular place to complete the work – the pizza delivery person needs to transport a pizza from a particular kitchen to a particular house. What is new here is that the work process can now be organized over the internet, usually through an app. All over the world there are now delivery riders, taxi drivers, cleaners and care workers finding their work in this way. In some cases, these workers are highly visible, if we think of the brightly coloured uniforms of food delivery riders or the stickers on Uber drivers' windows. In other cases – such as home cleaning services – this is work that continues to be invisible to many, hidden behind the closed doors of the household. The second kind of work we focus on is 'cloudwork'. This refers to online freelancing, as well as shorter digital tasks called microwork. Online freelancing involves work that can be completed remotely, like web development, graphic design and writing that happen on platforms like UpWork or Freelancer. Microwork, on the other hand, involves much shorter tasks like image recognition and transcription that are typical on platforms such as Amazon Mechanical Turk. Both forms of work are organized digitally over the internet, with workers completing tasks remotely for the requesting organizations or individuals. Workers live all over the world, doing work that can come from anywhere.

The use of digital tools in gig work also makes many jobs increasingly invisible. While some platforms bring workers into contact with customers, others are obscured behind apps and websites. In many cases, this means we know little about the new experiences and challenges faced by gig economy workers. These issues are compounded in many industries and places by a huge oversupply of labour in the market. As a result of this oversupply, individual workers have very little power to negotiate wages or working conditions with their employers. It is this lack of power that workers have relative to their employers that is one of the reasons why workers in many industries have traditionally grouped together in trade unions. A group of workers is much better equipped to collectively negotiate with their employer, or other powerful actors in the value chains of work, than a single one is. Yet, in most countries, the existing trade union movement lacks effective strategies to organize gig workers.

As there are an increasing number of workers finding employment through platforms, the relative lack of collective voice for platform workers poses important questions about their ability to collectively organize and bargain with platforms and employers. There are exciting examples of new forms of worker organizing on platforms that offer geographically tethered work – for example, the Deliveroo struggles taking place across multiple European countries, or the attempts by platform delivery drivers across Africa and Asia to collectively demand better working conditions. The location-specific nature of this sort of work offers the opportunity for workers to come together, organize and collectively withdraw their labour. But it is worth remembering that much of what is done in the gig economy has very little co-presence in either time or space. Online freelancing jobs can just as easily be done next door or on the other side of the world. It is therefore less clear what forms organizing can take in those contexts.

This book considers some of the key social, economic and political implications of these transformations of work – providing an account of the development, debates and operation of the gig economy. These themes are then further explored by looking at the experience of gig workers themselves, as well as considering emerging forms of resistance and pathways towards less exploitative forms of work.

Why did we write this book?

Both authors have studied work, and workers, in the gig economy in various ways since the gig economy took off, including extended periods of on-the-ground research in the UK, the Philippines, Vietnam, Kenya, Nigeria, Ghana, Uganda, Rwanda, South Africa and India.[2] In addition to our qualitative and ethnographic fieldwork, we have carried out large-scale surveys, and mapped quantitative datasets that reveal global-scale patterns of trade in work through gig economy platforms. However, what has struck us most in our research on the gig economy are the stories from the workers themselves. These stories should be at the centre of any discussion about the transformation of work. We would like to start with two that have particularly stuck with us.

Jamie has been doing research with Deliveroo riders in London since June 2016: observing, interviewing and using forms of co-research in collaboration with workers. Delivering food is an example of 'geographically tethered' work. One of the riders, who had been a participant in Jamie's research since the beginning, told a particularly revealing story about the experience of working for Deliveroo. At the end of an interview, Jamie asked the driver what he thought the most challenging part of the work was. Expecting the driver to mention the low pay, insecure contracts or threat of accidents, he was instead told the following story. The driver worked at two other jobs in addition to Deliveroo. In the morning he would wake up and go to the first job, trying to eat breakfast before he left. Over lunch he worked a shift for Deliveroo, making sure to grab something quick to eat on the way. In the afternoon he worked at the third job, before starting the evening shift at Deliveroo. The most challenging aspect of the work was making sure he ate enough food once he got home to ensure he had the energy to get up and repeat the process the next day. Deliveroo is marketed as a service for delivering food to stylish young professionals, but the reality is that many of his deliveries were to people too exhausted from working to make their own dinner. This is especially ironic given how Deliveroo brands itself. His story is therefore a damning indictment of the realities of gig work in London: a worker struggling to eat enough calories to deliver food to people who are too tired from work to make their own.

Mark has been studying and speaking with cloudworkers in Sub-Saharan Africa since 2009. In 2017, he and his colleague Amir Anwar spoke to an online freelancer in Takoradi, a medium-sized city in Western Ghana, who primarily sourced work through Upwork.com.[3] The worker, a university graduate with a family to support, previously worked at a local firm in Takoradi. After doing some freelancing on Upwork at nights and weekends, he decided to take the plunge and quit his job in the local economy. He now completes a variety of tasks (including app testing, data entry, technical writing and search engine optimization). While these tasks are fairly varied, they have two things in common. First, they pay better than his previous job in Ghana. Second, he is rarely told what they are for, or why he is doing them. He knows, for instance, that he needs to write a short article on gardening. But isn't told why the client needs it or how they create value from it. While the pay is good, the pressures to deliver are extremely high. In the online freelancing world, reputation is everything and workers are terrified of not receiving a five star review from clients Reviews from people the worker does not know have become an important part of management in the gig economy. Compounding this issue is the sporadic nature of work. When contracts are obtained by workers, they often need to be carried out very quickly. As such, the worker we spoke to ended up working extremely long shifts. He described multiple 48-hour marathon working sessions without sleep, simply in order to not disappoint his clients. Despite these gruelling work conditions, he maintained a positive outlook on his work: optimistically recalling that the other job options in Takoradi are also not perfect. His story highlights some of the key tensions in the global gig economy. Workers try to make a living in a hyper-competitive planetary labour market; clients and platforms take zero responsibility for their working conditions; and yet workers are often relatively satisfied with that state of affairs because of the lack of other good options.

What will the book cover?

These short accounts do not tell the whole story of the gig economy, but they are an important starting point for understanding what is at stake. These two positions, one of a significant erosion of working conditions, the other of hard work, but new opportunities, capture the complex and sometimes contradictory nature of the phenomenon. The gig economy is full of other such stories: stories of hope, success, desperation, exploitation and everything in between. In this book, we draw on a combination of these accounts – from our own research as well as that of others – to tell the story of how digital technology is changing the nature of work. Our assumption is that workers' own experiences can be a powerful tool to explain broader changes in society (Woodcock, 2014a).

In chapter 1, we discuss where the gig economy came from. This starts by looking at other forms of work that came before it, exploring how precarious work has a much longer history, including on the docks and in factories. We then introduce the political economy, technological and social preconditions that have facilitated the rise of the gig economy. In chapter 2, we explore how the gig economy works by examining the platforms that organize this work. This involves first exploring how work platforms serve as intermediaries, then using Uber as an example to illustrate the key dynamics of this kind of operation. We explain the geographically tethered and cloudwork models. The focus shifts in chapter 3 as we move on to explore what it is like to work in the gig economy. This draws on the voices of workers, across both kinds of gig work. We present stories and experiences of workers we have met through our research, showing the complex relationship that workers have to this new kind of working arrangement. In chapter 4, we continue the focus on workers to outline how they are resisting and reshaping the gig economy, tracing emerging forms and trends. In the final chapter of the book, we summarize and reiterate the arguments we have made about the gig economy and platform work into four alternative futures, involving transparency, accountability, worker power and democratic ownership – as well as what *you* can do.

1
Where did the gig economy come from?

In this chapter, we critically examine how the gig economy came into being. We begin by considering earlier forms of work that were marked by on-demand labour and precarious conditions, and explore how these dynamics have shifted and transformed into what is commonly referred to today as 'gig work'. In other words, contingent jobs that happen through, via and on digital platforms.

In the early stages, new kinds of gigs held ambiguous possibilities. As Sarah Kessler (2018: x) recounts in a story from a startup founder, the gig economy had a promise that 'we could work for our neighbours, connect with as many projects as we needed to get by, and fit those gigs between band rehearsals, gardening, and other passion promises.' At this point, some commentators began talking about the 'sharing economy' (Sundararajan, 2017), a term that sounds very optimistic in light of the evidence that followed.

Although there have been changes in the gig economy, it still involves work. At its core, paid work involves a relationship in which one person sells their time to another. This entails transferring the ownership of labour power (the capacity to work) from the worker to the owner of capital (the owner of the things needed to produce work). As Marx (1976: 272) noted, this relationship requires workers who 'are free in a double sense'. They are free to choose who to work for, but at the same time (lacking capital) also 'free' from any other way of making a living other than by selling their labour power. This means that the worker is put at a disadvantage when selling their time. They rely on work to meet their needs, and are under constant pressure to both find and keep work. From this simple starting point of one person buying the time of another, work has developed into vastly more complex forms. Relationships of work now spread across the world, bound in complex chains of supply and demand, and bringing people together in new and different ways. However, despite the organizational complexities of modern work, the fundamental relationship between the person who buys time and the person who sells it remains a core concern.

Work has always been a changing phenomenon, both evolving over time and changing as it is fought over. The transformation of work has become a popular topic of research, debate and discussion. It is, after all, the activity that most of us will spend the majority of our time doing. The gig economy, particularly mediated through new digital platforms, is at the forefront of changes in work today. However, before focusing on the growth of the gig economy and its implications, we must consider how it is connected to the kinds of work that came before. The recent changes in work relationships are often discussed as a break from the so-called 'standard employment relationship'. This term refers to the kinds of work found in the Global North after the Second World War. For workers, this meant the expectation of a 'stable, socially protected, dependent, full-time job ... the basic conditions of which (working time, pay, social transfers) are regulated to a minimum level by collective agreement or by labour and/or social security law' (Bosch, 2004: 618–19). These kinds of work involved a 'link' between the work relationship (i.e. between the buyers and sellers of time) and the 'wider risk-sharing role of the welfare or social state', which came to prominence by the middle of the twentieth century (Fudge, 2017: 379). This meant that the risks of work were increasingly mitigated through social agreements, particularly with social security nets that could cushion workers from some negative outcomes, such as lack of work, poor working conditions or illness and accidents. Of course, referring to 'the standard employment relationship' carries with it the implication that this is somehow the 'normal' state of affairs. It then follows that precarious work should be understood as a break from this norm, as an attack that newly undermines long-standing conditions and benefits.

Precarious work, however, has a much longer history than the standard employment relationship. Work that is precarious (unstable or uncertain) is 'not necessarily new or novel to the current era; it has existed since the launch of paid employment as a primary source of sustenance' (Kalleberg, 2009: 2). As Bent (2017: 3) has argued, when looking at work over time and across the world, 'the relative stability and security of employment in the West post-WWII, then, was an anomaly.' And even within this context, it was reserved primarily for white men in the Global North. The standard employment relationship simply was not extended to many women and minorities, and certainly was not something seen extensively outside of a few industrialized economies. The standard employment relationship is therefore a bit of a misnomer, with unstable and precarious forms being both older and more widespread. The relationships of work are determined by the relative power of workers (selling their time) and capital (buying that time), along with the societal contexts in which work is carried out. It is therefore no surprise that what we think of as work is continuously evolving over time and space.

An important historical example of this kind of precarity is the dock work that took place in the East End of London, following the rapid growth of shipping docks in the nineteenth century that brought commodities from the colonies into the heart of imperial Britain. The raw cotton, sugar and tea could not get themselves out of the holds of the ships and into the warehouses, so large numbers of workers were needed. However, this did not mean employing people to work on the docks. It was estimated that 'about two-thirds of dock labour was casual', and as Weightman and Humphries (2007: 41) note, 'there was no guarantee of work from one week to the next and the vast majority of labourers were hired or fired on a day-to day basis.' The arrival and departure of ships meant that dock work was not constant, with peaks in demand that needed to be met quickly. This was due to the strict timetables ships had to follow as they were caught up in a wider network of trade. Even before platforms, workers' schedules were shaped by global economic forces. Each day, prospective workers from London's deprived East End would queue up outside the gates of the docks, waiting to see if they would be 'called on' by a foreman. As Ben Tillett (1910: 8), a dock worker who later became a union organizer, explained:

> We are driven into a shed, iron-barred from end to end, outside of which a foreman or contractor walks up and down with the air of a dealer in a cattle market, picking and choosing from a crowd of men, who, in their eagerness to obtain employment, trample each other under foot, and where like beasts they fight for the chances of a day's work.

This is obviously a difficult environment for workers, who will be selling their time at a huge disadvantage. However, workers did not always passively accept this way of organizing work. In fact, it 'generated much anger among the dockers' (Tillett, 1910: 8). In the 1880s, other groups of workers were beginning to organize, most notably the 'Matchwomen' and their strike at the Bryant and May match factory in the East End of London (Raw, 2009). The strike was the result of low pay, long hours, fines, as well as severe health and safety problems related to the use of white phosphorous in the production process. After Annie Besant covered the conditions of the factory in a newspaper, the management of the factory tried to get the workers to sign a letter saying the claims were not true. After they refused, the managers tried to dismiss one of the workers. This triggered a strike of 1,400 women and girls. They elected their own committee to run the strike and successfully beat Bryant and May. As a result, they formed the largest female trade union. Louise Raw (2009: 224) argues that they were 'the mothers of the modern trade union movement'.

The success of the Matchwomen was then followed by the South

London Gas Workers strike in 1889. Then, in August of 1889, 100,000 dock workers went on strike over a reduction in 'plus' money – a bonus paid for unloading a ship quickly. The workers put forward a series of demands: wage increases, overtime pay, removing the 'plus' system, guarantees of minimum work and union recognition. The next month they won their strike demands. Their victory established strong, recognized trade unions on the dock, an important moment in the 'new unionism' movement in the UK (Duffy, 1961). Across different sectors, union membership rose from 750,000 members in 1888 to over 2 million by 1899. While the strikes did not end the precarious work on the docks, they proved that these workers could organize. This long period of struggle continued until the late 1960s, by which time 'virtually all dockers [were] on permanent terms' (Mankelow, 2017: 383). The London docks can therefore be seen as the 'ground on which the great battle against the most degrading forms of casualization was fought' (Mankelow, 2017: 384), and indeed – at least until the massive changes brought about by modernization and containerization in the late 1970s – dockers were able to win concessions from employers.

A similar story can be told of factory work. The development of factories entailed the movement of workers from the country-side to the city, with work concentrated within large workplaces like factories. Within the factory walls, 'employers could directly control when and how workers worked, adding new layers of insecurity to employment' (Bent, 2017: 4). In the early twentieth century in the US, for example, seasonal and peak demand pressures shaped the work relationship in many economic sectors. In the glass and textiles industries, workers would be employed for only three-quarters of the year to match demand, and broadly speaking, the numbers of jobs in industrial work could fluctuate by around 14 per cent, meaning many people risking loss of their employment. In the car industry, this fluctuation could be as high as 45 per cent (Jacoby, 2004: 16–17). However, by the end of the Second World War, in both the US and the Global North more broadly, these industrial jobs were highly unionized and workers had won much more stable employment conditions: protecting individual workers from down cycles, and placing more of the risk associated with doing business onto the firm rather than the individual worker.

There is a risk in seeing this development as a linear process – that is, one in which particular stages follow each other inevitably to a particular end. The thinking might go: first, industrialization introduces new forms of work, in which workers are made to accept unfair conditions. Next, industrial workers successfully organize and precarious conditions are overcome through the collective power of workers. However, because contemporary worker power is premised on the 'standard employment relationship' brought about by industrialization, all that workers have collectively achieved is threatened by waves of de-industrialization.

Although there are examples of the process developing like this, in many parts of the world the experience of industrialization was very different. For example, Bent (2017: 12) argues that large-scale industries were established in both Egypt and India under British imperial rule. This industrialization was deeply shaped by the exploitative relationships of the British Empire. Despite worker resistance, the industrialization that took place 'was highly disruptive to existing social and economic systems ... these changes resulted in the creation of working arrangements that were unstable, insecure, and contingent – in a word, precarious' (Bent, 2017: 14). However, as Webster et al. (2008) have argued, in low- and middle-income countries, the majority of workers were excluded from stable employment, unlike high-income countries. While there was a growth in more stable employment relations in low- and middle-income countries, the benefits of the standard employment contractor have never been widely felt by workers. Therefore, for most people, most of the time, work has been a precarious relationship. Precarity is the global norm.

The notion of precarious work is important for understanding the gig economy. A starting definition for precarious work can be found with the International Labour Organization (ILO, 2011: 5), which defines it thus:

> In the most general sense, precarious work is a means for employers to shift risks and responsibilities on to workers. It is work performed

in the formal and informal economy and is characterized by variable levels and degrees of objective (legal status) and subjective (feeling) characteristics of uncertainty and insecurity. Although a precarious job can have many faces, it is usually defined by uncertainty as to the duration of employment, multiple possible employers or a disguised or ambiguous employment relationship, a lack of access to social protection and benefits usually associated with employment, low pay, and substantial legal and practical obstacles to joining a trade union and bargaining collectively.

The problem, as Angela Mitropoulos (2005: 12) has noted, is that the term '"precariousness" is both unwieldy and indeterminate. If it is possible to say anything for certain about precariousness, it is that it teeters.' This is a useful starting point in 'emphasizing some of the tensions that shadow much of the discussion about precarious labour' (Mitropoulos, 2005: 12).

It is easy to observe the growth of this kind of precarious work, including temping, outsourcing, agency work and the gig economy. However, growth in the gig economy is not only driven by the private sector. In the UK, the largest employer of precarious workers is the state. There has been a huge growth of temporary workers across education, health and public administration, affecting both professionals and the lowest paid (McDowell et al., 2009: 9). The debate about precarious work is not just about whether or not there are workers with insecure contracts and conditions. However, the arguments about precarity really begin when the implications are considered. For Ulrich Beck (1992: 144), precarious work involved a break away from the system of either 'lifelong full-time work' or unemployment towards a 'risk-fraught system of flexible, pluralized, decentralized underemployment, which, however, will possibly no longer raise the problem of unemployment in the sense of being completely without a paid job'. In a similar vein, Pierre Bourdieu (1998: 95) argues that 'précarité' is a 'new mode of domination in public life ... based on the creation of a generalized and permanent state of insecurity aimed at forcing workers into submission, into the acceptance of exploitation'. Guy Standing (2011) goes even

further, claiming that this has led to the formation of a new class:
the 'precariat'.

What each of these positions is trying to argue is that there has
been a significant break from the 'standard employment relationship', meaning we are now entering a new phase of the organization
of work. The criticisms of these positions tend to focus on a rejection of two aspects – either the empirical basis or the implications
of what is being argued. For example, Kevin Doogan (2009: 91)
attempted to explain why there is a 'broad public perception of
the end of jobs for life and the decline of stable employment'
which operates alongside 'the rise in long-term employment'. At
its core, his argument is an attempt to counter the ideology of
neoliberalism by insisting that work is still really the same – and
therefore trade unions can continue to organize in the same way
that they have before. Similar critiques have been made against
Guy Standing's assertion that an entirely new class of worker has
been created. Perhaps the most useful of these comes from Richard
Seymour (2012, quoted in Woodcock, 2017: 136), who argues
that the concept of the precariat 'remains at best a purely negative,
critical concept', unable to actually describe or explain a social
class. Nevertheless, Seymour notes that it identifies something that
requires further attention: if people feel more precarious, then this
is an important dimension for understanding work.

Thinking about this in relation to the gig economy, it is self-
evident that these new kinds of work are more precarious than
established forms. Indeed, the gig economy operates in a context in
which 'social, economic, and political forces have aligned to make
work more precarious' (Kalleberg, 2009: 2). Kalleberg (2009: 6–8)
discusses five factors that contribute to this. The first is a 'decline
in attachment to employers', which can mean a greater number
of different jobs held over a lifetime, along with a willingness to
change jobs. The second is an 'increase in long-term unemployment', meaning more people are potentially seeking work. This is
much sharper in low- and middle-income countries, particularly
with large numbers of people who have never worked in 'standard'
jobs. The third is 'growth in perceived job insecurity', which
Seymour (2012, quoted in Woodcock, 2017: 136) identifies as

meaning that regardless of whether or not work is actually becoming more precarious, people feel that it is, and it therefore has an effect. The fourth is 'a growth of non-standard work arrangements and contingent work', which we have already identified in the gig economy. The fifth is an 'increase in risk-shifting from employers to employees', a process that we also argue is taking place in the gig economy. This leaves us with the question of the implications of the growth of the gig economy, a topic we return to later in the book.

We have outlined this brief history of work to make the point that the precarious nature of work in the gig economy is not new. However, the gig economy represents a transformation and reorganization of work significant enough for us to be concerned about it. In the rest of this chapter, we argue that there are three key factors that have facilitated the growth of the gig economy. Firstly, broad political shifts taking place in the economy including worker power, state regulation and globalization and outsourcing. Secondly, the technological changes and new networks of connectivity that have allowed for the recruitment and management of geographically dispersed workers. And thirdly, social changes (including consumer attitudes and preferences, as well as gendered and racialized relationships of work) that have resulted in both employers and workers seeking more flexible working patterns.

The preconditions that shape the gig economy

There is a temptation to focus simply on technology as the motivating factor that brings the gig economy into being. However, there are a complex and interconnected set of preconditions that shape how the gig economy emerges in practice. In this section we discuss nine preconditions that shape the gig economy (see figure 1). Each of the preconditions are connected to the underlying factors of technology, society, political economy, or a combination thereof. We have placed the gig economy in the middle of the figure to indicate that each of these preconditions and factors shape the outcome. The rest of the chapter is structured around the nine preconditions: platform infrastructure (technology), digital legibility of work (technology), mass connectivity and cheap technology (technology and social), consumer attitudes and preferences (social), gendered and racialized relationships of work (social), desire for flexibility for/ from workers (social and political economy), state regulation (political economy), worker power (political economy), and globalization and outsourcing (political economy and technology). These preconditions certainly vary in importance between places and times, but we would argue that, together, they influence how most people think about today's gig economy. Although we use the term 'gig economy' in its singular form, we acknowledge that there are actually myriad *gig economies* all over the world that are experienced in significantly different ways. In other words, the experiences, practices and labour processes within gig economies are far from homogeneous. Nonetheless, speaking about *the* 'gig economy' allows us to draw out broad similarities amongst those practices and experiences.

Platform infrastructure

While we will return to the concept of 'platforms' in detail in chapter 2, it is worth noting how important platform infrastructure is as a precondition to the gig economy. The basic idea in the architectures of platforms that mediate work is to create a digital context in which buyers of labour power are able to connect with sellers of labour power (what economists call a 'two-sided market'). Uber's platform connects people who want a taxi ride with people who are willing to provide taxi rides. Fiverr's platform connects people looking for a graphic designer or video editor with people offering those services. Unlike older ways of connecting buyers and sellers of work, digital platforms make much of the process relatively seamless for both parties. On many platforms, it only takes a few minutes for a client seeking a service to issue a request through the platform, connect to a worker, and the worker to begin to perform that service. This use of the platform as the mechanism to connect clients and workers is what has led many

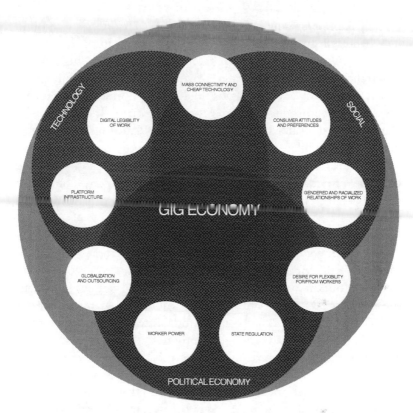

Figure 1 The preconditions that shape the gig economy
Design by Giorgio Marani

gig economy companies to attempt to claim that they themselves are not employers of the workers: that they simply provide a bridge between supply and demand. They claim, in other words, to be technology companies rather than taxi, delivery, home cleaning companies. Whilst this is certainly true, to some extent, for some platforms, the story is more complicated in other cases (a point we return to in more detail in chapter 2).

Current debates on the transformation of work often centre around technology, and imply that we are in uncharted territory due to the technological revolution that we find ourselves within. However, the idea that technology will change work is far from new. Take, for example, Marx's (1955 [184/]) often quoted line 'the handmill gives you society with the feudal lord; the steam-mill, society with the industrial capitalist.' The argument is not so much that the steam mill created the industrial capitalist, but rather that it would not have been possible to have an industrial capital-ist without the productive forces of the steam mill — the scale of production could not have supported this. Platform infrastructure operates in a similar way to the stream mill, providing the techni-cal basis for new organizations of work in the gig economy. The platform provides the ability for so-called technology companies to employ (or claim not to employ) large numbers of distributed workers.

Early platforms were set up around the turn of the millennium and were simply digital job boards that allowed workers to upload résumés or descriptions of their skills, and clients to upload infor-mation about the work that they needed done. Craigslist is perhaps the most well-known platform of this model. The architecture of the website influences the types of initial interactions that workers and clients can have with one another, but ultimately has little bearing on the labour process itself for most types of work.

Next came companies like Guru.com, vWorker and Elance, which allowed freelancers to upload profiles that highlighted their skills, leave feedback and bid for work. But it wasn't until the 2010s that platforms for geographically tethered work started becom-ing widely used. This was also not just a Western phenomenon. China's DiDi, India's Flipkart, and other copycats and genuine innovators developed infrastructures that could sit in between con-sumer demand and worker availability and skills.

What all platforms have in common is that they connect workers and clients who lack either proximity or synchronicity. In other words, they allow workers and clients to meet and transact who otherwise had no plans to be in the same place or share the same moments of co-presence. Today's platforms do this primarily through one of two mechanisms: negotiation-based matching and static-price matching. In the former system, clients and workers typically post information about their jobs and skills on a profile — allowing buyers to bid for workers and (more commonly) workers to bid for jobs. In the latter system, prices are fixed and no negotiation is possible. Uber and Deliveroo, for instance, don't allow drivers to negotiate their mileage rates. Fiverr conversely allows workers to set fixed prices for clients.

Uber's former CEO, Travis Kalanick, once noted[1] 'We are not setting the price. The market is setting the price ... We have algorithms to determine what that market is.' This selective framing conceals a lot of what platforms actually do. They are much more than just the matching infrastructure. Other core functions that they perform are facilitating payments, establishing trust mechanisms, surveillance of workers (and, in some cases, clients), and myriad sector-specific features like driver routing or panic buttons. The point here is that platforms are far from a simple marketplace in which clients and workers meet. They are designed with encoded features that impose rules and nudges onto all parties that they interact with. Platforms fundamentally shape the ways that gig work is carried out. But, as we will see, so too do many other factors.

Digital legibility of work

The ability to 'platformize' work – to use the platform infrastructure noted above – rests on an old problem of management: how to measure work. With the establishment of factories, workers were paid for their time in a workplace. This meant that managers wanted to ensure they got the most out of buying a worker's time. However, as most managers are not doing the work that workers do, it can be hard for them to understand whether workers are actually putting in enough effort. Not all workers want to work as efficiently as possible (especially when they are poorly paid or treated).

This deliberate slowing down of work – or 'soldiering' – became an obsession for Frederick Taylor (the 'father' of modern management theory). Taylor's solution was to meticulously record and measure the factory labour process. He argued that 'managers assume' the 'burden of gathering together all of the traditional knowledge which in the past has been possessed by the workmen and then the classifying, tabulating, and reducing this knowledge to rules, laws, and formulae' (Taylor, 1967: 36). This meant trying to make the work legible, making it visible so it could be understood by managers.

This managerial desire for legibility has developed with new forms of work. Factories became reorganized along Taylorist lines. Starting with time and motion studies, the factory floor would be investigated and measured in detail, calculating how much time each individual part of a task should take. The advent of the assembly line meant that production could then be sped up on this basis, trying to take control away from workers. Managers in call centres were able to use technological methods of surveillance to electronically measure the work process in great detail (Woodcock, 2017). Many work platforms follow on from these traditions, albeit without the physical supervision found in either factories or call centres. Some platform infrastructures allow the real-time location tracking and timing of every worker. This develops the forms of surveillance from the call centre, deploying them beyond the walls of a workplace (Woodcock, forthcoming). Some cloud platforms, in contrast, can monitor every digital activity performed by a worker on-platform.

The ability to organize work via a platform requires digital legibility. This means that some kinds of work are much more susceptible to this kind of 'routinization, reorganization, and rebundling' (Peck, 2017: 207). As we will discuss in this book, transportation, delivery and domestic work are proving comparatively easy to platformize. Similarly, forms of digital work that involve tasks that can be broken down and completed over the internet are, too. However, there are both forms of work and sites of work that are resistant to this kind of digital legibility.

It is worth thinking about labour in the gig economy as existing in a 'goldilocks zone' of legibility. Too little legibility and it becomes difficult to put work onto a platform in the first place. Here, layers of tacit rather than codified knowledge structure and govern the work process. Think of babysitters or security guards as jobs in which people tend to use personal recommendations, etc., that are hard to codify into platform ratings or databases. On the other hand, too much legibility and there is the risk that jobs become automated away. The Amazon dream of autonomous drones that can deliver parcels or the Uber dream of autonomous vehicles that can transport passengers are only possible in a world in which multiple overlapping spaces, activities and processes are highly digitally legible. Having a standardized addressing system, high-quality geospatial data, and the technology to produce and read those data has allowed large platforms to more effectively operate in some countries rather than others. For instance, a nascent delivery platform in Maputo, Mozambique, has to instead rely on a lot of human intervention and local knowledge to find delivery locations rather than automated geocoding to make their platform function.

Mass connectivity and cheap technology

Only a decade ago, the smartphone had just become popularized. Internet access was not something most people had in the palm of their hands, and most people used their phones for voice calls and SMS messages. Back then, internet penetration rates in many high-income countries were about 60–70 per cent – meaning that about a third of the population (and predominantly the poorest third of the population) in those countries had never used the internet. In most low-income countries, almost nobody was using the internet outside of elites, students and workers in a few select industries. For example, in 2006, the internet penetration rate in what the International Telecommunications Union (ITU) defined as 'developing countries' was 18 per cent.[2]

Much has changed since then! At the time of writing this book, over half of the world's population is now connected to the internet. So-called digital divides remain real, but in high-income countries almost everyone who wants to use the internet has at least some form of access. Penetration rates are lower in the rest of the world, with the ITU reporting that it is now 44.7 per cent for men and 37.5 per cent for women in the 'developing world'.[3] We are also in the midst of a 'mobile revolution' in many countries. The availability of cheap (<$20) smartphones and pay-as-you-go mobile plans have made the mobile phone an essential piece of technology to communities from Brazil to Burundi to Bangladesh. Urban regions of low- and middle-income countries are characterized by even higher levels of connectivity, and many of the working poor in cities as varied as Cairo, Bangkok, Nairobi and Rio all find ways of connecting.

As alluded to above, this connectivity for most people in low-, middle- and high-income countries is no longer confined to desktop machines plugged into a wall. A decade ago, internet access tended to be something limited to the home or the office, with many people still using dial-up modems. Today, the mobile phone is the device that most people use to connect. Instead of travelling to the internet, the internet now travels with many of us. The basic point here is that the world has very quickly become far more digitally networked than it used to be. Many of the populations of people who would be potential consumers and workers in the gig economy are no longer off the digital grid: they are integrated into the global network.

There are two primary ways in which this mass technologically mediated connectivity has been a key driver in moving work away from the traditional organizational structure of the firm and into the organizational forms of the contemporary gig economy. First, in their role as connectors, gig economy firms are now able to reach ever greater populations of clients and workers. This is especially important for the recruitment process (i.e. firms finding workers in the first place), but also for the day-to-day interactions that are a part of all gig economy labour processes. Drivers, delivery workers and data entry specialists are all continuously connected in order to carry out their jobs properly. Even though internet access is spreading rapidly across the world's population, many potential workers still only have access to 'feature phones' (i.e. pre-smartphones with no internet access). Some firms have therefore developed systems in which clients/consumers and workers require different technological affordances. In Maputo, Mozambique, for instance, there is a platform called Biscate that allows clients to request plumbers, builders, cleaners and other manual workers using a slick web-app, but the workers themselves receive requests through a more old-fashioned SMS system. The net effect is the same: that the world's workers are all being connected, and can potentially be enrolled into gig economy platforms.

Second, while most gig economy firms are focused on the provision of local services (for example, cleaning or food delivery), some gig economy firms have been able to set up global-scale platforms for services like data entry, graphic design or transcription that have fewer geographic limitations on where they need to be delivered from (see chapter 2 for more on this). These global platforms set up what you might think of as 'planetary labour markets' (Graham and Anwar 2019). In the words of Guy Standing (2016), they enable a mass migration of labour, but not of people. Clients suddenly have a world of workers to choose from, and workers from around the global are placed into competition with one another – all made possible because the majority of humanity has now been connected to the global network.

Consumer attitudes and preferences

New economic activity requires consumer demand. An important precondition for the gig economy is therefore preferences and desires of end users and consumers. In some industries platforms have to encourage entirely new demands and behaviours. In others, they simply build on pre-platform practices. Delivery platforms, for instance, build upon a pre-existing consumer attitude of buying food remotely over the phone and having it delivered. The shift to digital platforms does not require a significant change in consumer attitudes, often being easier to do via an app than calling a landline phone number. The changes wrought by the gig economy therefore fit with Teresa Amabile's (1983) understanding of creativity: the formation of something that is both new and meaningful. The platformization of many of these activities is 'new', but they also have to be 'meaningful' in that they make sense to consumers and they are prepared to use them. There is a risk here in making assumptions about consumers' (as well as workers') digital literacy and ability to engage with these platforms.

Platform companies have thus far been relatively skilled in

harnessing consumer preferences in the face of bad press and threats of regulations. When Transport for London announced they would not renew Uber's operating licence upon its expiration on 30 October 2017, Uber launched a Change.org petition to fight this existential threat to their operations in London. They claimed there were 3.5 million 'Londoners who rely on Uber', and called on customers to sign the petition and share with '#SaveYourUber'. The petition was signed by 858,111 supporters.[4] This level of consumer and citizen activism can be frightening for any elected (or unelected) official trying to impose regulation. Platforms can frame regulators as being anti-innovation: arguing that they are dinosaurs taking away services that the populace need. The outcome of this sort of strategy is that regulators in most cities want to tread lightly and not unsettle sectors of the economy that provide jobs and satisfy consumer demands.

Conversely, though, consumer power can be turned against platforms. All large consumer-facing platforms are aware of the implications of bad press and, as a result, spend enormous sums on public relations and advertising. This is one of the few significant leverage points to improve platform work, and an issue we return to in more detail in the final chapter.

Gendered and racialized relationships of work

The gendered and racialized relationships of work that pre-exist the gig economy shape its outcomes, while also being reinforced and rearticulated in new ways. As Hunt and Samman (2019) have argued, 'on the whole it represents the continuation (and in some cases deepening) of long-standing structural, and gendered, inequalities.' Although many commentators will claim that 'machines don't discriminate', the issue is that people – and the people that design and build machines – do. And, it is people who use algorithms, databases, machines and platforms to engage with workers. Platforms, in other words, do not operate in some sort of alternate digital realm (Graham and Anwar, 2018). They are both produced by, and produce, the social – and thus gendered and racialized – ways in which we economically interact with one another.

The gendered relationships of work (that we will explore in detail later) can be seen in the inclusion and exclusion of women from different kinds of jobs in the gig economy. The roots of this can be traced to the gendering of work under capitalism more generally. For example, domestic work has always been a central component of capitalism. Factory labour would not have been sustainable without unpaid work in the home, caring for the current workers, while raising the children who would become future workers. Too often, this work has been seen as 'unproductive' in relation to the productive labour in a workplace, undermining its importance, along with devaluing the skills involved.

While the gendered basis of capitalism has not always involved such a straightforward distinction between women in the home and men at work, the creation of the household under capitalism has shaped domestic work in important ways. For example, as Mariarosa Dalla Costa and Selma James (1971: 10) have argued, 'where women are concerned, their labor appears to be a personal service outside of capital.' This can also entail the additional gendered burden of emotional labour at work (Hochschild, 1983), as well as the 'second shift' after work (Hochschild, 1989). For the housewife, this means the work is devalued, both in terms of remuneration and also with how it is valued as work. Dalla Costa and James (1971: 34) conclude that inside and outside of the home, women:

> have worked enough. We have chopped billions of tons of cotton, washed billions of dishes, scrubbed billions of floors, typed billions of words, wired billions of radio sets, washed billions of nappies, by hand and in machines.

Work within the household is still work. As Anderson (2000: 1) has argued, 'domestic work is vital and sustaining, and it is also demeaned and disregarded.' The pressures of unpaid domestic work increase the likelihood of women working in 'non-standard' jobs (Fredman, 2003). This means that women are much more likely to end up in segregated jobs, with a gender pay gap and fewer social protections throughout the life course, amongst other negative outcomes. Similarly, when it is 'paid domestic work in private households', it is disproportionately performed by racialized groups' (Anderson, 2000: 1).

The racialization of work has its roots in slavery, which played a key role in financing the industrial revolution. As Eric Williams (1994: 7) has argued, 'slavery was not born of racism: rather, racism was the consequence of slavery.' This is not to say that racism did not exist before slavery, but rather that the specific racialization of work emerged as a consequence of the exploitation of slave labour. Williams (1994) explores how economic forces led to and then replaced slavery, rather than humanitarian concerns. Racism continues to deeply shape the experiences of work. For many workers, this is linked to migration status – and those without legal migration status are particularly at risk (Ryan, 2005). Migrants, for example, are 'often forced to accept the most precarious contracts, in jobs incommensurate with their skill levels' (McDowell et al., 2009: 4).

The majority of precarious workers are non-unionized and 'have been marginalized' (Pollert and Charlwood, 2009: 357), whether through gender, race or migration status. Therefore, those workers who find themselves in low paid 'non-standard' work are often not covered by any of the 'three regulatory regimes – collective bargaining, employment protection rights, and the national insurance system' (Fredman, 2003: 308). For example, migrant cleaners across London are often not covered by any of these regulatory regimes (Woodcock, 2014b). In the case of migrant cleaners, the gendered and racialized relationships combine to create a deeply exploitative workplace. More broadly, these relationships shape what kinds of work are available to a prospective worker, their likelihood of getting a job, along with their experiences of working it.

Desire for flexibility for/from workers

The next social precondition is also connected to political economy. It is a desire for flexibility that has come from both employers and workers, with the shifts in cultures and social practices that make flexibility desirable for both. This is not to argue that the structural changes we have discussed in the first set of preconditions are not important. Clearly, the changes within the broader economy are driving a restructuring of work, whether ostensibly as 'flexicurity' (European Commission, 2008) or more explicitly as a project to dismantle previous protections or benefits at work. However, this removes any sense of agency from workers themselves. Workers are not passive actors at work. While most workers might be free from any other way to meet their needs than through work, they are still (relatively) free to choose between different kinds of available work.

As both of us have found in our research, many workers in the gig economy are keen to stress that they appreciate the flexible aspects of the work, even if they then have other grievances. For example, a worker at Deliveroo explained that they preferred it as:

> you're not selling anything, you're not selling yourself so there's no emotional labour in it and I think that's why it's been like a job that I've stuck at longer than other shit jobs because I find it a lot easier to not do that sort of selling yourself side of things.

The alternative kinds of work that they described included service work based in a restaurant or working the phones in a call centre. This, despite the fact they still described Deliveroo as a 'shit job', made it comparatively better than the conditions in high-pressure call centres (Woodcock, 2017). Similarly, another worker explained that they 'wanted to work outside and with a bicycle, because it's my passion working with a bicycle'. For younger workers, the gig economy offers the potential – and it is important to stress that this is a potential, as we discuss further later in the book – for different ways of working. This is particularly important considering the rise of what David Graeber (2018) has called 'bullshit jobs', forms of work that appear to be meaningless busywork. The desire to escape from these kinds of jobs provides a ready supply of labour power to be put to work in new ways.

In low- and middle-income countries, even relatively high-skilled workers have tended to be quite constrained by the boundaries of their local labour markets. With most cities in the

Global South characterized by high unemployment rates and a lack of opportunities, it is not surprising that many workers in those places have jumped at the chance to find jobs in the gig economy. Furthermore, because the closed employment relations that have been the norm in much of the Global North were never that common in the South, the open employment relationships of the gig economy tend to be perceived less negatively by southern workers (Wood et al., 2019b).

It is also worth noting that gig economy employers are clearly pushing for ever more flexible forms of work. In many cases, employers refuse to even acknowledge their own role in the employment relationship. Uber and Deliveroo frame themselves as technology companies rather than taxi operators or delivery companies, respectively. Their drivers are referred to as 'partners', not workers, and certainly not employees. Constructing the relationship in this way has involved the widespread use of a different kind of relationship, far removed from the 'standard employment relationship'. Instead of an employment relationship, many kinds of gig work instead use versions of self-employment and independent contractor status. This goes further than the removal of stable employment that we have traced since the 1970s, representing a breaking of the employment relationship and the freeing of platforms from many of the responsibilities and requirements that used to be involved.

This feeling, or subjectivity, is also a key part of the debate on precarious work. For example, Mitropoulos (2005: 13) has argued that the 'flight from "standard hours" was not precipitated by employers but rather by workers seeking less time at work' and connects it to what 'the Italian Workerists dubbed the "refusal of work" in the late 1970s'.[5] Rather than seeing workers as passive recipients of the structural changes in work, the concept is part of politicizing work. As part of this, Anthony Iles (2005: 36) warns of the risks of considering struggles at work today only 'in terms of battles for better legislation'. The risk of only seeking to return to older forms of work 'misses the opportunity to investigate the tendency for self-organized (or "disorganized") labour to develop a more generalized struggle'. From this perspective, precarity becomes part of a political 'project to dismantle the mass worker as the central object for labour struggles and place it on the shoulders of the more encompassing but diffuse idea of the precarious worker' (McKarthy, 2005: 55). Here, too, attention is drawn to the heterogeneity of precarious workers, taking into account two kinds of precarious workers: 'BrainWorkers' who have specialist skills and relative bargaining power, and 'ChainWorkers' in the service industry and 'the only thing they have to sell is their labour' (McKarthy, 2005: 57). Meanwhile, gig economy employers find ever more ways to divide up the work process so that workers can always be called upon in an on demand way.

State regulation

In order to address the issue state of regulation, we need to start by making sense of 'neoliberalism'. However, the problem with using this term is that, as Jamie Peck (2013: 133) explains, it is a 'rascal concept'. While it is often used 'with pejorative intent' to refer to a wide range of economic problems, usually that is the end of the argument – as if without neoliberalism, everything would be fine. However, an important starting point for understanding neoliberalism is David Harvey's (2007: 2) argument, that it is 'in the first instance a theory of political economic practices that propose that human well-being can best be advanced by liberating individual entrepreneurial freedoms and skills within an institutional framework characterized by strong private property rights, free markets, and free trade'. However, as we shall discuss, the way in which this is put into practice is more complicated. Therefore, as Peck (2013: 153) notes, using the term 'must not be a substitute for explanation; it should be an occasion for explanation'. In order to explain how neoliberalism has facilitated the growth of the gig economy, there are two turning points to begin from.

The first is the economic crisis of the 1970s and the response, particularly in the UK and US in the late 1970s and 1980s. This 'structural crisis' saw the end of the economic growth of the post-war period (Duménil and Lévy, 2005: 9). The high-point of the 'standard employment relationship' discussed in the previous section was also now under serious threat as unemployment and inflation grew. In this turning point, as with the next, the crisis provided the opportunity for sweeping reforms, part of the 'shock doctrine' (Klein, 2008) of neoliberalism. In the UK, Prime Minister Margaret Thatcher dealt a serious blow to the trade union movement by defeating the miners' strike (one of the world's largest ever strikes that resulted in defeat for the workers). In the US, Ronald Reagan defeated the air traffic control workers. For both, this was followed with a programme of reforms that has come to characterize neoliberalism: attacking workers' terms and conditions, the rolling back of the welfare state and sectoral subsidies, and increasing privatization and use of market forces (Harvey, 2007: 12). In the UK, this also entailed tax reduction and significant deregulation, both financial but also relating to work (Woodcock, 2018a). As Thompson and Ackroyd (1995: 618) have summarized, from 1979 in the UK:

> Political action by a succession of Conservative administrations has also clearly shaped the broader landscape. Three significant dimensions of policy can be identified: a strategy of de-regulation of labour markets and promotion of a low wage, low skill economy as a means of attracting inward investment; competitive tendering and internal markets in the public sector; and the sustained legislative assault on union organisation, employment rights and collective bargaining.

This long period of change has shaped the current state of the employment relationship. In particular, the growth of the service industries since the 1970s has seen another phase in which workers have to sell their labour power without much ability to collectively bargain over the terms. At the same time, the labour market was '"deregulated" and labour made more "flexible"', as part of a political project to undermine workers' rights, restoring 'management's "right to manage"' (Munke, 2005: 63). A key part of this has been 'a general move away from the full employment goal towards activation policies' (MacGregor, 2005: 144). The result has been a growth in underemployment, and a decline of stable employment. It has also involved an increasing polarization of the types of jobs available (Kaplanis, 2007), with a growth in the number of low-paid 'lousy jobs' at the bottom (Goos & Manning, 2007).

If the first turning point put neoliberalism into practice, the second forced more action. The 2008 financial crisis, precipitated by a crisis of subprime mortgages, had its roots in the crisis of profitability that remained unresolved from the 1970s. As Peck (2013: 134) has noted, 'after doubling up' in the previous period, 'neoliberalism has doubled down' since 2008. The response from the European Commission (2008) was to focus on the labour market aspects of the crisis, stressing that 'EU member states should develop measures within a policy framework informed by the principles of "flexicurity"' (Heyes, 2011: 643). However, the reality was not a combination of flexibility and security, but rather the 'dominant trend has been towards less security' (Heyes, 2011: 643).

Since 2008 there have been many claims about an economic upturn or the beginnings of hopeful economic growth. However, as Paul Mason (2016) has argued, the years following have been a jobless recovery. Rather than the creation of new jobs and the sharing of the benefits of economic growth, there has been an increase in low-paid and insecure work. This has been facilitated by the rolling back of employment protections. There have also been aggressive changes to the welfare state including labour market activation policies that are forcing workers into low-paid work, often subsidized by the state. Alongside these policies, some countries are actively encouraging the gig economy as a potential source of economic prosperity and progress. South Korea, for instance, is investing public money in platforms in the hope that they will ultimately contribute to economic growth.[6] Kenya, likewise, is rushing to sign up people to its Ajira Digital programme: a scheme that intends to turn up to a million young Kenyans into platform workers as a way of tackling the youth unemployment crisis in the country.

The gig economy, particularly in the case of 'lean platforms', is successfully taking advantage of this context, which 'ultimately appears as an outlet for surplus capital in an era of ultra-low interest rates and dire investment opportunities rather than the vanguard destined to revive capitalism' (Srnicek, 2017: 91). The glut of money made by companies in the technology industry is increasingly being held outside of the home country of the firm, not brought back for fear of taxation and without anywhere profitable to invest. This is a continuation of the crisis of profitability referred to before, but under increased pressure as there is a vast amount of money needing to be spent on something. In essence, those with large amounts of capital were finding that their money was not growing in traditional bank savings or investments, and so they looked for avenues to invest. The fledgling gig economy became the perfect outlet for this through the growth of venture capital. In this way, the development of technology then feeds back into the gig economy as investment, as well as providing the tools upon which it is being built.

Worker power

This neoliberal context has greatly weakened employment protections, along with facilitating the growth of a pool of potential workers who are struggling to meet their needs through existing work opportunities. The changes in production identified by Ricardo Antunes (2012: 37) have had a significant impact on work:

> extensive deregulation of labour-rights, eliminated on a daily basis in all corners of the world that have industrial production and services; increase in the fragmentation of the working class, precarisation and subcontracting of the human force that labours; and destruction of class-unionism and its transformation into docile unionism, based on partnership.

The failure of the trade union movement to fully adapt to deindustrialization has also greatly reduced the collective power of workers relative to capital. In these contexts, trade unions 'face considerable obstacles to extending their presence in private services, not least from hostile employers' (Williams and Adam-Smith, 2009). In many contexts, as workers' power is reduced, and the deregulated environment allows for new kinds of employment relationships. Significant risks are shifted from employers to workers, while at the same time making workers bargain as individuals rather than as collectives. In this way, Ravenelle (2019. 6) argues that 'despite its focus on emerging technology', the gig economy 'is truly a movement forward to the past' in terms of conditions and protections at work.

These changes have limited the capacities for workers to shape their own work. In many contexts, workers have not operated within the institutional framework of trade unions that were integrated, at least in part, into capitalism in high-income countries. However, the decline of traditional trade unionism does not mean that workers do not resist, rather that the resistance is not expressed in forms that have been used previously. This does mean that many workers miss the protection of institutional forms of worker power. In most of the gig economy – despite some exceptions that we will discuss later in the book – there are no active trade unions. This means that management are more likely to act unilaterally, without the checks of collective bargaining or negotiation.

Globalization and outsourcing

The final precondition that has deeply shaped the gig economy in its current form is a combination of political economy and technology: the effects of globalization and outsourcing. This is a development and intensification of the outsourcing of call centres from high-income countries to low- and middle-income countries, for example, from the UK to India (Taylor and Bain, 2005). This laid the organizational basis for wider business process outsourcing that has become today's online outsourcing. However, globalization has not only meant the shifting of work and trade to different parts of the world, but also brought about a generalization of what Barbrook and Cameron (1996) have termed the 'Californian Ideology', referring to the encouragement of deregulated markets and powerful transnational corporations. While this is often linked to the rise of 'cognitive capitalism' (Moulier-Boutang, 2012) and the companies creating the software and platforms in Silicon Valley, it increasingly becomes a driver to open up markets in low- and middle-income countries too.

Alongside this ideological globalization, there has been a spread of common or shared technological infrastructures. For example, the IP addressing system, Visa/Mastercard/Amex (as well as new mobile) payment platforms, the GPS system, Google Maps as a base layer, and the Apple and Google Android phone operating systems, allow an increased internationalization of working practices. This globalization of technology has allowed platform companies to build their services on top of this globalized stack of infrastructures and scale relatively quickly. In some cases (such as platforms that rely heavily on GPS), it is also noteworthy that platforms are built on infrastructures that were made possible by early state investments. Firms can use these global infrastructures and standards to quickly scale up or down in response to changing market conditions, and quickly adapt existing models to new contexts.

The rise of the gig economy

This chapter has shown that the gig economy is characterized by not just firms using platforms to create two-sided marketplaces that connect buyers and sellers and services. It is also not just an extension of previous forms of labour market precarity. There is something new here. The gig economy is the combination of the nine factors which create an organizational form in which firms have an on-demand workforce that differs from previous types of precarious jobs. Dock workers could not be hired in intervals measured in minutes; they were still bound into local labour markets, needing to unload boats in particular places. The gig economy changes all of that with new controls over the temporality of work. Workers have the freedom to choose when they would like to work, but the other side of that bargain means that precarity exists at a much finer scale than ever before (down to the minute), and competition is expanded to a scale never before seen. This involves the expansion of the spatial scales of competition and the contraction of the temporal scales of the responsibility of the firm for its workers. This is outsourcing reconfigured for the new economy.

We should note that it is notoriously difficult to measure the size of the gig economy. There are two issues at play here: the data that are available, and how you define the gig economy in the first place. There have been claims that, in the US, contingent work and independent contracting is actually less common today than it was in the early 2000s.[7] Those claims have then been used to extrapolate that the gig economy is a shrinking phenomenon. In this book we take a narrower definition of the gig economy. We use the term not as a reference to all 'non-standard' employment; but rather in a way that is more in line with how it is deployed in everyday speech. In other words, as a reference to independent contracting that happens through, via and on digital platforms.

Using that narrower framing, reliable statistics on either the size of the market or the number of workers is extremely difficult to ascertain. In one of the few attempts to construct a headcount of gig workers, Richard Heeks (2017) estimates that up to seventy million people are registered on online outsourcing platforms. However, only about 10 per cent are likely to be active at any given time. Workers are also able to create accounts on multiple platforms: a fact that further inflates those estimates.

Data that capture more of the breadth of gig economy activities can be found in a survey conducted by Herman et al. (2019). The authors surveyed people in seven African countries, and found that 1.3 per cent of adults in those countries earned income from a platform. Using a very different estimation model, Heeks (2017) came up with a remarkably similar statistic. He estimates that there are between 30 and 40 million platform workers in the Global South (40 million would represent 1.5 per cent of the Global South workforce). In the Global North, there are huge variances in measurements and estimations of the number of platform workers (OECD, 2019). A McKinsey study of 8,000 workers in France, Germany, Spain, Sweden, the UK and the US found that 1.5 per cent of respondents had earned income from platforms (Manyika et al., 2016). A study by Huws et al. (2016) in seven European countries found much larger numbers. Their findings ranged from a low end of 9 per cent of the working population who had earned income from work platforms in the UK – slightly lower than the findings of Huws and Joyce (2016) discussed earlier   to 19 per cent in Austria. Eurobarometer similarly found that platform workers comprised less than 1 per cent of the population (in Malta) to 11 per cent (in France).

Ultimately, the reality is that all of these statistics are very rough numbers. But, however we slice the numbers, we do know that there are a lot of platform workers out there – probably tens of millions of them. And we also know that just a few years ago there were orders of magnitude fewer. Ever more work, in other words, is being mediated by platforms. Ever more work is entering the gig economy. We are in the midst of a profound period of economic experimentation into ways of organizing work that move beyond the traditional employment contract; ways of organizing work to be piecemeal, contingent and fragmented.

However, what we are not arguing is that gig work is the only kind of work that we should be concerned with. We have sympathy with Moody's (2017: 69) warning that focusing solely on this can 'trivialize the deeper reality of capitalism, its dynamics, and the altered state of working-class life' (Moody, 2017: 69). Gig work has to become numerically dominant to have far-reaching effects. As Callum Cant (2019) argues in his book on Deliveroo, the gig economy operates as a capitalist laboratory through which new techniques of management, control, worker exploitation and the extraction of profit are tested and refined. The success of these experiments, then, has much wider implications over the longer term as they are applied to other kinds of work.

There are now attempts the world over to introduce the gig economy model into almost every conceivable sector; to create the next Uber for X. As platforms expand into ever more sectors of the economy, we do not yet know which jobs will and will not become Uberized. However, by analysing what preconditions bring the gig economy into being, how the gig economy works, and who it works for, we can get a sense of how the gig economy might look in years to come and what effects might be introduced into other work. It is into this laboratory of the gig economy that we now turn.

2

How does the gig economy work?

This chapter is about how gig economy platforms operate. It takes examples from two fundamentally different types of gig work – *geographically tethered work* and *cloudwork*, to illustrate how they operate in practice (see figure 2). Through case studies of existing platforms, we explain the actual operation of the gig economy, focusing on how the work is organized, the practices of companies, how money is made, and we map the scale and spread of the phenomenon, to provide an overall picture of the gig economy worldwide. By examining business models and management practices that are either currently in use or in development, the chapter provides a combined view from the perspectives of the platform, the client and the employer. It therefore seeks to understand the motivations for the world of work they are each instrumental in creating. The ways in which platforms make a profit and organize their value chains have important implications for the experiences that follow in chapter 3.

What is a platform?

While the gig economy – or at least the prevalence of 'gigs' and precarious work – is not exactly new, platforms do represent a significant break with the past. As Nick Srnicek (2017: 6) has argued, the platform economy needs to be understood as a response to the economic crisis of the 1970s and the 'long decline in manufacturing profitability', which after 2008 saw the platform emerge 'as a new business model, capable of extracting and controlling immense amounts of data'. This connects platform infrastructure with other political economy preconditions discussed previously.

The designation 'platform' comes from its more traditional usage as a raised surface on which people can stand. In this context, the platform is a digital environment upon which other software can be run. In organizational terms, Nick Srnicek (2017: 48) argues that:

> Platforms, in sum, are a new type of firm; they are characterized by providing the infrastructure to intermediate between different user groups, by displaying monopoly tendencies driven by network effects, by employing cross-subsidization to draw in different user groups, and by having a designed core architecture that governs the interaction possibilities.

For the gig economy, as we have written elsewhere, 'the common feature of all digital labour platforms is that they offer tools to bring together the supply of, and demand for, labour' (Graham and Woodcock, 2018: 242). Similarly, Niels van Doorn (2017: 901) describes these organizations as 'platform labour intermediaries that, despite their self-presentation as tech companies, operate as new players in a dynamic temporary staffing industry.'

The platform therefore operates as a kind of intermediary for work. However, this intermediate function operates with a spectrum of control. For example, in figure 2, platform work is compared to traditional waged employment. In this case, there are (usually) high levels of temporality (workers are engaged for longer job durations) and the work has high levels of geographic stickiness (the work needs to be completed in a specific place). At the opposite end is cloudwork (microwork), in which there are very low levels of temporality and geographic stickiness: the jobs are of very short duration and can be completed from anywhere with an internet connection. As with online freelancing, which exhibits slightly more geographical stickiness, as well as the potential for longer job duration, platforms provide a way for a client to connect with a worker and set their own rates and conditions, following the model of Upwork or Amazon Mechanical Turk. The platform hosts the requests for work and the response of prospective workers. Geographically tethered platform work requires workers to be in a particular place. This means the platform exerts more control, often involving many of the same controls that a traditional waged employer would deploy.

Across both cloudwork types and geographically tethered work, platforms present themselves as different to traditional waged employment. At the core of the gig economy is a controversy over the classification of the people involved. In most countries, work can be categorized as conducted by an employee or someone who is self-employed. Self-employment means that a person runs their own business and therefore takes responsibility for its successes

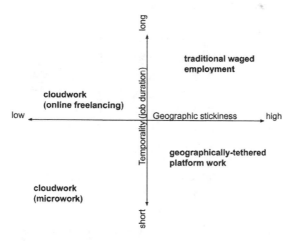

Figure 2 The spatiality and temporality of platform work

or failures, while also not having the rights or responsibilities of employees.[1] The issue at stake here is that being classified as self-employed means losing employment rights – although the protections that these afford can vary widely around the world. In most countries where there are binary employment statuses, this also makes it challenging to consider how gig workers fit within the traditional employee categorization.[2]

Platforms the world over prefer to use the self-employment classification as this allows them to contract work out to workers without meeting many employment regulations. It also means that workers have no access to rights around unfair dismissal or the right to organize in a trade union, issues that we will return to later. It is worth stating that we have not written this book as lawyers, and it is not our intent to get mired in debates about who is and is not an employee versus an independent contractor. We rather take the position that anyone exchanging labour power for money is a worker irrespective of their actual categorization. And that every worker deserves a set of minimum rights and protections. That said, it seems clear that many workers in the gig economy are misclassified as self-employed: a strategy that clearly offers more benefits to platforms than it does to workers. In the case of Uber, for example, this was supported by the employment judge in the workers' rights tribunal who stated: 'The notion that Uber in London is a mosaic of 30,000 small businesses linked by a common "platform" is, to our minds, faintly ridiculous.'[3]

This contractual outsourcing represents an evolution of a much older trend towards outsourcing. The trend towards outsourcing began in the 1970s as part of a push for lower costs and higher profits. It involved an organization taking parts of their operations like facility maintenance, cleaning or customer services and tendering them out to external companies. In the Global North, outsourcing became prevalent in both the private and public sector, driving down costs to either increase profits or meet internal targets. For example, in the UK it has become common for universities to outsource cleaning to private companies. This means a section of previously directly employed staff become employed by a private company. This creates a twofold advantage for university management. First, the responsibility for those workers (including how much workers are paid and their working conditions) is taken on by an external organization; second, by tendering out the contracts to the lowest bidder the university can drive down costs. Platforms have been able to take this project of outsourcing to a new level. What Srnicek (2017: 49) describes as 'lean platforms', are those 'which attempt to reduce their ownership of assets to a minimum and to profit by reducing costs as much as possible'. This was summarized by Tom Goodwin (2015) who noted that 'Uber, the world's largest taxi company, owns no vehicles. Facebook, the world's most popular media owner, creates no content.'

Despite the lean nature of these platforms, real people are still needed to drive cars for Uber, while Facebook needs people to serve as both content producers and moderators. The expensive capital costs are outsourced, retaining only the barest minimum of staff. This also extends to infrastructure costs, with many platforms running on Amazon web servers, renting the capacity needed. As Goodwin (2015) continues, 'the interface is where the profit is'. The elements that are retained by the company are the interface: methods to extract, analyse and use data. These aspects are not outsourced to any other company. Instead, the data are hoarded and put to work. Thus, the platform is like a shell, with just the 'bare extractive minimum – control over the platform that enables a monopoly rent to be gained' (Srnicek, 2017: 76).

The organization of the platform means that they are particularly reliant on network effects. The more workers and users on the platform, the greater the benefits of participating (Srnicek, 2017: 45). Conversely, if there is significant competition between platforms in any particular sector, those network effects are diminished. For instance, multiple taxi apps in a city will fragment both the driver and customer base, increasing waiting times and reducing the ease of access. Many platforms have been able to achieve these network effects relatively easily because of their relatively rapid expansion. In the case of Uber, there is no need for the platform itself to buy new cars. Instead, expansion is limited by server capacity, effective advertising and available workers. These two aspects combine to 'mean that platforms can grow very big very quickly' (Srnicek, 2017: 46).

The quick growth has meant that platforms have sprung up across different kinds of work. For the worker, this does not necessarily mean that their work process has substantially changed. A traditional minicab or taxi driver who becomes an Uber driver is still driving customers around, while a care worker moving onto Care.com is still providing care. However, a point that we will return to throughout the book is that this experience is differentiated between the Global North and the Global South. Some workers are moving from relatively formalized jobs onto platforms, whilst for others who have only ever worked in the informal sector, platform work is relatively formalized.

The case of Uber

The most recognizable geographically tethered platform is without doubt Uber. The platform has 3.9 million drivers across the world.[4] It holds so much brand recognition that the company is regularly used as a synonym for new platform ideas: the 'Uber for X' (Srnicek, 2017: 37), or even becoming a verb: to Uberize, meaning 'to change the market for a service by introducing a different way of buying or using it, especially using mobile technology'.[5] At its core, Uber provides something quite straightforward. The idea of transporting people as a job (i.e. taxis) has been around for centuries – albeit in a variety of forms such as drivers with horse-drawn carriages. Transporting customers for a fee has since been transformed through technology and licensing – moving from taxi-ranks and customers flagging them down in the street, to centralized controllers with radios, and medallion systems to limit driver numbers. What Uber provides is an app that connects drivers and passengers, in a straightforward exchange of money for transportation. It has neither invented the role of the driver, nor the need of the passenger, but rather a new way to connect them.

It is now possible to use the same app to quickly and reliably order an Uber in more than 600 cities around the world. Indeed, if Uber did not offer a genuine benefit to consumers, it would not have grown at such a rapid rate. This bringing together of workers and customers on geographically tethered platforms requires the building of trust by platforms. After all, the prospect of a stranger driving you around is a tough sell. Unlike pre-platform offerings, there is no obvious office or representative to complain to. Platforms instead rely on building consumer trust through rating systems and other forms of tracking.

Taking the example of London, the city has long had a two-tiered taxi arrangement. First, the famous black cabs, with drivers who learn 'the knowledge' of London streets.[6] These are taxis that can be flagged down on the street without prior booking. This is different to the second kind, minicabs, which had to be arranged by phone. These needed different kinds of operator licences to black cabs, along with no need to do 'the knowledge'. Minicabs had a reputation for unreliability, with the dispatcher often promising a cab was 'on the way' without any way for the customer to verify that it actually was. What Uber has been able to do is provide a customer interface that is appealing to smartphone users. No longer waiting on the phone to order a cab, but a slick designed app that orders the Uber car to the customer's location, showing not only the time until arrival, but also details on the driver and number-plate. This means no longer needing phone numbers for different local taxi companies, and no need for the customer to explain where they are. What Uber has achieved is a new way to intermediate a long-standing relationship between driver and passenger – something that has also involved huge amounts spent on advertising and branding.

Uber's initial offering was a high-end service. However, its main success has been UberX, a low-cost offering. In the US, the UberX version relies on 'unlicensed drivers with their own cars, many without commercial insurance' (Slee, 2015: 57). However, in the UK (as well as many other countries), Uber drivers have to have a private hire licence. In addition to UberX, the company has experimented with luxury services like Uber Black, pooling customers in the same car, as well as deliveries. This has been funded by astonishingly large tranches of venture capital funding, with $24.2 billion so far.[7] That funding has facilitated the rapid growth of the company, through its ability to run at a loss while spending venture capital money accrued through investment. From the start Uber provided special offers, bonuses and incentives to build the network effects needed to sustain its model. At first, a city with only a few Uber drivers could not sustain an Uber service for long, like a telephone network with few telephones. However, once 'it becomes established, Uber takes a bigger slice of each dollar and often cuts fares. Over time, Uber has taken a larger and larger slice of every fare' (Slee, 2015: 65). This is how Uber makes money with the platform: by taking a commission from every journey that a driver makes.

The success of Uber is also partly explained by its engagement with regulation and transport policy. As Travis Kalanick (2013) – the former CEO of Uber – explained:

> In most cities across the [US], regulators have chosen not to enforce against non-licensed transportation providers using ridesharing apps. This course of non-action resulted in massive regulatory ambiguity leading to one-sided competition which Uber has not engaged in to its own disadvantage.

This coyly phrased lack of 'disadvantage' has actually proven to be incredibly advantageous for Uber. As Trebor Scholz (2017a: 44) emphasizes: 'Uber is a labor company, not simply a tech startup, which means that it is reliant on the availability of an abundance of cheap labor and a permissive regulatory environment.' Despite its reliance on labour, Uber's business model involves avoiding sales taxes, the cost of vehicles, repairs, insurance, and meeting obligations for social security for its drivers. The main legislative loophole that Uber has taken advantage of is the categorization of its workers as self-employed independent contractors. In the process, 'Uber created a fundamental cultural shift in what it means to be employed' (Rosenblat, 2018: 4).

However, Uber has gone way beyond just taking advantage of lack of effective regulation, through its concerted public relations and lobbying campaigns. The company employs and is advised by political operatives such as Jim Messina (the former White House

Deputy Chief of Staff) and David Plouffe (Barack Obama's 2008 campaign manager). Pollman and Barry (2016) refer to this sort of strategy as 'regulatory entrepreneurship' – 'pursuing a line of business in which changing the law is a significant part of the business plan'. Kalanick has described the rise of the company as analogous to a political campaign in which 'the candidate is Uber and the incumbent is an asshole called "taxi"' (Kalanick and Swisher, 2014). Another documented tactic is the use of 'greyballing' to evade regulation. This involves the 'greyball' tool developed by Uber, which take the data collected by the app through its normal operation in order to 'identify and circumvent officials who were trying to clamp down on the ride-hailing service'.[8] The use of the tool was approved by Uber's legal team and has been running since at least 2014. For example, in Portland, Oregon, Uber was operating without approval. Uber gathered the details of city officials and 'greyballed' them, providing 'a fake version of the app, populated with ghost cars, to evade capture', including cancelling any rides they were able to hail. Uber justified this as part of its 'violation of terms of service' (VTOS) programme, aiming to prevent anyone misusing the service from accessing it. However, it has also widely been seen as a method for deliberately evading regulation by preventing officials from finding out whether Uber was operating within their jurisdiction.

The 'independent contractor' status frees Uber from many obligations to its drivers. Of particular importance are pay and rights to collective bargaining, which we discuss in chapter 4 and the Conclusion. Among the many concerns raised about the Uber platform is how much money its workers make. Uber's marketing campaign has worked hard to assuage fears, claiming at one point that Uber drivers in New York City earn over $90,000 a year (without giving a sense of the costs required to make this amount). However, as Trebor Scholz (2017a: 43) has noted 'nobody was able to verify' this claim, leading him to conclude that 'Uber's marketing campaign is falsifying the facts'. In an investor meeting, Uber's former CFO Brent Callinicos stated that it could easily raise rates to between 25 and 30 per cent. Mike Novogratz, a venture capitalist who was present at the meeting, asked a question: 'You've got happy employees, you've got happy customers, you've got happy shareholders. The holy triumvirate are all really excited about your company. Why are you going to risk that and push the employees' salary down 5%?' As reported in SF Gate, Callinicos simply responded 'because we can'.[9] As Slee (2015: 65) has noted, the experiment with taking 30 per cent actually means that Uber takes a bigger cut than most medallion owners.[10] What this also shows is a unilateral management attitude on platforms, particularly as they engage self-employed independent contractors.

Of course, the challenge of estimating how much drivers are paid is only difficult for those of us outside the platform. Within the platform, huge amounts of data are collected about the drivers and journeys. Uber knows where its drivers are, where they have been, the routes they have taken, the cost of each journey, and how it was rated by the passenger. Part of this hunger for data can be explained by Uber's ambition to introduce self-driving cars.[11,12] The huge quantities of data provide a training set that can be used to train artificial intelligence self-driving, meaning that the losses made in the short term could be offset by the potential for longer-term gains if Uber has the majority on self-driving vehicles.[13] Anyone in doubt about the granularity of Uber's data collection should note the so-called 'god view' that can be used to show all drivers and users in a city. At an Uber launch party in Chicago, a version of this was used as a party trick, showing the real-time movements of thirty users in New York – without their consent.[14] This highlights the lack of transparency around how data is used by the company – as well as what data it has access to – and reflects some of the claims about a 'toxic' atmosphere within the company.[15]

The geographically tethered model

The platform model has since been adapted to a range of different contexts and types of work. The model for geographically tethered platforms is one that takes existing forms of work that happen in particular places and reorganizes them through a digital platform. There is an ever-growing range of platformized work and services available to us today: from ordering a ride, having food delivered, having your house cleaned, arranging domestic care, getting your clothes washed and ironed, package delivery, to getting your dog walked. Each of these involve recognizable work processes: transportation, takeaways, cleaning, care, laundry and pet sitting existed before digital platforms did.[16] However, the use of smartphone apps to organize both the worker and the customer is a new way to organize work.

Your takeaway cannot make its own way to your door and your dog (probably) cannot take itself for a walk. Geographically tethered work thus tends to require spatial proximities and temporal synchronicities – it needs to happen in a specific place and time. You cannot outsource it to the other side of the planet. What this means is that geographic constraints (i.e. distance, and the local political economy) remain important. In other words, work cannot be completed solely over the internet, free from any geographic constraints (as we will discuss in the next section). Our internet use remains firmly constrained by the internet's physical infrastructure, with fibre optic cables laid across the planet along particular routes – often mirroring earlier communication networks, like shipping and telegraph routes.

The worker may need to be in the right place at the right time to complete a geographically tethered task, but the outsourcing process extends to ensure they are only paid for that productive moment, rather than the waiting time in between demand. Instead of the fleet of delivery drivers paid per hour with expensive equipment provided and maintained by a company, the gig worker is engaged for only the precise slivers of time required to complete a task. This relies upon contractual outsourcing which sidesteps many of the traditional obligations expected of organizations (worker protections and benefits), while still relying – as noted by Scholz (2017a) – on an actual worker.

The development of this model has meant breaking from traditional ways of organizing work. The taxi industry, for example, has many norms and regulations about how a prospective worker becomes a taxi driver. This includes 'the knowledge', the impact of criminal convictions, licensing arrangements, and so on. The geographically tethered model is based on the ability for a pool of potential workers to be called on to meet demand. This has required the development of technology that can do this efficiently, reliably and cost-effectively.

The preconditions that we have argued facilitate the growth of the gig economy can be clearly identified in this model. The changes in political economy have created a deregulated environment in which the platform can position itself as a 'technology company' rather than a cleaning company, taxi company, food delivery company or similar; all while using self-employed independent contractors to do the actual work. Neoliberalism enabled the deregulation of employment to support this model, while also creating an outlet for excess finance capital, allowing it to be poured into these platform companies. The technological factors can also be clearly identified here. In the case of Uber, the platform with its collection of data and automated back-end provides a scalability far beyond existing taxi companies. Building on this, the smartphone app has replaced the physical radio dispatcher as the interface. The use of technology – as well as huge amounts of marketing – provides powerful network effects that draw in both drivers and customers, further spurring this growth. The use of algorithmic management (Lee et al., 2015) keeps the costs low, while providing a new way to effectively manage a geographically dispersed and scalable workforce. Jobs are assigned and evaluated through code and data, without the need for human intervention. There is little chance of feedback, negotiation or the possibility of disputing decisions, resulting in very little transparency for workers. This is a continuation and intensification of the longer processes of outsourcing, minimizing the costs and risks to the platform. At the same time, the social factors that have led many workers to seek more flexible work are pushing many people onto these platforms.

The cloudwork model

Work has always been geographically tethered. As David Harvey (1989: 19) remarked, work is inherently place-based because, in contrast to capital, 'labour-power has to go home every night'. Farmers knew which fields to till, cleaners knew which houses to clean, and factory workers knew which factories to work in. Workers in other words have always had to be physically proximate to the object of their labour. This relationship between workers and place became more complicated once the raw material that workers were creating or transforming was information: something that, with the aid of information and communication technologies can be remotely manipulated.[17]

In other words, the spatial link between workers and the object of their work can be severed. For some types of work, workers need not be physically proximate to the customer, the manager or some of the physical manifestations of the work itself. This means that information-based work can, in theory, be done by anyone, from anywhere, with access to the right technological affordances. When you email customer support or report an image as inappropriate on your favourite social platform, the workers handling those tasks could either be in your city or on the other side of the globe. The untethering of work from place that this has allowed has meant that, for the first time, we potentially have a mass migration of labour without the migration of workers (Standing, 2016).

In order to adequately discuss why our expectations and visions about the relationships between work and economic development may have changed, it is useful to first outline what is and isn't new about digital work. Long, complicated global production networks have always existed. Workers on one side of the planet have laboured to make things for customers on the other without ever coming in contact with them. Two millennia ago, a Chinese silk weaver or Roman farmer might have little idea where the commodities that they made would end up. Today, technology has sped up relationships within global production networks. Workers putting laptops together in factories in Shenzhen could have those machines in shops in Brussels and Berlin by the end of the week. In both examples, it is worth noting that while the site of production can be spread to distant corners of the planet, some service work is necessarily spatially bound to particular places. Silk weavers and laptop assemblers can both perform work thousands of kilometres from European end users. But, until recently at least, shopkeepers are still needed to sell those goods. Some jobs are thus more geographically sticky than others.

Digital platforms have, however, made a lot of work less sticky. As work becomes ever more modularized, commoditized and standardized (Scott, 2001), and as markets for digital work are created, ties between service work and particular places can be severed. While the business process of outsourcing that emerged in the 1990s allowed large companies to take advantage of a 'global reserve army' by moving their call centres to cheap and distant labour markets, cloudwork changes the volume and granularity at which geographically non-proximate work can take place. A small business in New York can hire a freelance transcriber in Nairobi one day and New Delhi the next. No offices or factories need to be built, no local regulations are adhered to, and – in most cases – no local taxes are paid (Graham et al., 2017b; Irani, 2015). The switch in the production network of work happens by simply sending some emails or clicking some buttons on a digital work platform. And, in this way, the employer leaves behind no material traces in the places where it was once an employer. Its effects, however, are far from insignificant. And, as the following chapter will demonstrate, these changing economic geographies of work impact on the livelihoods of workers.

Two of the largest English-language platforms, Upwork and Freelancer, respectively claim to have 12 and 25 million workers signed up on them (Graham and Anwar, 2019). The number of workers signed up on cloudwork platforms is often a multiple of the number who actually find any work. But, if even 7 per cent[18] of those signups ever find jobs, these are staggering numbers on those two platforms alone. Even though certain types of digital work can now – in theory – be commissioned and carried out from anywhere on the planet with an internet connection, it still tends to be characterized by distinct geographies as can be seen in the map in figure 3(a). The map (produced by our colleague Sanna Ojanperä) visualizes a global index of online labour platforms. The index captures the five largest English-language cloud platforms, which represent 70 per cent of the market by traffic.[19] Almost three-quarters of demand for cloudwork on those platforms comes from the US and EU.[20]

We see a very different pattern if we look at the locations of workers (figure 3(b)). According to this data, over two-thirds of the world's crowdworkers live in Asia, and India and Bangladesh alone are home to 41 per cent of the world's population of freelancers. There is also a significant number of workers from the Global North signed up to cloudwork platforms. The US, for instance, is home to 12 per cent of the world's online freelancers (Ojanperä et al., 2018). Again, the data source is limited in its focus on only English-language platforms. Yet, even with that limitation in mind, it is noteworthy how workers from the Global North and South enter the same planetary market to compete for jobs that largely originate in the Global North (Graham and Anwar, 2019).

It is worth distinguishing between two different types of crowdwork: online freelancing and microwork. Online freelancing, which we have discussed so far, involves the platform as mediator introducing customers and workers often by allowing bidding and negotiation by either party. The work tends to be conducted off-platform, and can involve longer tasks like software development, web design, transcription or translation. The platform profits by taking a cut of the work transaction. Microwork involves the completion of short tasks on a platform interface that tend to be completed quickly, with the worker receiving a piece rate, minus the platform's cut. In a recent ILO study of this kind of work, Berg et al. (2018: xv) found that workers were engaged in a diverse range of tasks, 'including image identification, transcription and annotation; content moderation; data collection and processing; audio and video transcription; and translation.' These tasks were used by clients to 'post bulk tasks', which are split up into small fragments for individual workers to complete.

The Availability of Online Work

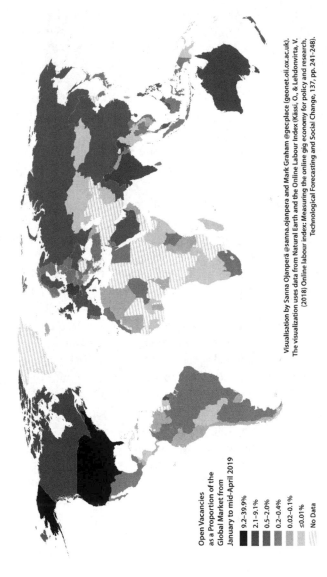

**Open Vacancies
as a Proportion of the
Global Market from
January to mid-April 2019**

- 9.2–39.9%
- 2.1–9.1%
- 0.5–2.0%
- 0.2–0.4%
- 0.02–0.1%
- ≤0.01%
- No Data

Visualisation by Sanna Ojanperä @sanna.ojanpera and Mark Graham @gecplace (geonet.oii.ox.ac.uk).
The visualization uses data from Natural Earth and the Online Labour Index (Kässi, O., & Lehdonvirta, V.
(2018) Online labour index: Measuring the online gig economy for policy and research.
Technological Forecasting and Social Change, 137, pp. 241–248).

Figure 3(a) The availability of cloudwork

Source: https://geonet.oii.ox.ac.uk/blog/mapping-the-availability-of-online-labour-in-2019/

The Availability of Online Workers

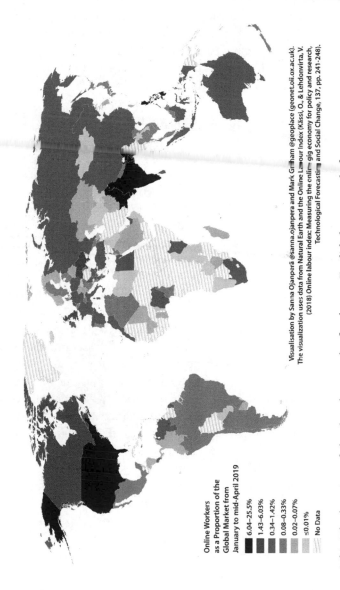

Online Workers
as a Proportion of the
Global Market from
January to mid-April 2019

- 6.04–25.5%
- 1.43–6.03%
- 0.34–1.42%
- 0.08–0.33%
- 0.02–0.07%
- ≤0.01%
- No Data

Visualisation by Sanna Ojanperä @sanna.ojanpera and Mark Graham @geoplace (geonet.oii.ac.uk).
The visualization uses data from Natural Earth and the Online Labour Index (Kässi, O., & Lehdonvirta, V.
(2018) Online labour index: Measuring the online gig economy for policy and research,
Technological Forecasting and Social Change, 137, pp. 241-248).

Figure 3(b) The location of cloudworkers on the five largest English-language platforms

Source: https://geonet.oii.ox.ac.uk/blog/mapping-the-availability-of-online-labour-in-2019/

Amazon's Mechanical Turk – the world's most well-known microwork platform – refers to these tasks as 'artificial artificial intelligence'. These are tasks that usually rely on a distinctly human ability to interpret things (for instance image recognition or sentiment analysis). These are tasks that might, in theory, be performed by AI, but are cheaper and/or quicker to simply outsource to human workers. For some types of task, it may not be a simple case of humans or artificial intelligence, but rather human microworkers embedded into otherwise automated systems through application programming interfaces (APIs). Here, workers are essentially treated as part of software, algorithms and 'automated' processes. The computer scientist Jaron Lanier (2014: 178) describes this as conjuring up 'a sense of magic, as if you can just pluck results out of the cloud at an incredibly low cost'. Ultimately, this is work that usually requires very little formal training, and – as a result – tends to be poorly paid (Hara et al., 2018). In both cases, what matters to the customer is the final product, not where the actual work was conducted.

Microwork is a clear extension of outsourcing, with roots in crowdsourcing. This term was coined by Howe (2006) to mean 'the act of a company or institution taking a function once performed by employees and outsourcing it to an undefined (and generally large) network of people in the form of an open call'. This provided a way to search for innovation and profitable ideas beyond the boundaries of an organization. However, microwork focuses this into 'a third-generation sourcing ecosystem', that provides a requester with a large pool of accessible workers (Kaganer et al., 2013: 23). The platform provides a way to mediate between customers and workers. This organization of microwork 'relies on dyadic relationships consisting of one buyer, one supplier and a well-defined final deliverable' (Kaganer et al., 2013: 25). This means that the kinds of tasks that are suitable for this platform are short and relatively simple. Larger projects of work can be broken into smaller tasks, but each needs to be completable by an individual working alone. This division of labour allows work to be completed quickly and cheaply. For example, rather than paying a trained expert for transcription, the audio file can be broken down into very small chunks and distributed out across a microwork platform. The quality can be assured by getting each small chunk completed twice and comparing the results. The end result can be achieved much more quickly as each part can be worked on simultaneously. Costs can be kept down by finding workers across the world prepared to work for lowest rates.

If Uber has become the emblematic example of geographically tethered platforms, Amazon Mechanical Turk takes that title for microwork platforms. The name of the platform itself is taken from the Mechanical Turk curiosity. The Mechanical Turk appeared to be a chess-playing automaton, playing against, and beating many prominent figures of the day. However, in its cabinetry, which can be seen in figure 4, was a concealed chess grandmaster who was in fact orchestrating the moves. Rather than being a successful

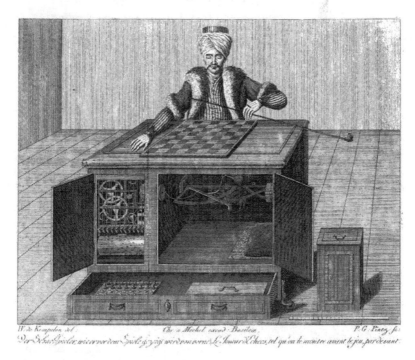

Figure 4 The Mechanical Turk (see https://en.wikipedia.org/wiki/The_Turk)

attempt at artificial intelligence, it was in fact a successful illusion of AI, underpinned by hidden human labour. The platform attempts to do something similar. For the 'requester', a task is put up on the platform and then they pay for and receive the results. The platform mediates between requesters and taskers, ensuring that the two do not have to communicate. Amazon's 'crowd sorcerers work with coolness and the spectacle of innovation to conceal the worker' (Scholz, 2015). In the process, Amazon distributes what it calls HITs (human intelligence tasks) to individual workers. These are separated out from the overall project and workers cannot collaborate on the discrete HITs. Microwork platforms therefore work like a 'black box', a 'system whose workings are mysterious' (Pasquale, 2015: 3). The odd turn of phrase that Amazon uses for tasks – HITs – indicates the connection to artificial intelligence with this kind of work. If Uber's dream is to replace drivers with automated vehicles, the work being conducted on microwork platforms is also key to this process (Gray and Suri, 2019).

It is technically challenging to develop products that are powered by artificial intelligence. The challenge is such that 'some startups have worked out it's cheaper and easier to get humans to behave like robots than it is to get machines to behave like humans' (Solon, 2018). For example, Expensify (an app for business expense management) claimed that its proprietary 'smartscan technology' transcribed receipts. However, scans were being posted as HITs to Amazon Mechanical Turk. As Rochelle LaPlante, a worker on the platform, pointed out: 'I wonder if Expensify SmartScan users know MTurk workers enter their receipts', including 'someone's Uber receipt with their full name, pick-up and drop-off addresses'. Echoing the Mechanical Turk example, Alison Darcy has called this the 'Wizard of Oz design technique', referring to the way the work is hidden behind an interface, like the man hiding behind the projection of the eponymous wizard in the story.[21]

This kind of work is also becoming an increasingly important part of content production on platforms like Facebook and YouTube. While much attention has been paid to the 'produsage' (Bruns, 2008) of users who both use and produce content, often the labour that this relies upon is obscured. A growing number of workers are now engaged in 'commercial content moderation (CCM)' to ensure that users can only upload and view content that is deemed acceptable. As Sarah Roberts (2016), who coined the term, explains, the 'interventions of CCM workers on behalf of the platforms for which they labor directly contradict myths of the Internet as a site for free, unmediated expression'. These workers are engaged in repetitive short tasks which involve viewing 'racist, sexist, homophobic, or sexually or violently graphic content' considered to be too disturbing or unpleasant for users (Roberts, 2016: 150). This work is closer to the often-invisible domestic work being transformed on geographically tethered platforms. In this case, it is the cleaning of content, required for platforms that make money from advertising – after all, advertisers do not want to be associated with the kind of content the CCM workers are deployed to keep off the platform. It is important to note that, in some cases, the tasks done by microworkers are being used to automate machine learning systems: systems that are designed to replace the very workers who train them.

Understanding how platforms work

This chapter began with the example of Uber as the archetypal platform in the gig economy. The Uber model has shown how a digital intermediary can manage the supply and demand of labour, paid for only when utilized by the platform. The existence of a transportation company that owns no vehicles shows how the longer trends of outsourcing have been effectively refigured through the platform to drastically lower the costs of labour. The platform has therefore become a new organizational form, stepping in as an intermediary in increasingly broader kinds of work, collecting both data and a cut of the payments made for services. Uber is an example of this at its most developed – both in terms of scale and use of business practices that seek not only to operate within grey areas of the law, but also to reshape them in the interest of the platform. This is now being replicated in different areas,

Table 1 Governance in the gig economy (inspired by Gereffi et al., 2005)

Buyer	Spatial control	Temporal control	Ability to set rates	Digital legibility	Barriers to entry for workers	Repeat transactions	Degree of explicit coordination
Taxi and delivery work (e.g. Uber)	High	Mixed	High	Mixed	Low	Low	High
Domestic and care work (e.g. SweepSouth)	High	Mixed	High	Low	Low	High	High
Microwork (e.g. Amazon Mechanical Turk)	Low	Low	Low	High	Low	Low	Mixed
Online Freelancing Platform (e.g. Upwork)	Low	Low	Low	Mixed	Mixed	Mixed	Mixed

Note: Because of the huge amount of diversity within the gig economy, this table necessarily over generalizes in almost every category. For instance, there will undoubtedly be cases of geographically-tethered self-employment with high barriers to entry, or online markets with low abilities of workers to set pay rates. However, we would argue that this broad model applies to the majority of work types within each category.

both within geographically tethered work as well as cloudwork.
Uber is not the only model in the platform-enabled gig economy.
Platforms are entering into increasingly diverse forms of work.

As the geographer Doreen Massey (1984: 8) has argued, organizationally and spatially separating work transformed 'relations between activities in different places, new spatial patterns of social organization, new dimensions of inequality and new relations of domination and dependence'. In order to make sense of this in the gig economy, we have distinguished between the different kinds of platforms and their relative spatial control, temporal control, ability of workers to set pay rates, task discretion, digital legibility, barriers to entry, complexity of labour process, and the degree of explicit coordination and power asymmetry. In table 1, we assess the relationship between these variables. The purpose of this table is not to develop a spectrum of governance types that run from high to low levels of explicit coordination and power asymmetry (as Gereffi et al. (2005) do in their analysis of value chain models). It is rather to illustrate some of the granularity in coordination and power asymmetry within the gig economy, and the diversity of models that can be deployed. There are undoubtedly limits to the spread of platform work, but – as shown in table 1 – there is also a multiplicity of ways of organizing work in the gig economy.

Spatial control

This category refers to the amount of control platforms exert over where workers do their work. Delivery riders and domestic workers have especially low levels of spatial autonomy. Spatial control by the platform is integral to the business model: workers are told which houses to clean, which houses to deliver to, and even which routes to take. Without exerting that control, the platform could not realistically conduct its business.

Cloudwork platforms, in contrast, tend to allow for an extremely high degree of spatial autonomy of their workers. Workers can, in theory, work from anywhere on the planet provided they have a stable internet connection. Cloud platforms also use that spatial freedom as an integral part of their business model. Companies like Upwork or Freelancer are so successful precisely because they bring together a world of workers on a single platform.

Temporal control

On the surface, it might seem as if platforms, by definition, do not exert any temporal control over their workers. Workers are, after all, free to log on and off whenever they choose. However, beyond that, there is a diversity of ways that platforms seek to control when workers work.

Starting from the least amount of control, cloudwork platforms tend not to get involved in when workers log on and off, and instead leave those sorts of negotiations to workers and clients. Workers on geographically tethered platforms likewise are rarely told that they have to work on any given day. In practice, however, platforms have a variety of ways of encouraging workers to be active at particular times. Ride-hailing and delivery platforms use variable rates to increase the available workforce at peak times. Once a worker has accepted a job, platforms then greatly increase the amount of temporal control that they exert. On some platforms, workers are tracked down to the second in order to ensure that work is effectively carried out.

While platforms do not have the ability to use employment contracts to force workers to work at certain times, it is usually a combination of an oversupply of workers and financial incentives to work at certain times that allow platforms to still have some influence on when their workers work. Cleaning, care work and cloudwork also inevitably usually happen on the client's schedule rather than the workers'. By ensuring a greater supply of labour than demand for it, platforms can avoid the messy business of scheduling work. Due to the oversupply of labour on those platforms, cloudworkers often have to complete any jobs that they get on tight schedules. You recall the story of the Ghanaian cloudworker who has to work all night that we mentioned in the introduction, as an example of this. This can mean that, when they find work, it has to be completed very quickly. With geographically tethered workers this often involves a freedom for workers to log on whenever they want, but only certain times of day have enough demand for work. For example, food delivery tends to be clustered around meal times.

Ability to set pay rates

For much geographically tethered work, platforms set rates of pay. Some platforms work on the basis of opaque pricing algorithms that leave workers with no real sense of how that gig would translate into an hourly rate. Others operate complicated bonus and reward schemes that have the same net outcome: workers are unclear about how exactly their time will be compensated.[22] And, in a few cases, there is an ability to accommodate individual workers who seek a higher rate of pay.

Cloudwork platforms tend to operate differently, as workers on those platforms tend to be able to set their own rates as either hourly rates or piece rates. Some platforms do, however, set minimum hourly rates. This act is likely driven less by altruism (or else why still allow some workers in some countries to work for less than their local minimum wage), and more by a desire to increase the commission that they take. Extremely low-wage work is not profitable for the platform for that reason. Even though most cloudwork platforms tend not to set rates, the nature of the marketplace pushes all workers who do not have specialized skills that are in high demand to accepting the going rate for that particular job. As the next chapter will show, going rates can be pushed sharply downwards by the planetary nature of a lot of cloudwork.

Digital legibility

By 'digital legibility', we are referring to the ability of automated processes to read, and ultimately replace key parts of the labour process. The legibility of gig work varies distinctly across the different types of platforms. Tied up in the platform model is the capturing of data from workers and users, and the developing of ways to turn it into a productive resource. For example, with Uber, the actions of workers provide data that is used to further the short-term aims of the platform, while also developing the possibility to replace workers with even cheaper (and more docile) artificial intelligence in the form of self-driving cars. While, in many cases, this level of automation may seem relatively far off, it impacts on the strategy of the platform and also informs the perspective that they take towards workers: why offer a steady and secure employment contract if you would prefer these tasks were automated anyway?

Automation is a concern that is increasingly on the policy agenda throughout the world. For example, in an influential study, Frey and Osborne (2017) analysed the susceptibility of 702 different occupations to computerization. Their key argument is that 47 per cent of employment in the US is at high risk of automation over the next two decades. While this focuses on production, transport and logistics, as well as administrative work, they also point towards the possibilities of automating service work. However, Nedelkoska and Quintini (2018) found that across 32 countries the risk varied significantly, but only 14 per cent of jobs were considered highly automatable. The McKinsey Global Institute (2017) estimates around half of all work could be automated, but again that there would be significant difference by country.

With microwork, many of the tasks may seem ripe for automation, even if at present this is difficult to do. Amazon Mechanical Turk already explicitly frames microwork as 'artificial artificial intelligence'. It is mostly work that could already be automated away (if it were not for an army of cheap labour able to do the same work for less cost than an automated system). Companies are currently experimenting with artificial intelligence solutions to the problems of image recognition, transcription, machine learning, moderation and a range of other needs. Automating those sorts of information-processing tasks, in most cases, entails less risk for the client and end user than, say, automated driving, but there is also less profit to be made by replacing low-wage workers. Domestic and care work, by contrast, is a long way off being automated.

This kind of automation develops at work, emerging out of the economic and power relationships that already exist there

(O'Neil, 2017; Noble, 2018; Eubanks, 2019) Gig work is par
ticularly susceptible to attempts at automation. Transport is an area
that is the focus of substantial investment in automation technologies, and many of the sorts of jobs on microwork platforms have
already been automated by some companies. With delivery work,
some parts of the labour process have already been automated,
through the use of GPS-assisted route planning and barcodes or
radio-frequency identification (RFID) tagging for inventory management. The second is that in all of these cases, workers are
contributing to datasets being used to train artificial replacements.
The data generated by drivers contributes to the training sets for
self-driving cars, while microwork allows for a much wider range
of training data. Often workers will not be aware of the role they
are playing, as the tasks are fractured and stripped of their meaning.

Barriers to entry for workers

Many platforms operate with limited barriers to entry for workers,
in part because of the relatively low levels of formal training needed
for workers to engage in the job. What this means is that platforms
can quickly scale up their workforces if needed. Taxi and delivery
platforms also have relatively low entry requirements for incoming
workers. Workers on many of those platforms need to be able to
drive and not have any major criminal convictions, but they do
need access to a vehicle. Although cleaning and care work tends to
require a high level of ability and skill, its manifestation as platform
work is likewise characterized by relatively low barriers to entry.

Online freelancing can incorporate a diverse range of job types:
ranging from jobs characterized by relatively low to extremely
high complexity. As such, some types of online freelancing can
have somewhat higher barriers to entry than other platform jobs.
Platform workers rarely have to demonstrate formal qualifications.
However, to get jobs in fields such as web development or graphic
design, they need to demonstrate both a portfolio of existing work
and a high rating on the platform that they work on (which they
will only obtain by satisfying their previous clients). Platforms
can compensate for relatively higher barriers to entry, and the

constraints on the supply of labour that those barriers create, by not
constraining the platform to any single local labour market.

Repeat transactions

For many types of platform work, workers tend not to encounter
the same clients across gigs. Many microworkers, and some online
freelancers, will never actually find out who their clients are.
Instead, the client is hidden behind the interface of the platform.
Delivery drivers may re-encounter some of the same customers,
but those interactions tend to be fleeting. It therefore makes little
sense for clients and workers to attempt to disintermediate the
platform – repeating their interaction, but without the platform
connecting to them. Ride-hail drivers may have long stretches
of time with some customers, but – for them too – it makes little
sense to attempt to disintermediate the operation of the platform.
It is precisely the multi-sided nature of the platform (connecting
workers and clients with many potential matches) that is of value
to both clients and workers in that case.

With domestic and care work there is an entirely different
calculation, however. Here there are both extended interactions
between workers and clients and repeated interactions between
those same workers and clients: leading to the danger of disin-
termediation for platforms. For those reasons, platforms such as
Homejoy in the US have struggled. Yet some platforms in this
line of work still thrive by reducing transaction costs and offering a
mechanism for trust to be built between worker and client.

Degree of explicit coordination

We then see that geographically tethered platforms tend to exert
a high degree of control over their workforce. Most platforms
need to control the locations of workers, manage the time it takes
for them to carry out their jobs, set the rates that they receive to
do that work. In controlling work in that way, platforms are able
to operate with relatively low barriers to entry for their workers.
Within these models, however, there are then a range of approaches

that grapple with varying degrees of digital legibility and varying levels of repeat interactions between the same workers and clients.

Cloudwork platforms, in contrast, tend to exert less explicit coordination over the labour process. Most platforms do not control the locations of workers, or manage when or how they do their work (even though some offer surveillance tools for clients to monitor their workers). Rate-setting also tends to be left to a negotiation between workers and clients. In most cases, cloudwork platforms attempt to remove barriers to entry for workers. They do this in large part by greatly expanding the geographic scope of where workers can work from and where clients can reach them from, but also by not structuring platform interfaces around formal qualifications or titles. While cloud platforms rarely seek to exert fine-grained control over the labour process, it is rather the contexts and networks that they bring into being that shape much of the nature of work on those platforms.

In sum, there are significant differences in how platforms organize work. However, what is missing so far is the actual experience of workers on these platforms, who – for now at least – do the work that provides the services and creates value for the platforms. It is to their experiences and the ways that they interact with these different forms of governance that we now turn.

3

What is it like to work in the gig economy?

In this chapter we turn to focus on the experience of workers in the gig economy. The preceding chapters have examined where the gig economy came from, discussed the debates that surround it and outlined the business models and operations that drive platforms. However, we cannot hope to fully understand the gig economy without also considering the experiences of the workers who support it. Trying to make sense of it without focusing on workers is like studying astronomy without ever looking up at the stars. And of course, the deep and ingrained knowledge of what it is like to work in the gig economy is already out there, held in the lived experience of workers across the world on many different platforms.

Drawing on extensive interview and ethnographic data, we turn to the voices of workers who do this work every day, and with whom we interact in both visible and invisible ways. We cannot claim to represent the voices of all gig workers in this chapter – it is far too short for that. The experience of working in the gig economy necessarily varies by place, by platform and by the myriad positionalities that each worker brings to the job. There are, as Alexandrea Ravenelle (2019: 1) has argued, 'strugglers', 'survivors' and 'success stories' in the gig economy. But by highlighting a range of case studies and examples that reoccur in the gig economy, we can begin to sketch out the good and bad of the gig economy.

Delivery work

Geographically tethered forms of gig work are often the most visible in major cities, as workers need to be in particular places to complete the work. The rapid growth of food delivery platforms has meant that large numbers of workers have been drawn into working as riders on bicycles, motorbikes and mopeds via platforms like Deliveroo. For many workers, the process of making money on a platform like Deliveroo is straightforward and it offers a particular kind of flexibility.

The desire for flexibility is something expressed by many of the workers we have interviewed, as well as one of the preconditions we have identified for the gig economy in chapter 1. For example, Mumit,[1] who drives a motorbike in London for Deliveroo, explained his choice to work on the platform: 'When I got insured on my bike I was like what do I do? I need to find myself a gig, I don't know what I'm doing now, you know, so then I thought ok, bikes [are] my passion, I wanted to make money riding my bike, so I found like a delivery job.' The flexibility of the job was a draw; however, it resulted in Mumit driving for 'six days a week. On a Sunday, my longest day, I do about from ten o'clock to half-eleven in the evening, so thirteen and a half hours. Mondays I do quarter to twelve to half-eleven. The rest of the week I do from five to half-eleven and Saturday is my day off!' This kind of schedule is common for a motorbike/moped driver, in which they need to work a large percentage of peak hours – over Friday, Saturday and Sunday evenings – in order to get access to priority shift booking. The fewer peak hours a driver works, the less access they have for shift booking, meaning they then have less flexibility in choosing when to work. The 'flexibility' of the work then becomes more nuanced – and often dependent on working large numbers of hours per week.

The platform's use of self-employed or 'independent contractor' status means that Mumit, like tens of thousands of drivers across the UK, does not have an employment contract with Deliveroo. The result is that while workers can choose when to work, they need to work the peak meal times of lunch and dinner to make enough money – as well as the majority of Friday, Saturday and Sunday evenings. This echoes Karl Marx's (1976: 272) observation that we discussed earlier about workers being doubly free. This 'freedom' and 'flexibility' is not sufficient for the workers themselves. For example, Alejandro explained that he used to be a chef before working for Deliveroo. In that job, he:

> had a contract, holiday pay sick pay … with Deliveroo there isn't anything, it's a problem. If I have an accident it's my problem, the company only care about if you deliver the order and that's it. I feel less secure absolutely. I feel alone with the company, you feel like you are a self-employed because you don't have bosses but at the same time Deliveroo is your boss, you can't see anybody but you work for a company.

Alejandro's self-employed status means that the usual benefits and social security are not available to him, with only the wage being paid to the worker. This is far from the promise presented by Deliveroo in their advertising to new riders. Mumit, who at the time of interview had already had bikes stolen, written off in accidents, and had broken bones while working, explained that when things go wrong:

> Deliveroo don't care, it's got nothing to do with them, because you're an independent contractor so you have to deal with your own things. They don't care, they'll sign you off for the shift until you can get back, they'll say get back in touch with us and that's all through the call centre as well, not through a person who's … even pretending to give a fuck [laughter].

For Alejandro, the result of working under these conditions was that:

we feel scared sometimes. I am young, I don't have any family to care for, it's not all that bad for me short term. But long term you're scared, you're scared. If I want to go holidays I need to keep money; if I crash or broke my leg so I can't work. If I can't work I can't pay the rent, I can't go holidays, so it's a process that's quite hard.

Alejandro – like many of the Deliveroo drivers we have spoken to – complained that 'we are not really self-employed'. At the time of writing in 2019, the Independent Workers union of Great Britain (IWGB) had brought a case to the CAC (Central Arbitration Committee), in which Deliveroo intervened and successfully argued that the drivers should not have worker status. This means that the platform has, so far, successfully freed itself from the responsibility to cover workers in the event of something going wrong. This is particularly important in driving work, given a recent survey of gig economy drivers, riders and their managers finding that '42% said they had been involved in a collision where their vehicle had been damaged and 10% of the total sample said that someone had been injured as a result and this was usually themselves' (Christie and Ward, 2018: 4–5). Furthermore, 'Three quarters of respondents (75%) said that there had been occasions while working when they have had to take action to avoid a crash.' The piece-rate arrangement also means drivers are 'chasing jobs', taking risks in order to get more work, which 'increases the exposure to risk'. Christie and Ward's (2018: 5) conclusion is that 'these faceless digital brokers take no responsibility for the health and safety of the people who accrue income for them.' This had fatal consequences for Pablo Avendano, working for Caviar (a food delivery platform) in the US. He was killed after being hit by another vehicle while working in heavy rain in Philadelphia. The callous non-response of the platform in response to Pablo's death was summed up by one of his friends: 'like risk and liability, Caviar seems to want to outsource even the emotional labor of mourning to its independent contractors and society as whole.'[2]

Despite this clear tragedy, it is important to stress that worker experiences of delivery platforms are not all negative. As Mumit explained, at Deliveroo: 'the work itself is really good, because it is the algorithm that's the boss, you do get that kind of a sense of freedom, even though it's not really [freedom].' He goes on to explain that because there is 'no interaction with Deliveroo' other than through the app and emails, this means no supervisor standing over your shoulder telling you what to do, or the experience of being 'bossed around' by a manager. Similarly, Fred, a Deliveroo rider in London argued that it is 'actually like a reasonable shit job because that illusion of freedom is really strong like you do kind of feel like your own boss because we can all stand around and talk shit about Deliveroo as much as we like'. Unlike other forms of low-paid service work, 'there's no reason to be extra nice to people like you're not selling anything, you're not selling yourself so there's no emotional labour in it.' On these platforms, the tip is mainly paid in the app before the delivery is actually made. While there are sometimes cash tips, these are rare. Compared to work in call centres, hospitality, and so on, this means not having to bring emotions to work and manage them throughout the shift, with all the stress that entails (Woodcock, 2017).

There is still the experience of surveillance for drivers, whether through the location-tracking on the app, or the visibility on the roads. For example, in December 2018 in India, a driver for Zomato (a food delivery platform) was spotted eating some of a customer's takeaway before delivering it. The video was widely shared on social media, leading to the driver being deactivated. As one commentator, Dushyant Shekhawat, noted: 'what made the man take a bite was, quite possibly, a horribly unfair system that had him working ungodly hours, to deliver food he could never afford for himself, to people who likely never tip.'[3] In our fieldwork in India we have found that many drivers work twelve hours a day, seven days a week, often in dangerous traffic conditions – something also echoed in our interviews in South Africa. In one group interview in Bangalore, drivers recounted how they had started receiving 60 rupees per delivery, which had then fallen to 40 rupees, and most recently down to 30 rupees.[4] At no point had the platform negotiated these changes – instead, they were announced to the drivers. At the end of the interview, we asked drivers what one thing they would like to be improved on the platform. They all replied 'more money', and when we asked if there was anything else, they shook their heads and pointed their fingers upward: 'more money'.

Taxi work

One of the key differences with delivering passengers rather than packages or takeaways is that there is a more direct interaction with customers. With delivery work, the customer can choose to tip the delivery rider through the app at the point of sale, meaning the interaction at the doorstep happens after the decision to tip, taking away the pressure of a positive service interaction. However, with platforms like Uber, the decision to tip happens at the end of the journey after the customer decides on the quality of the experience. This is accompanied with the use of a star rating system, which can determine whether or not a driver can continue to work on the platform. The rating system does not allow for much of a choice, given it has become customary for both drivers and customers to give five stars. This means dropping below that rating can put the driver at risk. On Uber, going below 4.7 in many cities can risk 'deactivation' of the driver – that is, being fired. This makes drivers vulnerable to demanding riders, as 'only a small number of complaints can lead to the driver losing their livelihood' (Slee, 2015: 73).

James Farrar – a co-founder of UPHD (United Private Hire Drivers), the Uber driver branch of IWGB – has explained what this process looks like in practice in an interview with James Temperton for Wired.[5] One Friday night Farrar picked up three passengers in London. As they had been drinking, they were demanding and difficult passengers, an experience for the driver just 'like any other Friday night as an Uber driver'. One passenger opened a door at a junction so she could vomit onto the road. Farrar stopped the journey, attempted to file a report to Uber, and would not set off again straight away. The group called another Uber which arrived. Following from his recent experience, James decided to warn the new Uber driver – something which his now ex-passengers opposed. One of them attacked Farrar, pushing and shouting anti-Irish abuse at him, and damaging his car. Due to his concerns about Uber taking the passenger's side – something reported by many drivers – he called the police to report what had happened, attempting to protect himself against a complaint from the passengers. As they had booked through Uber, he could only say it was 'my customer, but I don't know the name, or the address, but I'll ask Uber for it'. Uber refused to provide details for reasons relating to data privacy. Uber then refused to release the information without a court order.

What this event highlights is that despite their classification as self-employed, an Uber driver has little control over situations where something goes wrong. In response, Farrar contacted a law firm and began the process of challenging Uber on the basis of being misclassified, a process that at the time of writing in 2019 has already taken in excess of three years.[6] Farrar is not the only person to complain about the power passengers hold over Uber drivers. As Yaseen Aslam – another co-founder of UPHD – has explained, he had to 'keep my rating high to keep my job'. The result was 'always' being 'nervous of getting very low ratings from customers as it wouldn't take that many one-star ratings to put me at risk of deactivation. I felt that this system was inhumane.'[7]

These kinds of concerns are not only about the stress of deactivation, but can also have serious ramifications for the safety of drivers on the road, as already noted for delivery work. For example, in South Africa, Uber has faced serious – and sometimes violent – opposition from traditional metered taxi drivers. This risk of violence only increased as Uber began allowing cash payments to encourage users who did not have access to credit cards. While this grew the user base, it also exposed drivers to increased risks as they were now expected to carry cash. Whilst a limited number of taxis had existed beforehand, in cities like Johannesburg this meant there were now many potential robbery targets driving the streets, which could be ordered into dangerous situations via the app.[8] What followed was a spate of robberies and hijackings. Some of those attacks led to the murder of drivers.[9] A demand of almost all

Uber drivers that we spoke to in South Africa was for the platform to introduce positive identification for customers – something it already requires of drivers, whose photographs are shown to customers when they order a ride. Bolt, the rival platform in South Africa, allows cash journeys and even less identification from passengers – just a mobile phone number that can be obtained from a throwaway sim card. Many of the drivers we spoke to discussed how they could earn more with Bolt as the platform takes a smaller percentage fee, but the issues with safety made working for that platform much more of a risk, particularly at night.

The lack of any collective voice – or even individual channels – has meant that platforms like Uber and Bolt experience little, if any, pressure to implement changes. Even without the risk of robberies, many Uber drivers in South Africa have had their earnings significantly eroded due to rising petrol prices in the country. Uber and Bolt workers cannot change their rates to cover the additional costs, left only with the algorithmically determined price. Moreover, in South Africa many of the trips are short, reflecting users' fears of public safety. Drivers do not know how far a customer wants to travel until they have picked them up, as the destination is only revealed after this point. Drivers therefore complain that waiting for, travelling to, and carry out short trips can often cost as much – or in some cases more – than the fee the driver will receive. In both of these cases, self-employed drivers should have much more control over their work than they currently experience. This has led to protests and wildcat strikes in response to fuel price rises. As one striking worker explained to Times Live (a South African newspaper): 'at this time last year, after a hard day's work and after all expenses such as fuel had been paid, I could earn R3,500 weekly ... now, some weeks, drivers are barely getting R500 a week' (approximately £28 a week).[10]

Despite the wild claim that Uber drivers in New York earn $90,000 per year,[11] the reality across the world is that the platform is putting immense pressure on drivers' incomes, both on and off the platform. As James Farrar testified in the Central London Employment Tribunal in 2016 'in some months he earned as little as £5 per hour, well below the current national minimum wage for over-25s of £7.20' – the minimum wage at the time.[12] The latest case concerns claims that the '40,000 drivers are allowed almost £11,000 in wages and more than £8,000 in holiday pay', as Uber 'refuses to recognize a two-year-old ruling entitling them to holiday pay, a minimum wage and rest breaks'.[13]

In our discussions with Uber drivers across London, as well as in other parts of the world, they have confirmed that earnings are low. However, despite the evidence that making a living as an Uber driver is difficult, large numbers of workers are still choosing to sign up to the platform, something noted by author Tom Slee (2015: 67), who asks 'if the pay is really so poor, why do so many people drive for Uber?' The answer, he says, is that:

> For those who have a car, driving for Uber is a way of converting that capital into cash; some underestimate the costs involved with full-time driving; for some the flexibility is a boon; for many, driving for Uber offers what taxi driving has offered for years – a job that requires little skill and has a low cost of entry is better than nothing. And as Uber has cut into the demand for taxis in many cities, individual taxi driver income has fallen, leaving Uber as the best alternative.

In this way, Uber has become the quintessential example of gig work – that is, the idea of driving people around in between other jobs, adding another 'gig' to the worker's repertoire, while putting the asset of the car to profitable use. As Slee notes, it can indeed be difficult for workers to estimate the costs involved with full-time driving, particularly with fuel prices, but also the prevalence of what is effectively sub-prime car financing, along with complex estimations of car value depreciation. For a sense of the kind of calculations that drivers are faced with to make it in the gig economy, The Uber Game, published in *The Financial Times*, provides players with some interactive insights about how difficult it is to make money as an Uber driver,[14] particularly drawing attention to the hidden costs.

The point about cutting into the demand for taxis in many cities has also meant that Uber has changed the experience of work for taxi drivers who have never signed up to their app. In New York, which has operated a medallion system for limiting the number of taxis, Uber is having a deeply disruptive effect. At the start of 2018, Doug Schifter, a taxi driver in New York, shot himself in front of the City Hall in Manhattan. In a Facebook post he explained how he was having to work for over 100 hours a week to survive, while in the 1980s he had worked forty hours per week. The value of taxi medallions in New York had a peak of US$1 million before Uber, which is now down to US$500,000 and is continuing to fall. This means that some drivers have taken on debt at the peak value for something now worth half that, without the same availability of work to repay that debt. Schifter had lost his health insurance and run up debt, and declared he would no longer work for 'chump change'.[15] Similarly, Bhairavi Desai, the founder of the New York Taxi Workers Alliance, reports having received calls in 2017 from a community of Dominican taxi drivers, explaining how dire the situation had become, with two drivers also having killed themselves.

Domestic and care work

Domestic and care work platforms follow the model of acting as an intermediary between workers and customers, taking a cut from the worker's payment, while also sometimes charging additional fees on top. In this case, they can involve workers cleaning houses or providing care on demand, for example. There is a longer tradition of this in some parts of the world, whereas elsewhere new demand is being created. However, the high-profile nature of transport and delivery platforms, particularly Uber and Deliveroo, means that they often dominate discussions around the gig economy. The 'Uber for X' shorthand gives a good sense of how that model has come to dominate this kind of work. However, despite Uber (and Deliveroo) becoming the go-to examples, this can lead to us forgetting the other kinds of location-specific work. Ticona and Mateescu (2018) have argued that the narrative of 'Uberization' fails to capture how domestic work platforms operate. Domestic work is often described as 'invisible'; excluded from many employ ment protections, often carried out by migrant women workers, and lacking collective bargaining (Pollert and Charlwood, 2009). This lack of focus also points towards a gendered bias in the literature that focuses on forms of work that men are most likely to be involved in (Ticona and Mateescu, 2018). While the bulk of the research on digital labour has ignored domestic and care work platforms, the voices of workers across the gig economy are mostly absent too. Our research has so far focused on transportation and delivery, as well as microwork and online freelancing, but we have been conducting fieldwork with a range of platforms in India and South Africa since the start of 2018, including both domestic and care work platforms.

Anderson (2000: 1–2) argues that there are two factors that determine the living and working conditions of domestic workers. First, their relationship to the state, with regard to their immigration status. Second, their relationship to the employer, and whether they 'live in' or not. With work platforms, the former can become problematic when workers become more visible to the state through the need to present documents to register, while in the latter case they only visit the employer's home for a short period of time so the relationship to the employer is much shorter. However, unlike the clear labour (or task) objectives involved in driving or delivering food, domestic work can be far more complex. It often lacks specific job descriptions or definitions, as Anderson (2000: 15) found when interviewing domestic workers, who, when asked what they did, would frequently say 'everything'.

There are approximately 67 million domestic workers across the world, with women making up 80 per cent of the workforce (Hunt and Machingura, 2016: 5). In many countries this kind of work is being transformed by platforms like Care.com, Handy and SweepSouth. As Ticona and Mateescu (2018) explain, these platforms 'formalize employment relationships through technologies that increase visibility'. Workers create profiles and receive feedback and ratings, using this as the basis for repeat work. Care. com operates in twenty countries, with 12.7 million 'caregivers'

(Care.com, 2018). This is a significantly larger number of workers than the 3.9 million claimed by Uber.

The risk of complete automation is not so obvious with this kind of work. As Dalla Costa and James (1971: 11) have noted, 'a high mechanization of domestic chores doesn't free any time for the woman. She is always on duty, for the machine doesn't exist that makes and minds children.' Ticona and Mateescu (2018) point out that domestic work is both 'among the fastest growing and perhaps the most resistant to automation'. Large numbers of workers are being drawn in – still doing the same kind of domestic work, but now mediated via a platform rather than employment agency. Initial research on these kinds of platforms has found that there can be some positive outcomes for domestic workers, including 'choice over working times, tracking of hours worked and wages earnt, and potentially better remuneration compared with other forms of domestic work', while also identifying 'low and insecure incomes, discrimination, further entrenchment of unequal power relations within the traditional domestic work sector, and the erosion of established labour and social protections as key challenges' (Hunt and Machingura, 2016: 5). The increased visibility of domestic workers on platforms can facilitate both the positives and the negatives.

What few findings there are, however, are beginning to draw attention to the experiences of this kind of work, giving voice to workers who have been marginalized both historically and structurally. In Hunt and Machingura's (2016) important research on domestic work platforms, they interviewed workers in South Africa. One worker they spoke to, Busi, explained that SweepSouth (a major domestic work platform):

> takes R13 [$0.90] for every R38 [$2.63] ... per hour. So, for example, if I work for three hours, instead of getting R120 [$8.29], all I get is R75 [$5.18]. On that R75, I have to cater for my own transport no matter how far the place I go and work is. Usually, that only leaves me with R20 [$1.38] [for the whole job].

The experience of working piecemeal by the hour meant that Busi had to travel to different neighbourhoods, often those she was not familiar with. Given the limited public transport in South African cities like Johannesburg, this meant she would often have to walk and could arrive too late to make the appointment. At the time of the study, the minimum wage for domestic workers was R13.39 per hour (in metro areas, working less than 27 hours per week), which is less than the minimum wage for all other workers (Hunt and Machingura, 2016). While SweepSouth paid above the minimum wage, the worker still needs to take into account costs involved in the work. For example, Busi explained:

> this is really sad for me because I have a family to look after, I am a single parent. At the end of the week when I look at how much I have worked for, I ask myself why I am killing myself like this. (Quoted in Hunt and Machingura, 2016: 23)

This experience is also detailed by another worker, Susan, who was also interviewed by Hunt and Machingura (2016: 24):

> I came from Zimbabwe straight into someone's home as a domestic worker. I worked as a full-time house maid ... When I realized that the money was too little ... I moved over to the next person ... until I realized that stay-in jobs are not well-paying. I started doing part-time jobs [through the platform] and that really paid me well because I would get R200–R250 [$14–$18] per day. So I brought my children from Zimbabwe because I could now afford to take care of them and send them to school here. I could also even afford the day care course I was talking about. But honestly, it's very hard because all the [extra] money goes back to transport, airtime, bundles and some [clients] are rude and delay payment, or lie that you have stolen something, among other things.

This kind of work is clearly 'very hard' and low paid, and workers also lack formal channels to improve their situation. To focus on South Africa again, while there are relevant unions like the South African Domestic Services and Allied Workers Union (SADSAWU), they are yet to make any major inroad into organizing these platform workers. SweepSouth employs, or rather contracts, a workforce that is overwhelmingly black African and female. They have an estimated 8,500 registered workers in South Africa. A recent survey by SweepSouth indicates some of the structural barriers these workers face (SweepSouth, 2018). For example, in their survey of 500 domestic workers, they reported that 84 per cent were the sole breadwinners in their family, and on average supported three dependents. Thirteen per cent reported that they 'suffered physical or verbal abuse from someone they worked for'. There is also a separate lower minimum wage for domestic workers, which means that these workers are only entitled to a minimum of R2,625 (£145) per month, rather than the R3,500 minimum that other workers are entitled to. However, the surveyed workers spent on average R900 on food, R400 on electricity, R500 on school fees, R1,000 on rent, and R100 on airtime for a total of R2,900 per month (SweepSouth, 2018). However, this does not include the substantial transportation costs that these workers need to travel to appointments, which according to the research company Numbeo, could be as much as R500 per month (quoted in SweepSouth, 2018). Aisha Pandor (the founder and CEO of SweepSouth) has argued that 'it's easy to say let's increase salaries across the board but the reality is that we face high levels of unemployment in the country.'[16] With the example of domestic work, low wages also combine with the historical under-valuing of this kind of activity, resulting in damaging outcomes for workers – now mediated via an app.

Microwork

In a different vein to either taxi, delivery or domestic and care work, many people are now finding and completing work through the internet, without the need to be in any particular place. In the US, up to 5 per cent of the population have made money from a work platform by completing digital tasks. This figure rises for workers under 30, and is higher than the equivalent figures for taxi driving (2 per cent) or delivery and cleaning (1 per cent) (Smith, 2016).

In most other places, it is difficult to get hard statistics on the number of people engaged in microwork. Microwork is usually carried out behind closed doors in the home. As such, it is typically hidden from the end user, making it difficult to get a sense of what its value chains look like and how the job of microwork is structured and organized. Whenever we use a digital service, product or even an algorithm that was trained using digital labour, there is almost no way to know whether an exhausted worker is behind it; whether they get laid off if they become sick or get pregnant; whether they are spending twenty hours a week just searching for work; how precarious their source of income is; or whether they are being paid an unfairly low wage.

In the Global North, this kind of work is growing within a context of deindustrialization, becoming an option for people who may have seen alternative kinds of jobs disappearing. As Alana Semuels (2018) has uncovered in interviews with microworkers in the US, this kind of work is increasing. One of her interviewees, Erica, explained that she started working for Amazon Mechanical Turk after struggling to find work in her 'economically struggling town'. She noted that 'here, it's kind of a dead zone. There's not much work.' In the county where she lives, only half of people over the age of 16 have a job, and a quarter are below the poverty line. Erica spends around thirty hours a week completing simple tasks, surveys and questionnaires, earning around US$4–5 per hour, but often much less. Much of the working time can be unpaid. For example, Erica recounts examples of tasks that requesters claim will take twenty minutes, but that actually take an hour. Often this can only be discovered after putting in enough time that it is worth completing anyway. Erica explains, 'I've felt so ripped off that I've walked away and cried.' A significant amount of unpaid time can also be spent by workers simply searching for and applying for jobs.[17] Another interviewee, Valerie, explains that she started working for Mechanical Turk after her car battery died, forcing her to work from home to try to make the money for repairs.[18]

A question that might come to mind with these stories is how workers can be paid so little to do these tasks? As with geographically tethered work, microworkers are organized as independent contractors, rather than workers or employees. So, when Erica receives US$4 an hour, which is US$3.25 below the federal minimum wage of US$7.25, Amazon is not breaching any local laws (Semuels, 2018). Emerging evidence shows that the stories of Erica and Valerie are not outliers, but rather representative of the trend for earnings on Mechanical Turk. In a recent study, it was demonstrated that workers earned a median hourly wage of only around US$2 per hour. At the upper end, only 4 per cent of workers earned more than the US$7.25 per hour federal minimum wage in the US. As the average requester paid over $11 per hour (indicating that requesters who pay much less also offer far more work), this demonstrates how the actual hourly wage is lower, taking into account the amount of unpaid work needed to find and complete the job (Hara et al., 2018).

On platforms like this, it is not possible to be productive (in the sense of doing paid work) for 100 per cent of a worker's available time. Significant time is spent searching for tasks, or working on tasks that do not convert into pay. The ability of requesters to 'reject work that does not meet their needs' is built into the Amazon platform, and 'enables wage theft' (Irani and Silberman, 2013). As another study has found, workers who used the online rating website Turkopticon to evaluate requesters on Amazon Turk, could avoid wage theft, given requesters who were badly rated committed wage theft about five times more than highly rated employers. For workers, choosing to only work for those higher rated requesters would mean making 40 per cent more (Benson et al., 2015). This highlights how wage theft is, as Irani and Silberman (2013) have argued, a key part of these platforms.

For those of us who have never worked for a microwork platform, it can be hard to imagine what the day-to-day work is like. Eric Limer, a reporter who decided to try Amazon Mechanical Turk for a story assignment, described how the experience is one of fractured and hard-to-understand tasks. In his first task – an experience he says stayed with him long afterwards – he was asked to track people on social media, trying to link user accounts across different platforms. In another odd task, he was requested to perform expressions in front of a webcam to help 'teach ...

computers how to detect these kind of expressions'.[19] Across a range of these experiences, Limer explains that

> If I've made Mechanical Turk sound like a disturbing hole that sucks up countless dazed hours clicking away pondering the world as a strange unimaginable shape, that's because it is. Or, it's a relatively fun way to make a couple bucks playing around on the internet ... I did this shit for hours. It's addictive! Mechanical Turk is like gambling's alternate universe cousin. It's a bizarre cephalopodan slot machine, a thousand-armed bandit that pays you for the trouble of pulling one of its many strange levers. I found it alarmingly easy to slip into a Turking daze. Each strange task leaves you with a brief glimpse of some larger whole, and it's easy to find yourself looking for just one more.

It leverages the 'gamification' that is a feature of many forms of work today (Woodcock and Johnson, 2018) in order to encourage people to work for an amount that may not hit minimum wage.

In the process, it unveils parts of modern society that are often hidden: the work that goes on behind the scenes to develop AI and run services that many of us rely on. In some cases, the work that is being requested can be much more sinister than the tasks that Limer describes. For example, in his ongoing PhD research, Adam Badger (2018) has traced where some of his writing tasks have ended up. For one, he was asked to rewrite an article for Russia Today on Russia stockpiling gold, with the task setter noting that 'our readers are into conspiracy theories'. The payment for this was US$3, with an additional US$1 for an image to go with it, plus a bonus of US$1 for 'exceptional work'. As Badger explained, as 'a writer, lefty, and general critic of the role of the internet and the press on our contemporary psyche, the job made me deeply uncomfortable'. Ethics is not something that most microworkers get much of an opportunity to reflect upon when selecting work, particularly as 'once the tasks are done, they also often shoot-off into the ether with no follow-up apart from the payment (if you're lucky).' However, in this case, Adam was able to track down the article afterwards as he could search for parts of the text via Google. The result was finding the article published under someone else's

name, and Adam explained, 'if that wasn't creepy enough, there
was a video made for the "Alternative News Network" (ew...)
which is just a narrated version of my article as read by a robot
from the dystopian future' (Badger, 2018).

Another glimpse into the experiences of microworkers can be
found with the 'Dear Mr. Bezos' letters organized by Mechanical
Turk workers to the founder and CEO of Amazon. This followed
an article in *Business Insider*, which noted that 'Jeff Bezos may run
Amazon and he may be a billionaire, but he is very accessible to his
customers with an easy-to-find email address, jeff@amazon.com.'[20]
Through Dynamo,[21] a workers campaign was organized to send
emails to Bezos with three aims: first, to point out that 'Turkers
[workers on Mechanical Turk] are human beings, not algorithms,
and should be marketed accordingly'; second, that 'Turkers should
not be sold as cheap labour, but instead skilled, flexible labour
which needs to be respected'; and third, that 'Turkers need to have
a method of representing themselves to Requesters and the world
via Amazon'. In each of these emails, which can still be found on
the internet,[22] the experiences and concerns of these workers are
made clear, all starting with 'Dear Mr. Bezos' – or close to it. For
example:

Dear Mr. Bezos
I am a Turker: middle age, entrepreneur, university student, mom,
wife, reliant on my mTurk income to keep my family safe from foreclosure. I don't Turk for $1.45 per hour nor do I live in a developing
country, I am a skilled and intelligent worker, and I Turk as my main
source of income and it is currently my chosen career. I am a human
being, not an algorithm, and yet Requesters seem to think I am there
just to serve their bidding. They do not respect myself and my fellow
Turkers with a fair wage, and in fact say that we should be thankful
we get anything near to minimum wage for the 'easy' work we do.
Searching for work all day isn't easy. Having to find and install scripts
to become more efficient isn't easy. Dealing with unfair rejections isn't
easy. Being a Turker isn't easy.
Kristy Milland (Turkernation Forum)
...

Hi Jeff,

I am from India, I am so grateful that you build such great platform for online jobs, it makes my life little more easier than others.

I am not just writing for me or Indians, but every single turker who are so much depended on income from AMT. It is time to upgrade your system, countries other than India and USA, only have payment as gift vouchers, which is not enough, please try to introduce new ways to get paid or improve Amazon Payments. If you can introduce Direct Deposit methods for us, it will be great.

Create a better platform for the workers, AMT need both Requesters and Workers, so make it equal. Try an inbuilt review system for every Requester, so that we can avoid cheaters.

And lastly, introduce a minimum wage system, all of the workers in AMT are well educated and experienced people, we deserve the right pay for quality work we provide.

That's all from me, once again thanks for everything you have done for us.

Bayon

In sum, microwork can often feel like the ultimate in alienated labour. Workers are rarely told why they are asked to do what they do. Work and workers are treated as entirely interchangeable, and disembedded from local laws and norms. As a result, platform-based microwork tends to be traded in small chunks, with workers given a take-it-or-leave-it offer on whether or not to accept any given job. Microwork platforms offer the promise of maximum productivity for clients who can pay workers only for the minutes (or even seconds) that they spend on the job. For workers, despite the fact that many workers rely on microwork as their primary source of income, there is no illusion that microwork offers a sustainable career path.

Microwork, at its essence, harnesses many of the computational and sensory skills innate to the human brain. Many workers are hired not because they have a deep domain knowledge, a long career, or formal qualifications in a particular domain of work or knowledge. They are, rather, hired because they are a human being willing to perform a relatively interchangeable task for a certain amount of money. And yet, despite its reliance on its workers' core human-ness, it remains the fact that microwork is severely lacking in humanity and attention to human dignity. Microwork, in its present state, offers a bleak look into a world of commodified jobs that are sliced up, and shipped off to a microwork platform, with little attention or care to the individuals carrying them out.

Online freelancing

The rise of online freelancing offers a case that is unprecedented in human history. While the practice is a clear extension of offshoring and outsourcing for service jobs, we now see global labour arbitrage happening at a scale that was never before possible. At the time of writing, the world's largest freelancing platform, Freelancer. com[23] claims to have connected 'over 30,325,814 employers and freelancers globally from over 247 countries, regions, and territories', and their Twitter account lists their location as 'everywhere'. Upwork.com, which hosts 12 million registered workers, likewise talks about their worker pool as being global in scope: 'online work can happen wherever there's a reliable Internet connection – an office, home, café, or rooftop. This also means you can choose who you work with, among a larger pool of people from around the globe.' Online freelancing is a broad term that can encapsulate all manner of jobs. Workers writing essays, doing 'lead generation', designing presentations, building websites, working as personal assistants, and carrying out all manner of other jobs all get their work through online freelancing platforms that allow workers and clients to connect in a planetary labour market (Graham and Anwar, 2019).

For many workers, the planetary scale of the market affords workers a significant amount of freedom in choosing where to work from, and in many cases allows them to escape from relatively constrained local labour markets. There are workers in places like Manila in the Philippines or Lagos in Nigeria who simply want an escape from the horrendous local traffic conditions (it is not uncommon to hear stories of three-hour commutes to work in both places). Working as online freelancers allows those workers to work from home or nearby cafes or Wi-Fi hotspots.

Other workers sign up because there are simply not enough good jobs close to home. Examples include young Kenyans who struggle to find any work because of the extremely high youth unemployment rates in the country; Palestinians with few options because of the economic entanglement of their economy;[24] and migrants around the world who lack the requisite work permits to find jobs locally. For all of those groups, online freelancing opens up opportunities that would not otherwise be there for them. Online freelancing allows workers to escape some of the fundamental constraints of the local labour market, and access jobs that would likely otherwise not be available to them.

Especially important to many workers is that salaries for online freelancing jobs can often be higher than wages they would receive in the local labour market. Angel, a transcriber in Manila, left a job in nursing in order to work for American and European clients that could be found on a large freelancing website. The pay that Angel received transcribing text was significantly higher than wages for local nurses. So, despite having spent years training to be a nurse, Angel moved to solely focus her working hours on transcription. Similar stories exist in low- and middle-income countries around the world, and the ability to earn wages that are significantly higher than those that can be obtained locally is an alluring draw for many people and leads people to forge entirely new career paths.

The freedom to work from wherever you want is especially appealing to young women across the Global South because of the ability to work from home, combining childcare duties with work. This seemed especially productive when other family members (parents, siblings and occasionally spouses) could look after children during work hours. While such arrangements are undoubtedly empowering for many, it is worth paying attention to the ways in which crowdwork is essentially subsidized by the reproductive labour of the rest of the household. Many other workers choose to freelance from public spaces in order to take advantage of free Wi-Fi (in most low- and middle-income countries, few people have unmetered internet connections at home). Yet others work from schools, universities and physical offices in order to take advantage of the computers and fixed infrastructures in those places. In all these cases, the infrastructure, connectivity, childcare and other domestic work that are carried out in the household are not treated as business expenses, and yet all serve to facilitate the freelancing that is carried out.

For every worker who realizes significant opportunities in online freelancing, there are many more whose goals go unrealized. A study of Upwork.com shows that globally, less than 7 per cent of people who register for jobs are ever able to secure one (Graham and Anwar, 2019). This oversupply of labour power is fiercely experienced by workers.

It is a rare online freelancer who feels that they have significant bargaining power in relation to the clients who source their work (Wood et al., 2018). Workers are well aware of the fact that if they try to raise their rates, there are thousands of people from around the world who are willing to do the same job, sometimes for a fraction of their own wage (Wood et al., 2019a). Indeed, engaging in any sort of bargaining is out of the question for many workers. This is not only because workers understand the futility of trying to bargain in the context of labour oversupply, but also because the digital architectures of platforms lend themselves to showing clients just how many workers are out there at any given time. As such, it is not uncommon to actually hear stories from workers about the ways in which they had to progressively reduce their rates over time. This happened to James who used his freelancing income to pay rent on an apartment in Nairobi. However, once his rates started going down because of market pressures, he could no longer afford to live there.

The global geography of workers serves to not just create enormous downwards pressure on wages through market forces, it also encourages workers to see themselves as competitors rather than colleagues. As such, when we asked online freelancers if they would ever consider being part of a trade union, the most frequent response we received was laughter. Factory workers or office workers have found much success in the past through the strategy of setting up picket lines. The spatial proximity inherent to pickets allows collective action by workers to grow in size and reduces the ability for workers to break ranks with one another. But for cloudworkers, there is no ability to use the spatial proximity deployed by those doing geographically tethered work. Workers in Ghana talk about Filipinos ready to do their jobs should they try to withdraw their labour, and Filipinos spoke of Indians willing to do their jobs for a fraction of the price. There's always a sense that someone else somewhere else will do the work for less money, and there's always a sense that the sort of solidarity needed to collectively withdraw labour is an impossibility. Cloudworkers therefore remain relatively atomized in how they interact with clients.

This atomization of cloudworkers, in turn, leads to a situation in which many workers have no choice but to accept whatever work they can find. The online freelancer in Ghana that we mentioned in the introductory chapter spoke of the multiple 48-hour stints that he went without sleep in order to deliver work on time for clients. The reason why he, and others like him, are willing to do this is because they are scared about getting anything other than a perfect five-star feedback score. In the context of an oversupply of labour power, workers know that they need to do everything in their power to avoid bad feedback. And almost every online freelancer has at least one story of an unsavoury client who realizes this and uses it as a threat should the worker not agree to extra hours, extra deliverables or lower rates.

4

How are workers reshaping the gig economy?

The aim of this chapter is not only to shine a spotlight on the new moments of resistance that gig work is creating, but also to understand that work is a phenomenon that always is shaped by both employers and workers – along with other preconditions that we discussed in chapter 1 like the role of the state and regulation. By examining how workers are resisting, organizing and shaping the gig economy, we can draw out different potential futures of work. However, when the gig economy and platform work was first recognized as a growing phenomenon around ten years ago, many commentators noted that traditional forms of worker representation would no longer be appropriate or adequate to protect these workers. The widespread use by platforms of self-employed independent contractor status not only creates the conditions of low pay and precarious work that we have discussed so far, but it also creates significant barriers to traditional forms of trade unionism.

Emerging forms of resistance in geographically tethered work

Geographically tethered work, as we have seen in previous chapters, shares many characteristics with the jobs that it has either replaced or displaced. When looking for examples of worker agency, some of these forms also share characteristics with more traditional forms of resistance. Worker resistance has historically covered a range of different activities, from the everyday activities of gossip, toleration and resignation, to the less common theft, sabotage and non-cooperation, as well as formal complaints and legal action (Tucker, 1993). The more open forms of collective action include strikes – the archetypal form of worker resistance (Hyman, 1989). The most effective forms of resistance come from the way the labour process is organized. For example, on assembly lines, workers found that they could shut down the line by only striking at particular points, using this to minimize lost pay. In new forms of work like digital labour, innovations are required to successfully organize, finding new weaknesses in the control of work (Woodcock, 2018b). There is therefore a learning process taking place in the gig economy, as workers find new and emerging forms of resistance and organization.

Worker resistance and organizing has historically drawn on the fact that workplaces tended to bring together groups of workers, put them in the same place for extended periods of time, and subject them to identical conditions. For example, factories were traditionally large workplaces, occupied by workers on shifts, working the same machines for the same pay. The time spent together meant that collective identities and grievances could form alongside the other social bonds that people make at work, providing a strong basis for collective action. The dispersed nature of platform work breaks down the possibilities of building networks and trust. For example, with Uber there is no reason why drivers need to spend time with each other. Compared to the minicab company with its shared garage and waiting area for drivers, there is no opportunity or reason for Uber drivers to meet. However, it is not the case that gig workers operate in a social vacuum – after all, the geographically tethered nature of the work means they work within the shared space of the city. This means sharing a workplace of sorts, albeit one much larger than a factory or office.

This meeting of workers can be seen clearly with the example of Deliveroo. Walking around many other European cities, Deliveroo workers are a common sight due to their bright turquoise bags and uniforms; similarly, the red of Zomato and orange of Swiggy across India, and the black and green of Uber Eats in New York City and the US. In some cases, the app directs drivers to a meeting point. This is an algorithmically determined location in each delivery zone, meant to ensure the driver is likely to be able to deliver the next order in the shortest possible time (Woodcock, forthcoming). From a computational perspective, this makes sense: analysing data and pushing for the greatest efficiency. From the workers' perspective, this means drivers finding themselves together in the same place. These become a stand-in for a more traditional workplace, providing the basis for the organizing that followed.

In 2016 in London, these meeting points became a focus for self-organization of Deliveroo workers. Workers met each other in these algorithmically determined meeting points, swapping numbers and starting WhatsApp groups (Waters and Woodcock, 2017). This led to the formation of overlapping networks that were used to share grievances, keep in contact and later build support for a strike (Woodcock, forthcoming). WhatsApp became an example of what Alex Wood (2015) has called 'mass self-communication networks'. As Kurt Vandaele (2018: 16) has noted more recently, these 'networks are serving as a "breeding ground" for self-organized courier associations boosting their associational power'. In June and July 2016, these networks clearly had a latent capacity for organizing in London. In August 2016, Deliveroo sent a message to drivers that it would be ending the hourly-rate payment scheme, moving instead to pay drivers per delivery. There was no option for workers to negotiate or discuss the changes. This left the workers with one option to voice their concerns about the changes: going on strike.

The UK, like many countries, has strict laws governing strike action. The issues of self-employment mean that in many contexts, workers cannot join a trade union – let alone have it recognized – or organize a legal strike. However, this also creates a kind of 'illusion of control' for platforms like Deliveroo (Woodcock, forthcoming). While they are able to use forms of 'algorithmic management' (Lee et al., 2015; Rosenblat and Stark, 2016; Rosenblat, 2018) to control the work, this becomes much harder when workers decide to resist. As Deliveroo riders were classified as self-employed, independent contractors, the regulations and laws governing strike action did not apply to them. If they choose not to log in for a shift, there was no way Deliveroo could challenge this, other than by discontinuing all of their contracts. This is an example of 'unauthorized walkouts – or the threat of them – the most dramatic of disruptive tactics' which previously have been 'a familiar and even routine part of grievance negotiations in such industries as coal mining, city transit, construction, automobile, steel, metalworking, and longshoring' (Kuhn, 1961: 50–1). Therefore, this first strike at a food delivery platform showed that 'stopping machines in the twentieth century corresponds to collective logouts in the twenty-first century' (Vandaele, 2018: 15). Strike action had not disappeared; instead, workers were in the process of mutating it into a new form.

From the starting point in London, these strikes spread across Europe in 2016 and 2017. As Callum Cant (2018) has argued, the 'official strike statistics do not sufficiently describe worker resistance in food platforms' as they don't capture this kind of action. Drawing on the same mass self-communication networks that were used to organize these strikes, Cant sourced reports of strikes from the UK, Netherlands, Germany, Spain, Belgium, France and Italy. Across the two years, he found '41 incidents across 18 months in 7 countries involving an estimated 1493 workers'. This led Cant to conclude that there are three features to food platform strikes: 'first is an increase in incidents over time. Second is a sporadic month by month but consistent quarterly increase in the total number of workers mobilized. Third is an increase in the synchronicity of mobilization across all seven countries.' This means that these strikes are not isolated occurrences, but rather part of a wave of struggles that are emerging in food delivery. There have since been strikes by Deliveroo workers in Hong Kong, as well as large strikes on other food delivery platforms in South Africa and India. Across each of these incidents are the stories of workers delivering food without the employment protections they may have had previously. Each incident also has the stories of workers meeting each other, discussing, planning and then carrying out strikes – with no protection from mainstream trade unions. The strikes themselves have been creative, energetic and inspirational. What the strikes also show is that, despite the structural barriers to organizing, workers 'do have a certain workplace bargaining power'. As Vandaele (2018: 14) continues, workers' 'disruptive capacity stems from the delivery, transport and logistics system's key importance in the interaction between producers and customers'.

Following the strikes in 2016 in London, a section of the workers involved joined the IWGB. This is a small trade union that began organizing with mainly Latin American migrant workers in universities in London, but has now grown to represent couriers, Uber drivers, foster care workers, self-employed electricians and, most recently, videogame workers. The IWGB 'is a non-bureaucratic, grassroots, "bottom-up" organization'.[1] It is a registered union, but not affiliated to the TUC (Trade Union Congress). Outside of London, food delivery workers have joined the IWW (the Industrial Workers of the World), a radical union with a long history of organizing precarious workers (Fear, 2018). This model of grassroots trade unionism has been followed in different parts of Europe. For example, in Germany, riders have organized with FAU (Freie Arbeiter Union – Free Workers Union); with CLAP (Collectif des livreurs autonomes de Paris – Paris Autonomous Deliverers' Collective) in France; the Riders Union (FNV) in the Netherlands; and the Riders Union Padova and Riders Union Bologna in Italy, amongst others. These different groups are now coordinating across Europe through the Transnational Federation of Couriers. As one of the IWW members of the network explained: 'these companies operate on a transnational level, so we need to resist them on a transnational level.'[2]

Some of these struggles across Europe have evolved into pro-tracted legal battles over the employment status of gig workers. The problem of self-employment status has made it difficult for workers to organize in traditional forms of trade unionism. As of 2018, the IWGB is engaged in two legal battles to overturn the self-employed independent contractor status at Deliveroo and Uber. The argument for doing so has been clearly articulated by Jason Moyer-Lee,[3] the general secretary of the IWGB. He points out that there are two sides in the public debate at present:

> [One side claims] the problem is confusion in the law, or the inability of the law to keep up with the times, which can result in workers being inadvertently deprived of rights to which they're entitled. On the other side of the debate, you have those of us who have been submitting and repeatedly winning tribunal cases establishing the 'gig economy's' labourers as limb (b) workers, in particular the Independent Workers' Union of Great Britain (IWGB), and of course the judges who are writing these decisions. We say the law is pretty clear and the companies are clearly on the wrong side of it.

Regardless of the decisions over employment status, workers are finding ways to resist and organize on platforms across the world. For example, when we were interviewing drivers in Bangalore, India, we would regularly hear stories of resistance. Every time we asked drivers (who worked for the largest food delivery platforms, Zomato and Swiggy, in Bangalore) if they were members of a union, they always answered 'no'. However, when we asked if they spoke to other workers about problems they had, we would hear stories of large WhatsApp groups of workers, or meeting places that workers would organize. In one stage of our fieldwork, we set off to find a meeting point for Zomato workers with our local research collaborators. After interviewing an autorickshaw driver (who now worked via the Uber app), he agreed to drive us to a popular meeting point in central Bangalore.

We were led to a row of restaurants with wide steps in front, as well as plenty of parking. Over the course of an hour, we sat on the steps discussing working conditions with a shifting group of around a dozen Zomato 'two wheeler' (or motorcycle and moped) drivers. Some of them spoke to us the whole time, while others dropped in and out as the orders came in. The majority of the conversation was held in Kannada, with occasional English, and translated by our colleagues Pradyumna Taduri and Mounika Neerukonda. The drivers' zone had around 600 workers, delivering across a busy part of the city. When we discussed what they thought about their work, the replies centred around the falling piece-rate for deliveries. The workers explained they had set up WhatsApp groups and tried to complain to the platform, who did not respond to their grievances and refused to meet anyone claiming to be a representative of the drivers. As a result, the workers had recently gone on strike, with an estimated 400 workers taking part across their zone. The strike did not win any concessions, nor was it coordinated with any other delivery workers in the city. It is one glimpse of the bubbling resentment that platform workers were feeling, something that could otherwise be missed without talking to workers.

We heard similar stories in South Africa during our fieldwork. None of the drivers we spoke to were members of a trade union. There were, like the previous examples, large WhatsApp groups of workers, sharing experiences and grievances. In Cape Town we spoke to Ayanda, who worked for three different delivery platforms simultaneously. He explained how he would 'stack' orders, but always made sure to deliver the food before the packages, as 'the food has got to be warm by the time you deliver it!' While he said there were few problems with the package deliveries he made, there were more complaints with OrderIn for food delivery. Ayanda explained how the drivers formed a WhatsApp group to discuss what to do. He talked us through the example of a strike they had organized. The strike was pitched on the WhatsApp group and the majority of workers agreed. They then made sure to talk to other drivers they met on the street to prepare. When the strike day arrived, they all logged off from the app. We asked how they made sure that other drivers did not break the strike, tempted to 'boost' earnings from the platform. He replied that if other drivers went against the majority, 'we smashed up their bikes, that's democracy'. These tactics worked; the drivers had gone on strike multiple times over the last year, winning concessions from the platform each time. We asked whether they would form or join a union. Ayanda thought that there was no need to. He explained that there were no leaders, but they also did not need any: when they wanted to go on strike, they did. While we did not hear any other examples of strikes as widespread as on this platform, there were examples of smaller strikes and collective organizing across other platforms in South Africa.

Strikes in China show another example of workers finding new ways to resist and organize in a quite different context. In China there is technically only one union: the ACFTU (All-China Federation of Trade Unions), with around 303 million members. However, there is little opportunity for workers' autonomy as it is constitutionally subordinated to protecting national interests, does not hold elections, and is tied to the ruling party within a one-party state (Taylor and Li, 2007: 707). As has been argued by Bill Taylor and Qi Li (2007: 703–7), the ACFTU 'is not a legitimate trade union because it fails three tests of unionism'. First, its constitutional role includes protecting the 'national interest' not workers' interests; second, there is no election of officials by the rank-and-file membership; and third, the union is tied to the state ruling party within a one-party state, meaning there is little opportunity for workers' autonomy (Taylor and Li, 2007: 703–7). While the right to strike was removed in China in 1982, as noted by Taylor and Li, 'there is no legal prohibition on workers taking strike action'. This means that strikes operate in a grey area. Despite this, as the China Labour Bulletin has documented, there have been at least 10,000 strikes in China since 2011, including strikes of food delivery workers (China Labour Bulletin, 2018a). With grievances echoing those in Europe, Meituan workers struck across China because they were being 'paid less per delivery, penalized for not completing impossible orders, forced to risk their lives, sacked for talking about it' (China Labour Bulletin, 2018b).

While there have been strikes like these across the world, many of which have gone unreported, the UK was the starting point. In October 2018 these strikes changed in form again. Uber Eats riders went on strike against a change in payment terms that would reduce the amount they received per drop. Across the UK, riders had begun organizing with the IWW. They had success organizing riders outside of London, but following the spontaneous strikes on 20 October 2018, they called for a national strike to coincide with strikes at McDonald's, TGIFridays and Wetherspoons pubs in London, Cambridge and Brighton. This represented a significant shift in the organizing of food delivery platform workers, with coordinated strike action up the supply chain. There has also been organizing of Uber drivers, who in the UK formed the UPHD (United Private Hire Drivers), now a branch of the IWGB. While they coordinated with these other groups of workers, they also called their first ever strike in the UK on 9 October 2018 for 24 hours from 1pm. They demanded an increase of fares to £2 per mile, Uber to reduce commissions to 15 per cent, an end to unfair deactivations and bullying, and worker rights protection. As the branch chair, James Farrar argued:

> After years of watching take home pay plummet and with management bullying of workers on the rise, workers have been left with no choice but to take strike action. We ask the public to please support drivers by not crossing the digital picket line by not using the app during strike time. (IWGB, 2018)

This positioning of the app as a picket line represents a new way of understanding workplace struggle, re-pitching the picket line in more contemporary, digital terms.

It is not only Uber drivers in the UK who have started organizing against the platform. Across countries the kinds of resistance have differed, with action taken by existing taxi drivers against Uber in countries including across Europe, as well as Brazil, China, Indonesia and the US. However, this is not so much resistance by platform workers, but rather action against platforms (and therefore the workers who choose to work on them). While this kind of opposition has been incredibly widespread, there are emerging patterns of strikes by Uber drivers in different countries, including strikes in Bangladesh, India, Kenya, South Africa and the UK.

In India, there have been large strikes of Uber drivers, including drivers for Ola – the Indian-based competitor. For example, in October 2018 there was a combined strike of Uber and Ola drivers in Mumbai and Delhi, with demands for higher fares to meet rising fuel costs. These were coordinated by existing union organizations like the Mumbai Taxi Drivers' Union.[4] In Bangalore, we met with Tanveer Pasha, the President of Ola, Taxiforsure and Uber drivers and Owners Association, to discuss organizing at these companies. While there was little participation in Bangalore in the previous strike, the union represents around 55,000–60,000 drivers.[5] While they are yet to win concessions from Uber, it shows that sustained organization is possible.

The picture is complicated by the fact that Uber has been banned in a number of countries (while remaining to operate in some). Similarly, Uber has pulled out of China, leaving Didi Chuxing as the dominant company, while selling to Grab in Singapore and neighbouring Southeast Asian countries. In June 2018, drivers at Didi Chuxing went on strike across China. The action took different forms. For example, in Shaodong, Hunan, hundreds of workers were involved in a strike that lasted six days. They posted their grievances online, citing lost bonuses, high commission and long journeys for pickups. In Hangzhou, Zhejiang, workers were offered a new scheme that would provide a guaranteed income but required them to work for ten hours per day. Those drivers who did not join the scheme then started to receive less work, triggering the strike. The strikes were so large that transport workers accounted for 20 per cent of all workers on strike in China during that month (China Labour Bulletin, 2018c).

We have focused specifically on food delivery and taxi platform work, as this has seen the sharpest and most coordinated workers' action. However, only minor concessions have been admitted to by companies so far. For example, in 2017 riders working for Notime platform in Switzerland organized protests backed by the Unia union. They were successful, winning improvements to terms and conditions, as well as no longer being classed as independent contractors (Vandaele, 2018: 15).

There are also emerging stories of resistance on other kinds of

platforms, many of which face significant barriers to organizing
For example, Juliet Schor[6] points out that on TaskRabbit, workers
taking customers off-platform 'is very prevalent'. TaskRabbit allows
customers to request location-specific tasks from workers, while
charging a 20 per cent fee. Rather than continuing to have their
pay docked by TaskRabbit, Schor notes that 'once the relationship with the client is established, they don't feel like TaskRabbit
should take such a high fee.' The reliance on independent contractor or self-employed status makes the issue of worker retention
difficult for platforms. To maintain the illusion of self-employed
status, platforms cannot be seen to direct the work too closely
or exert too much control. Otherwise workers can (successfully)
challenge the status in court. This taking of work off-platform is a
form of individual resistance. While not comparable to a collective
strike, it points to the frustrations on the platform.

A story of how this kind of process can affect the platform
can be found with the cleaning company Homejoy. At first the
platform grew quickly, taking advantage of venture capital funding
and aggressive discounts for customers. When Homejoy collapsed
in 2015, the co-founder Adora Cheung claimed that the 'deciding
factor' was the lawsuits brought by cleaners against the independent contractor status (Huet, 2015). However, much of the blame
was also placed on how Homejoy acquired customers – particularly
how the discounts were not converting into repeat customers – the
model arguably did not work to keep workers on the platform. In
fact, one former employee noted that 'maybe our retention was
a lot better, but it was retention off the platform'.[7] For workers,
it made sense to move off the platform after the introduction.
After all, the platform took a significant cut of the cleaning fee,
sometimes almost half. As one former worker explained, 'a lot of
people who initially hired me through Homejoy have mentioned
that they could hire me outside.' The platform charged $60 per
hour, taking a cut of $25 per hour. Instead, the worker continued,
'when I work directly, I bill people at $40.'[8] This means that both
the customer is saving money and the worker is making more.
This process of work migrating off-platform was exacerbated by a
failure of the platform to facilitate repeat relationships – the feature

allowing a customer to hire the same worker again was only added just before the platform folded (Farr, 2015).

Cloudwork and resistance

As we have discussed with delivery and taxi work, some gig workers share the same workplace – even if that shared space is somewhere as diffuse as a city district. For cloudworkers, however, there are no necessary shared spaces of co-presence. With microwork, the labour process of each individual worker is fractured into many parts. Workers often do not know much about the purpose of the work that they are doing. Image taggers know that they are tagging images, but not why those images need to be tagged or who else is working on the project. Many workers have no idea how many others might be working on the same job or for the same client. This means that while they are often working as part of a group, they might never come into contact with other workers. This is no accident. Platforms are designed to facilitate some types of cooperation (for instance the negotiations between clients and workers) whilst limiting others (for instance providing any way for workers to identify or communicate with each other).

Online freelancing can also be deeply individualized. Many forms of freelance work are completed by a single worker in communication with the client. On the biggest platforms, freelancers only win contracts by bidding against other potential workers. This has an isolating tendency, setting workers against each other, rather than building bonds of solidarity over shared conditions. These factors lead to especially challenging barriers to organizing, as workers do not pass each other in the street, nor are they likely to live in the same neighbourhoods (even if they did, most wouldn't have any way of knowing). However, that is not to say that online freelancers are totally atomized. Many find and offer mutual support through forums, Facebook groups and other digital media. As Wood et al. (2018) have argued, 'internet-based communities enable workers to support each other and share information.

This, in turn, increases their security and protection. However, these communities are fragmented by nationality, occupation and platform.'

The risk here is that the technological innovations of this work are overemphasized, leading to a determinism that sees the ability of workers to resist and organize as already being defeated before they even start. As the previous section on geographically tethered work has demonstrated, resistance can – and does – take a wide range of forms. Resistance is taking place with cloudwork, but the emerging forms that it takes remain mostly below the surface. This does not mean that they are not important, but it can make them much harder to find – particularly for people who do not work those jobs. Even in the hardest conditions, workers are finding a voice in the gig economy. There have also been moments when this latent potential can be seen, showing how cloudwork could be reshaped in workers' interests.

Cloudworkers on Upwork, for instance, have developed ways to resist the surveillance methods forced upon them. On Upwork, screenshots are taken of the workers' computer screen at random intervals every ten minutes (this is only for work that is paid hourly rather than per task). In other words, the screenshot can be taken between second 0:01 and 10:00. If a client sees something unrelated to their job (say, the use of social media during work time), they can flag the image and the worker will not be paid for that ten-minute period. In response, workers have figured out two strategies to escape this surveillance. The first is setting up a second monitor and using that for games, social media and general internet browsing. The screenshot monitoring system only ever takes screenshots of the first screen – meaning they can do whatever they want on the second screen. Second, if a screenshot happens early enough into the ten-minute slot (e.g. at minute 5), the worker knows that they have five minutes before another screenshot is going to be taken. Some use this to not work on the client's job. These tactics are only used by a minority of workers, as many freelancers have internalized a need to be efficient for their clients and consider this sort of strategy to be unethical. However, the existence of these sorts of practices show that cloudwork is not as efficient and as free of resistance as it might at first appear. Even in the most controlled of environments, workers are able to push back against their labour being treated as a commodity.

One of the most powerful examples of the ability for workers to resist and organize comes from an intervention made on the Amazon Mechanical Turk platform. Workers in Mechanical Turk, and similar platforms, face a host of challenges: the disciplinary use of ratings, the prevalence of non-payment for work and the lack of communication channels for workers. As a response, the Turkopticon project was developed by Lilly Irani and Six Silberman. It is 'an activist system that allows workers to publicize and evaluate their relationships with employers. As a common infrastructure, Turkopticon also enables workers to engage one another in mutual aid' (Irani and Silberman, 2013: 611). Turkopticon provides a browser plug-in that produces an overlay for workers while they are on the platform. It allows workers to share their rating of the requester – thus reversing the Panopticon-like relationship between platform and workers[9] – to try and hold employers accountable for their treatment. Turkopticon then included a forum through which workers could meet and discuss online.

The importance of Turkopticon is that it shows workers can collectively organize on the platform. Although it began as an outside intervention, the design promotes workers' self-activity through its use. Rather than workers being organized from outside, it provides a way for workers to begin to organize themselves. In this way, it is an embryo of new forms of digital worker organization, subverting the tools that are used in the work process and finding new uses for them. This was later iterated with the 'Dynamo' platform that aimed to 'support the Mechanical Turk community in forming publics around issues and then mobilizing' (Salehi et al., 2015). One part of this was the letter-writing campaign, which we discussed earlier in the book, which drew attention to the working conditions on the platform (Dynamo, 2014).

What Turkopticon also provides is a way for workers to come into contact with each other. It shows that, despite not needing to share the same geographical location to complete the work, workers can still collaborate. Like the Deliveroo workers who share the same streets and hang around by the restaurants, microworkers too share the same communication channels and hang around on forums. Digital communication is a key part of this work (Gupta et al., 2014; Gray et al., 2016), and forums have been shown to be important (Yin et al., 2016). The forum acts as a place for workers to share tips and grievances, operating in a similar way to the WhatsApp groups. For the cloudworker, the forum is the equivalent of the street corner for the geographically tethered worker, which is broadly equivalent to the gates at the dock for the prospective docker. Clearly there are differences between these three meeting points. The forum lacks material co-presence, building comparatively weaker connections. The street corner may bring platform workers together, but only at that corner, and not across the whole city. The gates of the dock bring together a critical mass of workers. However, the dock gate was also not the perfect environment to organize – after all, workers are competing against each other to be 'called on' (whether directly or indirectly). Nevertheless, each is a location in which workers can potentially meet and start collectively organizing for better conditions. In online work this is becoming widespread. A survey by Wood et al. (2018: 100–1), for instance, showed that 58 per cent of cloudworkers in their sample communicated with other online workers at least once a week, either through social media, SMS, email or on forums. Communication is an important first step towards collective resistance and organizing.

Towards a new kind of trade unionism?

The evidence so far is that workers on geographically tethered platforms the world over are increasingly fighting to reshape platform work. There are visible – as well as more hidden – examples of strikes and organizing now spreading across the planet. Even at this early stage, there have been some limited successes for those workers. While the struggles of cloudworkers to reshape and control parts of their work also remain at a nascent stage, there is emerging evidence that worker resistance is also present in – what on the surface – appears to be highly controlled and atomized worker processes. At this point it is important to remember that while cloudwork is new, it builds upon histories of other kinds of precarious work – indeed, cloudworkers may already have experienced precarious work, and perhaps developed tactics to deal with it.

This resistance is happening within structurally difficult conditions, often in grey areas of legality, or even taking place illegally. This is because, in many locales, the self-employed are not allowed to form trade unions like workers or employees are. In those places, doing so is seen as operating like a price-setting cartel rather than simply providing a means for workers to bargain over their pay. In fact, the US Chamber of Commerce, of which Uber and Lyft are members, has argued in a Seattle court that 'by allowing drivers to bargain over their pay, which is based on fares received from passengers, the city would permit them to essentially fix prices in violation of federal antitrust law.'[10] This measure has been seen as an attempt to prevent the Teamsters from organizing Uber drivers in Seattle.

The threats of legal injunctions mean that workers are not only having an effect on the gig economy, but are redefining what organizing and trade unionism mean today. It is worth noting here that the kinds of trade unions that exist today have come quite far from the early forms of unions. The struggles of textile workers have been traced as far back as 1675, then later linked with Luddism and the smashing of machinery in England, but their actions can also be read as a response to their economic conditions, rather than just an opposition to machinery per se (Binfield, 2004). Many textile workers participated in the demonstration in Manchester in 1819 calling for parliamentary reform – now infamous as the Peterloo Massacre, after cavalry charged the protestors, killing 15 people and injuring hundreds more. In 1833, six agricultural labourers swore a secret oath to join The Friendly Society of Agricultural Labourers in the Dorset village of Tolpuddle, with the aim of protesting their falling wages. After their discovery, they were sentenced to penal transportation to Australia, becoming famous as the Tolpuddle

Martyrs (Marlow, 1971) It took until 1871 for trade unions to be fully legalized in the UK, less than twenty years before the struggles of the London dock workers that we discussed in chapter 1.

It is important to remember, therefore, that many attempts by workers to organize activities start out neither as legally allowed nor institutionally accepted. Organizing in groups, formal trade unions, collective bargaining, strikes, picketing, and so on all began as illegal activities. It was only through the success of these tactics and the collective strength of workers that they became legitimized (at least in part). Even now, many of these activities are highly regulated or even prevented in some sectors (such as the armed forces or other areas deemed important to national security). In the UK, for example, workers cannot simply decide to go on strike for any reason. The strike must be a 'trade dispute' related to terms and conditions, and cannot be 'secondary action' in support of other workers. A postal ballot has to be organized among the union members, overseen by an independent party, and the employers informed. The ballot then must return a majority in favour, and the turnout among the members is required be over 50 per cent. The results need to be announced and the employer can apply for a court injunction to prevent the strike. If it goes ahead, the employer must be informed at least seven days beforehand. While this may then allow a legal strike to go ahead, the bounds within which such action can be taken are relatively narrow.

It is important to note that there is much more to workplace struggle than legally sanctioned industrial action, and indeed we have identified a range of different forms of worker resistance throughout this chapter, including forming of networks, unofficial strikes and protests. The vast majority of these do not have the support of legal trade unions – IWGB and other alternative unions in Europe are the exception here – and are often technically illegal. And we should also note that networks of workers or smaller unions have far fewer resources than larger official trade unions. This means that while there may be exciting developments at the workplace level (however we define that in the context of the gig economy), these remain on a relatively small scale, and isolated from the wider workers movement.

This isolation can be explained in two ways. First, many unions are simply not trying to organize with these workers. Although mainstream trade unions would not admit this publicly, one UK organizer has observed to one of the authors that it was not possible to organize drivers, because: 'how would you even find them?' Without wanting to castigate that particular union, it is not beyond the stretch of imagination to actually use the platform to place an order to come into contact with a worker. What this highlights is that some older unions appear to be unwilling to organize these new groups of workers. From an organizational perspective, this makes sense. Gig economy workers are far less likely than workers in traditional waged employment to pay consistent dues to the union, meaning that recruitment is not a solution to the ongoing crisis of membership and funding that many unions face (or will face in the near future). Most mainstream unions also simply do not have the 'boots-on-the-ground' understanding needed to organize with gig workers. Successful organizing of these highly distributed workers takes time, commitment and resources. If there is an expectation of a quick return on investment through union dues, organizing in the gig economy does not make immediate sense – an outcome that leads many to argue that gig workers are unorganizable.

These kinds of arguments have been made, and proven wrong, before. For example, workers in the car industry in the early twentieth century, as well as those 'working seasonally across a range of industries' were 'regarded as unorganizable' (McIlroy, 1995: 9). However, during the Second World War, car factories became a focus of organizing, with strength continuing to build afterwards. The car industry became a bastion of trade unions in the UK (Beynon, 1973), until their decline with changes after the 1970s, with the greater use of technology and fewer jobs as much of the production moved overseas.

The work we have discussed so far is clearly very different to the car industry. However, it is still work, and work still involves the buying and selling of people's time. This creates a tension between the buyer and seller, particularly when the seller pushes to drive down the costs of their 'self-employed' workforce. What

We have tried to draw attention to is the activity of workers trying to change their conditions in various ways. While on a surface level there may not be widespread organized resistance, the same process that Harry Braverman (1998) identified in factory work can be found too:

> But beneath this apparent habituation, the hostility of workers to degenerated forms of work which are forced upon them continues as a subterranean stream that makes its way to the surface when the conditions permit, or when the capitalist driver for a greater intensity of labour oversteps the bound of physical or mental capacity. It renews itself in new generations, expresses itself in the unbounded cynicism and revulsion which large number of workers feel about their work, and comes to the fore repeatedly as a social issue demanding a solution.

This is not to say that we are on an inevitable march towards effective resistance and organization of workers, but rather that this work still contains tensions between employers and workers (however defined) and that both sides will push to get a better deal from the relationship. No matter how work is organized, workers will always have power. As Kim Moody (2017: 69) has noted 'a new terrain of class struggle has emerged' beyond the gig economy, 'which in many ways is more favorable to working-class initiatives'. The trick is figuring out how it can best be harnessed in our new world of work.

Conclusion:
What next for the gig economy?

The gig economy is not just a synonym for algorithmic wizardry, large datasets and cutting-edge technologies. Whenever we think (or indeed research or write) about work, it is important to remember that work necessarily involves workers. This means actual people with complex lives, working in relationships with each other.

When talking about the numbers of workers in the gig economy across the world, the everyday lived experiences of these workers can fade into the background. After all, with millions of stories, we cannot possibly as individuals relate to all of them. However, when thinking at the macro scale of millions of workers, it is more than just individual stories or experiences that are harder to grasp. When workers become numbers that are graphed or plotted, their agency – whether collective or individual – fades into the background. The gig economy thereby risks being understood as something that is done to workers, rather than something they engage with, create and produce, in different ways.

While we still need a macro-level analysis and mappings of the gig economy, that sort of work needs to be combined with stories about workers' own experiences, both as a redress to the anonymizing character of platforms, and to centre their voices in any proposed changes. Furthermore, many of the stories that we hear about the gig economy – from the budding entrepreneur on Upwork in the slums of Nairobi to the single mother in Nebraska taking advantage of the scheduling flexibility that Uber affords her – only paint part of the picture. If the gig economy is coming to define ever more of the economy, it is not good enough to focus just on those who thrive in it. Such feel-good stories, so often shared in the media by the PR arms of platforms, policymakers who don't have the sense to know better, and academics who have been bought off with privileged access to proprietary platform data, distract from the real winners in changes to labour markets that shift risk in one direction and reward in the other. The gig economy is built by design to convenience consumers, to return profit to platforms and, ultimately, to disempower workers. We therefore need a concerted effort to understand the cracks that many fall through. We need to focus on those that are excluded, those that are disadvantaged, and the ultimate winners and losers in what has become a profound reorganization of how many people work.

Workers are never passive participants in work. They bring with them a range of experiences, expectations, relationships and desires to work. While the role of management is to try and control work, workers too can reshape it. Work is therefore a site of constant contestation between the different interests of workers, managers and owners. As we have shown in chapter 4, it should therefore come as no surprise that there is significant resistance in the gig economy. Too often we consider resistance to just involve trade unions and strike action, but the reality is that resistance takes place across a wide spectrum of actions.

Anyone who claims that there is no worker agency or resistance in the gig economy is simply not looking in the right place. That resistance may take many forms, including the delivery drivers complaining about work outside a restaurant, the spreading of WhatsApp groups, joining trade unions, burning tyres and vandalizing bikes during wildcat strikes, sharing scripts that automate menial tasks, and other new forms of organization that are only just beginning to emerge. What the examples of resistance show is that the gig economy is already being contested every day across the world. What is less clear, however, is how that contestation will be resolved, and whose interests will be benefitted.

The gig economy that we know today only exists because of the digital transformation that we are in the midst of. Mass connectivity, the almost ubiquitous availability of phones and computers, the digital legibility of work, the pressure from an economically globalized world combined with outsourcing, and the emergence of platforms that harness vast databases to match supply and demand for labour power have ushered in a world of work that represents a departure from older ways of organizing the labour process.

But today's gig economy is not just enabled by technology. Particular political and social circumstances – consumer attitudes and preferences, gendered and racialized relationships of work, permissive regulatory environments, ineffective trade union resistance, and a general desire for flexibility from both employers and workers – have also allowed for employment relationships in which workers are atomized units competing for jobs in open markets. Within the economic transformation within which we find ourselves, work is becoming temporary, unstable, mediated, patchworked and persistently contestable (Peck, 2017). This is happening across sectors and around the world as a result of particular technological, social, political and economic preconditions.

Work, for those in the gig economy, is on demand, no longer embedded in organizations, and mediated by platforms that capture significant rents. It is often characterized by informational opacity and asymmetry, with workers knowing little about the production networks that they are embedded into. It is an individualized pursuit with few opportunities to build a stable cohort of colleagues. It is becoming ephemeral, with today's work not necessarily resembling yesterday's. It is highly fragmented, with some jobs measured in minutes or even seconds rather than months or years. It is relatively unregulated and tends to evade much labour law through a re-classification of the relationship between the employer and worker. And it is almost always defined by a relationship in which the burden of training and risk is put onto the worker rather than the client, the platform or the state. Workers who become injured, need time off for caring duties, or want to save up for retirement need to make sure that they have planned appropriately. Where once it might have been unthinkable – and certainly unfeasible – to have entire industries defined by contingent work, it now seems increasingly possible to Uberize yet another profession.

What is important to note here is that most workers in the gig economy actually want a level of flexibility. We have spoken to workers who talk emphatically about how platforms allow them to work in ways that would simply not otherwise have been possible; whether this means escaping some of the constraints of the local labour market, or doing jobs they would not have been able to access previously. These people like the anonymity, they like the flexibility, and they are happy with the pay.

Indeed, gig economy firms like Uber and Deliveroo waste no time in sharing case studies of happy workers when faced with demands to improve working conditions. They remind workers that the last thing they want are nine-to-five jobs on traditional employment contracts in which they lose the ability to control their schedules. In many of the international-level policy meetings we have attended, the response from the well-dressed men sent to represent the interests of those platforms is usually to revert to anecdote – for example, about the single mother who needs the flexibility afforded by platform work to schedule jobs around her caring duties. Here they are careful to frame platform work not as something that her livelihood depends on (otherwise we might want to subject the relationship to a bit more scrutiny), but rather as a means for her to earn a bit of extra income in a relaxed way. Indeed, in many of those same meetings, when we speak about our own research with gig workers, one of the first comments from the platform representatives tends to be: 'these people aren't workers'. We need to have this discussion outside of these discursive boundaries. As we argued earlier in the book, these are workers. And these sorts of responses are just part of a fantastically powerful public relations machine that is reshaping how we think of work – by framing it as anything but work.

This is obviously only one part of the story. The dependence of workers on platform jobs varies by job type, but we do know that across sectors significant numbers of people rely on platforms for their livelihoods. While we have spoken to gig workers in India and South Africa who regularly work over twelve hours a day, seven days a week, evidence is increasingly showing that it is becoming harder to work full-time as incomes fall. We also have to ask ourselves who ultimately benefits from these arrangements. We should be asking not just whether workers like their jobs, but rather what are the political, economic, technological and social preconditions that have brought these activities into being, and whether those enablers ultimately mean that ever more jobs will fall under the shadow of the gig economy.

It is also worth noting that the sorts of conversations mentioned above about the virtues of platform work tend to be with people who have found ways of succeeding in their corner of the gig economy. And they are conversations with people who have not yet fallen upon misfortune as most of us do at some point in our lives. People in the prime of their lives who have a flexible job are, of course, going to value those jobs. What we have to ask ourselves is whether we would hear the same stories from the workers who tried and never made it onto the cloud platforms because of the lack of jobs?; would we hear the same stories from the Uber drivers accused of something by customers and deactivated from the platform with no due process; would we hear the same stories from food delivery riders who suffer an injury and have to go two months without pay until they can ride a bike again? The gig economy represents a way of organizing work in which the strong and the able can thrive, but in which the weak can fall through the cracks. It is all of our responsibility to remember who the gig economy does not work for, and why it does not work for them, when thinking about the benefits that it offers to workers.

Do we want a society in which long-term employment contracts are increasingly a thing of the past and in which ever more work is mediated by platform intermediaries? Do we want to shift even more risk onto workers? Do we all really want to trade our job security for flexibility – and the precarity that often follows? Few would disagree that flexible contracts are needed in some instances and some sectors. But how many jobs in the economy should actually be defined by gigs?

In this book we have shown how the gig economy involves an organizational form that is beginning to characterize ever more sectors of the economy. We have done this through a focus on a range of activities in a range of places. The gig economy is not just an extension of previous forms of labour market precarity. It is a reshaping of the spatialities and temporalities of work through particular enablers.

The Fordism of the assembly line changed the place and time of work, seeking to treat workers like machines, transforming not only the factory, but society more broadly. Now the gig economy is changing the places and times of work too. The economic geographies and temporalities of the gig economy make it challenging for workers to build effective and lasting structural power, hinder the ability of regulators to apply labour law, entrench the monopoly power of platforms as key intermediaries between supply and demand of labour, and ultimately bring about high levels of opacity that prevent the various actors in production networks from holding each other accountable. Unlike the Fordist era, today's workers are expected to be not machines, but rather entrepreneurs and atomized individuals. Although it may not be apparent at first glance, today's gig economy workers are also part of a bigger machine, albeit one held together by fibre optics, databases and algorithms.

Rather than accept that this is just how the machine works, we want to try to envision some alternative mechanics. We have done this framed around four problematic characteristics of the gig economy: a lack of transparency, accountability, worker power and democratic ownership. In some cases, we propose tweaks to the machine; in others we propose a fundamental rebuilding; and in yet others, we are simply suggesting places in which spanners might be effectively inserted to stop the cogs. For each of the four issues in this conclusion, we tried to rethink the political, economic, technological and social reconfigurations that would be needed to bring into being alternative and fairer futures for the workers of the gig economy. In all cases, we see each of the four futures as inherently intertwined. Each of them supports each other And each of them is less effective when considered in isolation.

If we acknowledge that today's gig economy is not just a natural and inevitable outcome of technological changes, and instead is a particular mode of organization that was nurtured and brought into being by specific human and organizational actors with specific vested interests, then we can also acknowledge that alternative outcomes are possible. There is not enough space here for a full exposition or a detailed roadmap of any of these paths. We hope merely to expose the beginnings of a range of strategies and ideas; and by focusing on these four issues, their preconditions and enablers, and then four alternative futures, we can see that the undesirable aspects of today's gig economy are neither inevitable nor irrevocably locked in. We can no longer turn back the clock to some idealized past. But, by reflecting on the nature of gig work, we can still shape its futures.

Future #1: Transparency

Many of the problematic production practices in the gig economy are shielded by the opacity that is present within almost all digital production networks. Users, clients and consumers often know little about what is behind the screen or the app. This opacity is articulated in Susskind's (2018) piece on 'outcome thinking'. He argues that we should all be interested in the outcomes that workers bring, rather than the outcome of work on workers: 'clients don't really want us. They want the outcomes we bring', he notes. Indeed, most platforms encourage this state of affairs. When you use a platform to outsource a task, order food or even contract with a house cleaner, you are not encouraged to build long-term bonds with workers. They are instead presented as largely interchangeable beings in the market for talent. The entire model of most platforms in not premised on connecting clients to the perfect worker for them, but rather on indicating that clients and consumers have choice from a vast pool of workers.

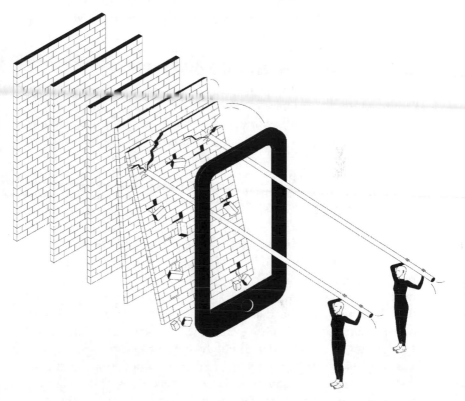

Figure 5 Transparency
Illustration by John Philip Sage

This de-personalization (and some might say de-humanization) of workers is not the norm in non-platform gig work around the world. In Britain, it is common to invite tradespeople in for a cup of tea and a chat about the weather or the football before they get down to work. In Kenya, it is not uncommon for people to pay for school fees or medical costs for the families of cleaners or gardeners that service their homes. Everywhere else in the world, we altruistically share time, stories, food and drink, advice and resources with the myriad workers that we encounter on a daily basis. We do this because of our social nature: feeling empathy, concern and care for people we barely know.

The efficiencies of platform services deprive us of much of that. Our relationships with workers are turned into a simple ranking and reputation system designed to regulate the performance of workers (Gandini, 2016). As we strip away the possibilities for social bonds and empathy, users, consumers and clients have few opportunities to get to know about the working conditions that define what it is like to work in the gig economy. We know little about whether workers enjoy their jobs, how precarious their income is, how vulnerable they are to change, whether they are paid a living wage, or whether they face discrimination or dangerous working conditions. The gig economy, in short, is defined by opacity and alienation.

But it need not be that way. We agree with Susskind that clients want outcomes. However, they also want more than that. How many of us would knowingly support companies that we know are actively engaging in destructive production practices? Indeed, a central reason why large companies spend so much money on corporate social responsibility is to ensure that they are not perceived as unethical. This desire for companies to be seen to be doing the right thing in order to avoid the reputational damage that could come with bad press has sparked an immense range of kitemarks, schemes and standards, all with the intent of informing consumers that the commodities that they buy are produced in ethically sensitive ways. There is always a danger here that such schemes can simply de-link the relationships between consumerism, capitalist production and global poverty (Cook, 2004; Richey and Ponte, 2011).[1] However, on the whole, it appears undeniable that individuals and businesses are more concerned than ever about what lies on the other side of the supply chains that they embed themselves into as consumers.

This brings us to our first future. We think there is a need for more transparency in the production networks of platform work, precisely in order to re-link capitalist production practices and poverty in the minds of consumers. In other words, we need a movement to help users, consumers, clients and platforms perceive the moral responsibility that they have for the livelihoods of workers. The first step here is to demystify the production process, and to build mechanisms so that platforms can no longer conceal what happens behind the app.

Platform companies may well fear the consequences of greater transparency in their production networks. It is worth remembering Tom Goodwin's now famous observation of the platform economy: 'Uber, the world's largest taxi company, owns no vehicles. Facebook, the world's most popular media owner, creates no content. Alibaba, the most valuable retailer, has no inventory. And Airbnb, the world's largest accommodation provider, owns no real estate.'[2] These companies, in other words, rely solely on their ability to control flows of information and act as intermediaries between clients and workers. If Uber and Upwork were to collapse tomorrow, the drivers, cars, computers and customers previously enrolled into their platform would still exist.

The move to deny platforms total control over information flows between suppliers and consumers can be achieved in a number of ways. The first is through research. Here we need to go beyond the numbers. It is not enough to simply scrape, map and model the economics of large platforms. We instead need to recall Marx's (1845) famous '11th thesis', that while 'philosophers have hitherto only interpreted the world in various ways; the point is to change it.' Inspired by that mission, and examples of action research in the gig economy (e.g. Irani, 2013; van Doorn, 2018), we have begun a broad-reaching research project to address issues of opacity in the gig economy.

The Fairwork project is a response that we developed to address many of the challenges that platform workers face across the world The core mission of the project is to give a rating to every gig work platform that reflects the fairness of working conditions on the platform. The project began in early 2018 with a grant from Germany's Federal Ministry for Economic Cooperation and Development, and the convening of a large meeting at the International Labour Organization in Geneva to which we invited a diverse group of workers, trade unions, platforms, policy makers and academics. In that meeting, and follow-ups in Johannesburg and Bangalore, we were able to establish a set of five principles for 'fair work' in the gig economy. The principles cover fair pay (paying at least a minimum wage in the worker's jurisdiction), fair conditions (protecting worker health and well-being), fair contracts (at a minimum following national law and having a clear contract, and not engaging in the misclassification of workers), fair governance (having an appeals process for disciplinary procedures, and policies that ensure equality in the ways workers are managed), and finally, fair representation (having a process through which worker voice can be expressed, and recognizing collective bodies like unions where they exist). These five principles are converted into a possible score of ten for each platform. This involves two points for each principle, the first for achieving a basic level of fairness (for example, reaching a minimum level of fair pay), which if achieved, can result in a further point for a higher level of fairness (for example, guaranteeing a higher level of fair pay).

Through the ratings that are being produced through the project and put into an annual league table, a degree of transparency will be infused into the gig economy. Platforms and clients will no longer be able to hide behind the veil of the app, and instead can be held accountable by consumers. By utilizing the same rating scheme for all platforms, and allowing best (as well as worst) practices to be highlighted, it lessens the opportunities for anyone to shrug away problems with the statement that 'that couldn't work for our business model'. We do not see this as a panacea for the gig economy. Rather, it is a way to take inspiration from progressive organizations like the Living Wage Foundation in order to establish a clear set of fair work principles for the gig economy which could ultimately be used not just by platforms and clients, but also by workers: as benchmarks to embed into future campaigns and bargaining with platforms.

The second strategy through which platforms can be made more transparent is through the establishment of 'counter' platforms that seek to allow workers a degree of control. This involves countering the level of informational control that existing platforms have over the activities that they mediate. We have already discussed Turkopticon as an example of a counter platform, and will revisit the example in 'Future #3' below. But there are many other examples of hubs for platform workers to engage in collaborative information sharing and horizontal communication outside of the walls of the platforms that they work for. The Fair Crowd Work website (http://faircrowd.work/) run by Germany's largest trade union, IG Metall,[3] Sweden's white-collar union, Unionen, and the Austrian Chamber of Labour, is a platform that allows workers to rate platforms using a five-star rating system (mirroring the ways that workers get rated on most platforms). However, by far the most used counter platforms by workers are groups that workers set up on commonly used platforms like Facebook, WhatsApp and reddit. On those groups, workers are no longer constrained by the limited affordances that platforms seek to create for horizontal communication amongst workers, and they are no longer constrained by the limitations on the types of information that platforms allow workers to post about their jobs, their clients, their pay or anything else (also discussed in more detail in 'Future #3'). Workers, in other words, are finding ways to share the information that they want to share about the ways in which their jobs work.

We have seen how the opacity of digital production networks can allow for problematic upstream outcomes. If clients and consumers know little about working conditions, there is an incentive to cut costs to the end user at the expense of the wages and job conditions of workers. Yet by making work practices more visible, a combination of human empathy on the side of consumers, the reputational fears of firms, and the demystification of work processes that can help to develop shared worker consciousness about their jobs, can be harnessed to bring about fairer futures in the gig economy.

It is undeniable that many people enact 'outcome thinking' in how they approach the world. Yet, there are probably at least as many who embed an ethic of care and empathy in how they interact with others. This is not a simple argument that somehow ethical consumption decisions can fix everything that is wrong with platform capitalism. They cannot and they will not. We are not all equally responsible for the problems baked into the gig economy, and we do not have equal power to change those problems. But, together, we can impose change by insisting on knowing more about the impacts of our actions. Building mutual understanding about work and working conditions is a starting point for larger structural change. Narratives about what the gig economy is need to be taken away from its current gatekeepers. By building more transparency about the nature of platform work, workers and their advocates lay the foundations for a more just world of work.

Future #2: Accountability

Our first future is about trying to better understand the networks that platforms mediate – from sites of work to sites of consumption, and everything in between. The lack of publicly available knowledge about how platforms work has meant that, in most parts of the world, they are faced with very little accountability. From Lagos to London to Los Angeles, platforms are making the case that they are a new, special type of technology firm. 'We're a technology company, not a taxi service, says Uber', reads the headline of a South African newspaper reporting an interview with a company spokesperson.[4] Uber's argument, made at an employment tribunal in London in 2016, is that it is a technology company because instead of providing a transport service to customers, 'it merely puts them in touch with drivers'.[5] In response to this, the following quote was heard during the *O'Connor vs Uber Technologies Inc.* case in the US in 2015:

Figure 6 Accountability
Illustration by John Philip Sage

Uber does not simply sell software; it sells rides. Uber is no more a 'technology company' than a Yellow Cab is a 'technology company' because it uses CB radios to dispatch taxi cabs.

To which the judge responded: 'we respectfully agree'.[6]

Despite this, platform companies deploy this kind of framing to argue that they have little responsibility to the millions of workers who rely on them for a daily income. If you, as a worker, want to take a holiday or need to take sick leave, the 'technology company' that simply connected you to your clients certainly is not going to help you out. But platforms are no more just technology companies than a shop or a factory is just a building. Platforms reap huge rewards from the positions they occupy as infomediaries, and so it does not seem unreasonable to expect them to shoulder a certain amount of accountability and responsibility for the lives of the workers that fuel their businesses.

The issue is that most platform managers are not just going to wake up one day and miraculously decide to become more responsible, putting at risk delivering profit to shareholders. Platforms can use regulation that was not designed with the platform economy in mind in order to have the best of both worlds: rewards without risk and responsibility.

Our first step here is therefore a discursive one. We need to stop imagining that platforms inhabit some sort of separate 'technological' realm of society. Taxi companies, cleaning companies, delivery companies and outsourcing companies are, and have always been, companies that use technology. For platform companies to now fetishize the information and communication technologies that power their business is clearly a strategic and self-serving move. Yes, platforms use technology. But no, they are not technology companies. They are transport companies, delivery companies and employment agencies, and so on. We need to start talking about them in that way.

Despite the efforts of platform lobbyists arguing that ministries of labour are against progress or that outdated labour laws no longer work, there has been a range of successes in trying to regulate platform work. Much effort has been expended here to get limited protection for workers via the courts, by arguing that gig workers are employees and that they therefore deserve the protections traditionally afforded to employees. For instance, a Valencia court, in June 2018, noted that Deliveroo riders are employees because they are 'subject to tight control by the platform monitoring their delivery rides, with GPS features, and to the laying down of the main terms and conditions, including prices' (Aloisi, 2018). Control is considered to be a key index of employment status. Those riders will therefore have all of the rights that employees are entitled to under Spanish law. In Australia, a Foodora food delivery worker was reclassified as an employee by the country's Fair Work Commission who noted that the platform 'had considerable capacity to control the manner in which the applicant performed work, and it fixed the place of work and the start and finish times of each engagement or shift' (see De Stefano 2018).[7] At The Doctors Laboratory in London, the IWGB won a union recognition agreement, with a range of employment statuses for riders previously part of a gig economy set-up (from full employee through to worker and self-employed). The benefits of this include representation, secure wages and increased bargaining power management.[8]

As these examples demonstrate, turning to the courts can be a useful means to secure protection for gig economy workers – at least those who have succeeded. Unfortunately, for most, this is ultimately a losing battle (Aloisi, 2018). Today's victory can quickly turn into tomorrow's loss, should the platform companies decide to tweak their policies to ensure that the next court decision deems platform workers are not entitled to the rights and protections of employees after all.

Even more troubling is the fact that some platform companies even seek to evade the rules that clearly do apply to them. Uber's South African entity (Uber Technologies SA) was recently taken to the Commission for Conciliation, Mediation and Arbitration (CCMA) by a trade union on behalf of some Uber drivers who were 'deactivated' from the platform.[9] The union demanded that Uber Technologies recognize drivers as employees and so give workers the protections afforded to employees under South African labour law. Uber appealed the decision at the Labour Court. The court decided that the case could not proceed not because it had no merit, but rather because the claim was made against the wrong Uber entity. It turns out that Uber International Holding(s) BV, a company based in the Netherlands, owns the Uber software application, and, as such, all South African drivers are in a contract with Uber BV rather than Uber SA. South African Uber drivers would therefore have to take up their case in a court in the Netherlands.

There is no predestined reason why Uber drivers in South Africa should have a contract with the Dutch parent company rather than the local company. But the way Uber has structured the relationship is that Uber BV controls the drivers in South Africa and Uber Technologies SA provides support services to the drivers (for instance recruitment and onboarding) (du Toit, 2018). This use of multiple jurisdictions in order to operate a taxi company with an app is simply a way of ensuring that there is even more of an arm's-length relationship between the company and its workers.[10]

These decisions mean that, in order to hold platforms truly accountable through the courts and regulation, changes are needed. The first step is supporting workers and their advocates who have taken the fight to the courts. The second is identifying the cross-cutting needs and conditions of platform workers across sectors in order for broad protections to be brought into being. For instance, the South African Labour Relations Act and the Australian Independent Contractors Act both go some way to extending rights to all platform workers, irrespective of their employment status. We also need to look beyond existing labour law that, in most places, was designed for white-collar workers in offices and blue-collar workers in factories. In many places, the law simply is not designed to meet the needs of gig workers. If the platform as an intermediating party between clients or customers and workers is here to stay, and if we acknowledge that there are some cases in which the relationship between workers and platform looks substantially different to a traditional employment relationship, we then require protections that are either tailored to platform workers or exist independent of employment status.

Across Europe, both workers and unions have fought in the courtrooms to clarify employment status – either as employees, or in the UK with the application of 'worker status', in order to gain employment rights and protections. Although there have been test cases, Countouris and De Stefano (2019: 57) have argued that 'This relative quiet at a national policy level can be usefully contrasted with the more lively debate currently taking place at the EU level particularly around the draft Directive on Transparent and Predictable Working Conditions in the European Union.' This has the potential to extend rights, as Countouris and De Stefano (as well as the European Trade Union Confederation, ETUC) note that its stated aim is 'to provide protection for the widest categories of workers and in particular the most vulnerable workers'.

In the UK, the government commissioned a major report into the realities and futures of contemporary work. The results were published in *The Taylor Review of Modern Working Practices* (2017), with Matthew Taylor as the lead author. While the report itself has some critical internal issues – for example, Greg Marsh, a lead panel member held Deliveroo shares while the report was being researched and written – it does highlight a desire by the British government to tackle the issues of employment regulation. The result was proposals for a seven-step plan that encourages a mixture of worker empowerment, harnessing of previous law (promoting a National Minimum Wage, for example) and organizational cooperation in the future. The report was accused of not going far enough by those who have been fighting for improvements (see the 2017 response from the IWGB: 'Dead on Arrival.'[11]) and providing little beyond encouragement for stakeholders to change their actions. The struggle over employment classification continues in the UK, as well as whether new regulation is needed or how existing implementation can be achieved.

The lack of effective regulation for gig workers does not only have to be approached by thinking of new labour law specifically for the gig economy. Instead, one solution being discussed by the ILO (2019: 39) is the call for two 'universal labour guarantees' for all:

(a) fundamental workers' rights: freedom of association and the effective recognition of the right to collective bargaining and freedom from forced labour, child labour and discrimination; and

(b) a set of basic working conditions: (i) 'adequate living wage';[12] (ii) limits on hours of work; and (iii) safe and healthy workplaces.

The idea here is that 'all workers, regardless of their contractual arrangement or employment status, must equally enjoy adequate labour protection to ensure humane working conditions for everyone' (ILO, 2019: 38). Rather than seeking to update laws to deal with each new contractual permutation in the gig economy, this solution instead reasserts the rights of all workers. Drawing on these ideas, we – along with our colleagues Sandra Fredman, Darcy du Toit, Richard Heeks, Jean-Paul van Belle, Abigail Osiki and Paul Mungai – have produced a broad outline of a Convention on Platform Work, incorporating the Fairwork principles, which can be found in the Appendix.

Future #3: Worker power

While we need transparency in production networks and knowledge about the ways in which platform work is pieced together and governed; and while we also need genuine protections for workers and the ability for urban, regional, national and transnational regulatory bodies to hold them to account – what is really needed for genuine positive change is for platform workers to have, create and take more power in their collective destinies.

Workers in the gig economy have potential 'associational power' (Silver, 2003). This power comes from the ability of workers, brought together at work, to act collectively in their interests. This is often thought of as something that happens through unions, but it can also include campaigns, political parties or other kinds of organizations. While the gig economy has changed many of the processes at work, it still involves the buying and selling of workers' time. Workers enter into work at a structural disadvantage: they

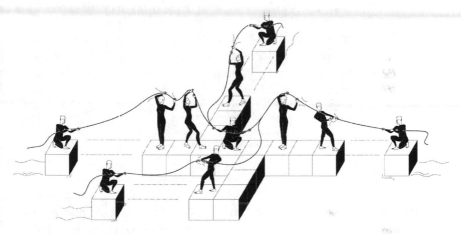

Figure 7 Worker power
Illustration by John Philip Sage

need to sell their time to earn a living, but have very little bargaining power as individuals. However, work brings together workers
– whether in factories, or increasingly now on the same streets,
waiting outside the same restaurants, or communicating together
on the same websites – with common interests. Often these interests can turn into shared grievances and complaints. In chapter 4,
we began to sketch out these formative moments of associational
power being recognized and flexed – often starting on WhatsApp
or face-to-face where workers' paths cross.

While most individual workers have next to no effective bargaining power, platform workers have the power to cause massive
disruption to economies and cities should they choose to collectively withdraw their labour. Imagine cities without on-demand
taxis, food delivery, platform-based care work, and the myriad
digital services offered by cloudworkers (often we would not
realize the effect this would have until it happened). Life would
go on, but it would no longer be business as usual. Some types of
workers (such as drivers) even have the power to affect non-users
of platforms. In cities around the world, they have blocked roads
as part of their protests.

One of the problems is that workers' interests can be set against
each other during periods of strikes or protests. For example,
transport platforms can offer increased surge pricing or boosts to
greatly increase pay rates. The often anonymous nature of the work
means that the traditional picket line outside of a workplace can
be harder to enforce, with other workers continuing to work on
the platform. If gig economy workers are to build a better future
as allies, collaborators and colleagues rather than competitors, and
if they are to ever exert any effective collective power, what best
practices, successes and visions should we look towards?

First, we at a minimum need strategies and platforms that
can support more effective horizontal communication between
workers. It is worth recalling here that most gig platforms are – at
most – designed for workers to speak to their clients. Very few
offer the affordances for workers to speak with one another. But,
because most people in most jobs want to be able to speak to people
in similar working conditions, gig economy workers from around

the world have found ways of connecting. Most of these efforts occur within corporately owned tools that can be repurposed for worker organizing around the world. From Uber drivers in India to package delivery riders in South Africa, and from food delivery riders in the UK to online freelancers in the Philippines, Facebook and WhatsApp groups are the channels of choice for workers who wish to speak to one another.

On a Facebook group for Kenyan freelancers who work on platforms like Upwork and Freelancer.com, there are frequent posts by people selling each other computers, sharing news, and asking for advice. On WhatsApp groups used by delivery riders in the UK, workers post jokes and memes to pass some of the idle time while waiting for work, but also share tips on how to increase earnings. In all cases, what we are seeing is people refusing to accept the idea that they are atomized workers, and refusing to accept the idea that connectivity only runs vertically rather than horizontally. Even if workers like drivers and domestic workers rarely if ever see each other, they can start to collectively challenge ways of structuring the work processes that they are enrolled in.

The Turkopticon project is probably the most successful initiative to do this. Started in 2008, the platform allows Amazon Mechanical Turk workers to see and submit client reviews. Because wage theft is such an endemic problem on Mechanical Turk, Turkopticon found an important use amongst workers seeking to avoid some of the worst culprits. As of 2018, the platform hosted over 420,000 reviews of over 59,000 requesters. The benefit of Turkopticon is that it is integrated into the workflow of Mechanical Turk workers. However, there have also been a range of suggestions floated for worker-run, or at least worker-oriented communication platforms. Often these are additional programs or apps for workers to use. There are risks with using a platform like WhatsApp or Facebook, as they are not designed for worker organizing and lack safeguards against management surveillance or infiltration. While alternatives have their benefits, the real challenge in encouraging their use will be getting people to switch away from existing channels like Facebook and WhatsApp which rely on network effects to keep people using them. If the majority of the people you already want to speak to use Facebook and WhatsApp, then it is always going to be hard to switch an entire network to another platform.

Our discussion thus far has focused on the technologically mediated ways that workers communicate with one another. This is because, for many job types, there is simply no convergence in time and space that happens between groups of workers. But this is not always the case. In large cities, cloudworkers meet in co-working spaces and social meetup events. In many parts of the world, app-based taxi drivers congregate in places like malls and airports whilst waiting for rides. Co-presence is especially common for delivery riders who tend to have long stretches of wait-time in front of clusters of restaurants, shops and off-licences.

It is likely no coincidence that it is delivery or taxi platform workers that have had the most success in collectively organizing around the world. When the IWGB organizes Deliveroo riders and Uber drivers in the UK, The Movement organizes taxi drivers in South Africa,[13] or different unions mobilize across India, collective organization has been built on workers convening in the same times and spaces.

This brings us to our second point. Once workers have first established a foundation upon which they can effectively communicate and coordinate, we can then look to successful efforts to collectively organize and bargain. In some cases, this means workers setting up or joining official trade unions. But, in others, many workers seek to set up groups that fulfil many of the same functions of unions without the official designation.[14]

Once these groups of gig workers are established in either existing unions, new unions or groups that don't call themselves unions, they can engage in an eye-level discussion with platforms in a way that is impossible for individual workers to conduct. In Denmark, the 3F trade union signed an agreement on behalf of domestic workers with the platform Hilfr.dk that allows workers to be reclassified as employees after they have performed over 100 hours of work (Hilfr, 2018).[15] It also grants these workers an hourly minimum wage of 141 DKK (US$21) and the right to unemployment benefits and holidays, and protection against unfair dismissal.

Importantly for domestic workers, it also obliges customers to pay half the agreed wage if jobs are cancelled without sufficient notice.

The platform economy is not the only area where workers have faced precarious contracts, as we have argued in this book, both historically and in other sectors. Within the entertainment industries (as we mentioned with the origins of the term), there has been a long history of gig work. From a more recent example, the International Arts and Entertainment Alliance (IAEA) is the global union that represents workers in the Arts and Entertainment sector, bringing together three global federations. It has organized a campaign to reach out to 'atypical workers'. This involved developing 'fundamental principles and rights at work [that] apply to all workers in the media and culture sector, regardless of the nature of their employment relationship' (ILO, 2014: 25). Rather than seeing the contracts themselves as the problem – with many workers engaged in project-based work – this focuses on how to improve the rights of workers in a way that works for them within the industry. One of the member federations of the IAEA, the Media, Entertainment and Arts division of UNI, negotiates framework conditions for workers on this basis.

Similarly, in 2002 the Screen Actors Guild (SAG), which later merged with the American Federation of Television and Radio Artists to become SAG-AFTRA, passed the Global Rule 1. This required members 'to ensure that a producer is a SAG signatory and to get a SAG contract wherever they work in order to get the protections of SAG's agreements, even when working outside of the United States'.[16] This acted as a starting point to drive up working conditions, both in the US and more widely. While there are many challenges for understanding how workers and trade unions can cooperate across national boundaries and jurisdictions, positive examples like this can be taken as inspiration.

What is needed here is more visibility about the ways in which collective bargaining can be successful. Indeed, the terms and conditions offered by platforms should be seen as a starting point for negotiation rather than something that workers need to take or leave. Of course, underpinning any negotiation must be the ability for workers to collectively withdraw their labour. This is our third point Across our fieldwork we have heard stories of workers striking and winning local concessions, often without any coverage in the media. Below the surface changes are beginning to happen in the gig economy. These stories need to be heard much more widely.

In summary, there are multiple pathways to worker power. As a start, gig economy workers need visibility. They need to be able to see and communicate with fellow workers, and they need physical places and digital networks that are conducive to building deeper collaborations. Those collaborations might happen through small and nimble local unions, groups of workers that refuse to call themselves a union, big tent domestic unions, international union federations like UNI Global, or unions like the Industrial Workers of the World. What matters is simply that gig economy workers find ways of collective bargaining, and that they are able to build the associational power, symbolic power and structural power that would be required to collectively withdraw their labour should they need to. Platforms design their digital connectivity to atomize their workforce and reduce potentials for disruption, but workers can make use of alternative connectivities to push for better working conditions. The roots of the trade union movement lie in trying to get rid of harms in the workplace, and it is possible that the rise of the gig economy will serve as a call to arms for unions and associations to build new solidarities and new strategies to improve the nature of work.

Future #4: Democratic ownership

Throughout this book we have explored the ways in which the current model of platforms is creating many negative outcomes for workers. So far in this chapter we have discussed the ways that workers are beginning to shape and reshape gig work in their own interests. In all of these cases, we see workers pushing back against the owners and managers of platforms. However, in none of the cases do we see a situation in which workers are ever truly taking

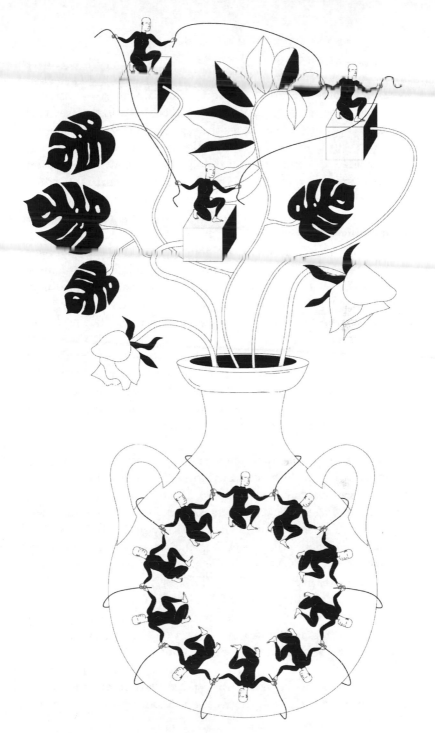

Figure 8 Democratic ownership
Illustration by John Philip Sage

control over the means of production or distribution. In this final section, we therefore wish to explore potential ways to do just that.

At the core of the platform cooperative idea is the fact that platforms operate as mediators: bringing together workers and customers. In the process, they take a substantial cut of the transactions – sometimes as high as 30 per cent. However, once the infrastructure has been set up, these platforms essentially become rent-seeking. Rather than providing anything new to either party using the platform, they collect a cut of other people's work, often driving down wages to do so. As the costs of producing apps used by platforms have fallen dramatically over time, they are no longer the sole preserve of multi-billion-dollar companies. Trebor Scholz (2017b: 47), who argues for 'platform cooperatives' (platforms that are democratically governed and cooperatively owned), proposes an alternative model for the gig economy that begins with a thought experiment:

> Just for one moment imagine that the algorithmic heart of any of these citadels of anti-unionism could be cloned and brought back to life under a different ownership model, with fair working conditions, as a humane alternative to the free market model.

The idea here is that the centuries-old cooperative model can be updated for the gig economy: drivers could come together to make and run their own taxi app, cleaners their own cleaning app, and translators their own translation app. By pooling their resources – and perhaps with the help of politically sympathetic software developers – they could start their own platform and keep more of any income taken from the client, and have more of a say of how their work is carried out. The idea has been promoted by Trebor Scholz and the Platform Cooperative Consortium based in New York.[17] The major strength of this project is that it presents an imaginary for how platform work could be organized differently. In fact, as Scholz (2017b: 50) has reiterated, 'the inability to imagine a different life is capital's ultimate triumph'. The idea of platform cooperatives connects this different vision of digital work to the long history of cooperatives: the Mondragon Corporation

In the Basque Country, the long history of cooperatives in the UK, or even the example of workers taking over struggling factories and running them as successful cooperatives in countries like Greece[18] or Argentina.[19] In the current context of low-paid work in which many people have little control, just pointing out that there is a (potentially) viable alternative model for running platforms is a huge step forward. And, indeed, the platform.coop website now lists over 300 platform coops around the world who are actively trying to put into practice this alternative model for the gig economy.

While getting rid of the boss is, without doubt, an exciting idea for many workers in the gig economy (it is, after all, one of the main reasons people choose platform work), there remain inescapable economic pressures for cooperatives. This risk is acknowledged by Scholz, who notes 'the problem of competition with global corporations that are rolling in money' (Scholz, 2017b: 47). For example, a worker-owned alternative to Uber would still have to contend with Uber (and, remember, that Uber currently operates at a massive loss), regardless of how well it was structured internally. While we could hope that the millions of users in a city like New York or Johannesburg might choose to move onto a new platform that upheld workers' rights, at a more basic level there is the challenge of effectively advertising with little or no budget. After all, no one will choose the worker-friendly version of Uber if they have never heard of it. Many of these companies not only take a cut of existing transactions, but also drive down wages to unsustainably low levels. If a platform cooperative for taxis was established, you would hope the drivers would earn a decent wage. However, they would still need to operate and survive in a deeply competitive environment.

Platform cooperatives are not the only way that we could imagine a more democratic and equitable system to govern platform work. We could also think about platforms as a civic utility: the platform as a local infrastructure similar to how internet, electricity or public transport is managed in much of the world. The network effects at play in the platform economy already mean that it is unviable to have more than a few platforms focusing on the same industry in any given city. Because of these inevitable monopolistic tendencies, platforms could be regulated in a similar way to many public utilities: placing priorities such as decent jobs, environmental and social impact as necessary conditions for a licence to operate.

This idea could even be taken one step further by thinking about platforms as publicly owned and run utilities. For instance, why not find a way to have a taxi platform or a delivery platform not run by a private company with its headquarters on the other side of the world, but instead by an organization with local priorities baked into its DNA? The platform as a locally run, locally managed, and locally owned utility.

We could envisage a city setting up a ride-hailing platform, owned and managed by the city government. If we use the logic of the platform company here: this is not about a city starting, say, a taxi company; this is about a city providing opportunities for tens of thousands of drivers. It is the city (or the state, region or country) establishing a civic monopoly over the platform. Through this civic monopoly, it could ensure that decent work is the starting point for any services offered. To the end user, does it really matter if you hail a car from a city-run platform or from a privately owned one? But, to the worker, this could make a world of difference. Unlike a cooperative, this does not put the pressure on workers to offer a viable service, backing it with public resources. If it was a success, it could even cross-subsidize public transport.

There are undoubtedly significant legal and operational challenges that such organizations would face, and we shouldn't downplay those challenges. In many countries, for instance, it would be illegal for a city to set up a rival to Uber or Deliveroo. However, if we are serious about wanting new regulation to curb the damaging outcomes of platforms (Future #2), then we could also envision new regulation that facilitates and enables alternative forms of governing, organizing and managing platform work. We need to envision our desired end states that have the rights of workers and democratic ownership and governance at their core, and then work backwards from those visions. Once we do that, these alternative futures appear much more achievable.

What can you do?

Technology alone has not brought about the gig economy, and there is nothing inevitable about its current or future state. For these reasons, it is important to not just reflect on what the gig economy is and where it comes from, but also to present a series of more desirable futures. More transparency and accountability, more worker-friendly regulation, greater structural power for workers, and the democratic ownership of platforms are all futures that help to build each other. No single one of these futures alone will likely bring about meaningful change in the quality of platform jobs. What use, for instance, would the democratic ownership of platforms be, if there is no transparency about working conditions, little worker-friendly regulation and no collective body representing workers? It would likely only bring about a situation in which local government ends up running a platform for low-paid, precarious and dangerous jobs.

If we are rethinking what the gig economy can evolve into, then we need a renewed effort to encourage all four of those futures. We need more transparency about the workings of the platform economy in order to try to impose more accountability through both pressure and regulation. To see lasting changes, we need to find ways to foster, build and support the structural power of workers. And, if we want lasting and sustainable organizations committed to equitable and fair outcomes, we need to embed that power, and focus that regulation, on building more democratic institutions that occupy key nodes of information exchange in the digital economy.

Multiple gig economy models have emerged, ranging from general online freelancing platforms, which are necessarily limited in the amount of control that they can exert on work, to transportation and care work platforms, which are characterized by extremely high levels of explicit coordination and power asymmetry. But what all gig economy models have in common is a defining logic that seeks to shift maximal risk and minimal reward onto workers. Platform companies achieve this through technologies and infrastructures of connectivity that allow work to be organized via two-sided markets, political environments that impose few regulations, a zeitgeist that values flexibility, and a backdrop of increasing inequality that leads ever more workers to make the calculation that a bad job is better than no job.

The gig economy is big, and around the world there are powerful interests who only seek to make it bigger. Yet nothing about the gig economy is inevitable. If we want to make sure that we avoid yet another industry in yet another place becoming organized by the logics of the gig economy, then we all have a part to play in resisting some of its worst characteristics. What, then, can we all do?

As a start, we can begin by revisiting part of the International Labour Organization's (1944) Declaration of Philadelphia: 'labour is not like an apple or a television set, an inanimate product that can be negotiated for the highest profit or the lowest price. Work is part of everyone's daily life and is crucial to a person's dignity, well-being and development as a human being.'[20] While using an app to order a driver, a takeaway, a cleaner, a babysitter or a dog walker can remove the need to ever speak to, or meaningfully interact with, the person performing that service, a crucial first step to decommodifying work is to get to know each other, to ask questions about the people and the processes that we are interacting with, to never take the work that someone is doing for us for granted, and not to treat it as a commodity that we are buying. It is from that foundation that we can build the solidarities needed to bring about lasting change.

If we are committed to learning about the processes that we are all embedded into, then we must also be committed to adjusting our own behaviours to support some practices and avoid others. This is not about launching individual boycotts and imagining that you can change the world alone. It is rather about acting out our responsibilities to those that we are connected to and impact upon. In practice, this could mean avoiding companies engaged in some of the most egregious violations in order to be part of an economic disincentive for them doing so. But this is not just about individual actions. For strikes and boycotts to be effective, we need to collectively respect them. In other words, don't cross picket lines! If the delivery drivers in your city are on strike for higher pay, do not use the app. Platforms will continue to ignore the demands of workers if their strikes are seen as being ineffective. So help to make those strikes effective. We can do even more though. In much the same way that some platforms use their international reach to evade local accountability, we can use that same global reach of some platforms to put pressure on them. If drivers or cleaners for a large international platform are on strike in Boston, Bangalore or Bangkok, show solidarity with them in your home town by respecting the picket. At the end of the day, striking platform workers are local actors taking on a global company. Help to give their actions some global reach.

That is only the beginning though. One of the most important things that all of us can do to change the future of work is to join a union or a worker's association. This need not be a formal traditional trade union, and indeed your job and your industry may not have one. But all unions have humble beginnings. If there is not one relevant for your job, start a chat channel for your colleagues. Get together outside of the job to discuss ways of improving your work and strategies for achieving those aims. And get in touch with already existing unions to ask them for help. They usually will. Many have resources they can share, as well as advice on how to get started. The most common concern that most people have is that it feels wasteful to spend a fraction of your already small paycheque on union dues. It's hard enough to pay the bills as it is. But this is again where we have to think about our power as a collective rather than our power as atomized individuals. Chapter 4 showed how effective it can be for workers to come together for collective action and collective bargaining. Union dues are a small price to pay for an economy in which the private sector sees labour as a partner to be negotiated with at eye level rather than an inconvenience to be dealt with on an individual basis. Even if you do not work in the gig economy, join a union. Your job may be next, and strength in numbers will be needed if work is to be reshaped into fairer directions.

Because of the problems that most gig economy unions and

workers' associations have in raising dues, a lot could be done by supporting those that are on the cutting edge of cases and conflicts that will reshape the gig economy for years to come: from the IWGB and IWW in the UK, to CLAP in France, the Transnational Courier Federation across Europe, The Movement in South Africa, the New York Taxi Worker Alliance, Rideshare Drivers United, and Gig Workers Rising in the US. Their battles in the courts are often costly and they tend not to have strike funds, so donate to their causes so that they have the opportunity to win, and the resources to keep going should they lose.

Last but not least, we need to make sure that the energy, compassion and power that can be built amongst groups of workers can transition into the domains of regulation and law. The places in which we live all have parties and politicians who claim to want to remove regulatory red tape so that they support local businesses and avoid choking off innovations that are good for everyone. These are appealing ideas; after all who wants to get left behind or left out of the digital revolution. But, as we have shown, the gig economy is a petri dish for theories of limited regulation. It is precisely within a laissez-faire approach to workers' rights that the concerns we outlined in chapter 3 take form. Platforms are not going away; we will continue to have on-demand taxis and app-based food delivery, and people will continue to innovate whether or not the workers who make it all possible have decent jobs (and, indeed, we have to ask ourselves if we want those innovations if the only way to bring them into being is on the back of indecent work). We therefore all need to look to local, regional and national political parties and politicians who stand for decent jobs and who stand up for the rights of workers. We need to vote for them, campaign for them, support them, write to them and hold them to account.

The gig economy is the battleground in a set of conflicts being waged that will determine the futures of work. You may think that your own job is safe from some of the changes described in this book, but the processes that define the gig economy could come to transform almost every type of work. The balance sheet thus far is deeply worrying, and should be a cause of concern for workers the world over. And it will continue to be a concern unless we find ways of taking what we already know about how the gig economy works and who it works for, to collectively build a more equitable and fairer future of work.

Appendix:
Draft Convention on
Platform Work

A broad outline of a Convention on platform work, incorporating the Fairwork principles, and written by: Mark Graham, Sandra Fredman, Darcy du Toit, Richard Heeks, Jamie Woodcock, Jean-Paul van Belle, Abigail Osiki and Paul Mungai.

1. **Coverage**
   a. It should cover all workers, regardless of classification. A model for this is Convention 181, which states: 'This Convention applies to all categories of workers and all branches of economic activity [except seafarers].'[1] For the avoidance of doubt, it should specify that the term 'worker' refers to everyone who provides personal services mediated by the platform, including independent contractors.

2. **Pay**
   a. All platform workers should be paid for their work regularly and in full in accordance with their agreements. Platforms should ensure that such payments are made timeously.[2]
   b. Member States should take the necessary measures to ensure all workers receive just and equitable remuneration allowing

them and families to lead an existence worthy of human dignity, supplemented, if necessary, by other means of social protection.[3]

c. After consulting with representative platform owners and platform workers' representatives, Member States should establish procedures for determining minimum remuneration for platform workers, or include platform workers in existing procedures for determining remuneration for workers.[4]

d. The level of remuneration should take into account the nature of platform work;[5] the needs of platform workers and their families, taking into account the general level of wages in the country, the cost of living, social security benefits and the relative living standards of other social groups,[6] as well as economic factors such as the desirability of attaining and maintain high levels of employment.[7]

e. Appropriate measures should be put in place to ensure the effective implementation of the provisions relating to minimum remuneration.[8]

f. Minimum remuneration must not be subject to abatement by individual agreement, nor, except with general or particular authorization of the competent authority, by collective agreement.[9]

g. Workers should be given clear and regular statements as to how their remuneration is calculated, including which components are counted in the minimum, the costs paid by the worker, how the minimum is calculated for piece-rate pay, and if the minimum is an hourly or monthly rate.[10] Workers should be given a statement which sets out, in an appropriate, verifiable and easily understandable manner, the remuneration, method of calculation and periodicity of payments.[11]

3. **Health and Safety**
a. 'Workplace' covers all places where workers need to be or go by reason of their work and over which the platform has direct or indirect control or is in a position to influence by contract or otherwise.[12]

b. Where the worker works at home, national laws and regula tions on health and safety must apply, taking account of its special characteristics.[13]

c. The enforcement of laws concerning occupational safety and health and the working environment for platform workers must be secured by an adequate system of inspection.[14]

d. Representatives of platform workers must be given adequate information by the platform on health and safety; workers and their representatives should be given appropriate training in relevant occupational health and safety; and should be consulted to determine their health and safety concerns.[15]

e. Adequate compensation in case of occupational accidents or diseases should be provided as and where appropriate,[16] either directly by the State or by compulsory insurance to be taken out by platforms.

f. Workers who remove themselves from a work situation which they have reasonable justification to believe presents an imminent and serious danger to their life or health must be protected from penalties.[17]

g. Employers should provide, where necessary, adequate protective clothing and protective equipment to prevent, so far as reasonably practicable, risk of accidents or adverse effects on health.[18]

h. Occupational health and safety measures must not involve any expenditure for workers.[19]

4. **Hours of Work**

a. Platforms should not be permitted to require or allow workers to work more than 48 hours a week, with a maximum of 8 hours a day, in order to achieve the level of wages referred to in paragraph 3(b).[20] Hourly earnings should be sufficient to make this possible. If they are not, this will breach the principle that they should not be required to work more than the maximum weekly hours.[21]

b. Workers may only be permitted to work a limited number of additional hours above the maximum and at a higher rate of earnings.

5 Contracts

a. In recognition of the risk that there can be attempts to disguise the employment relationship, and that contractual arrangements can have the effect of depriving workers of the protection they are due,[22] there should be a legal presumption that an employment relation exists where one or more relevant indicators is present.

b. Such indicators should include the fact that, expressly or in effect, the work: is carried out according to the instructions and under the control of the platform; involves the integration of the worker in the activity or the business of the platform; is performed solely or mainly for the benefit of the platform; must be carried out personally by the worker; is of a particular duration or has a certain continuity; requires the worker's availability; or involves the provision of tools, materials and machinery by the platform.[23]

c. Platform workers should be supplied with a written statement of terms and conditions of work which clearly state all the terms of the contract.[24] Platform workers should be informed of their terms and conditions of work in an appropriate, verifiable and easily understandable manner. This should state at the very least the name and address of the other contracting party or parties, who must be subject to the local jurisdiction; remuneration, method of calculation and periodicity of payments, and terms and conditions relating to termination, including deactivation or other penalties, whether temporary or permanent.[25]

d. Adequate procedures should be in place to investigate complaints, alleged abuses and other practices of the platform.[26]

e. Platform workers' terms and conditions of work must be agreed to by the platform worker under conditions which ensure that the platform worker has an opportunity to review and seek advice on the terms and conditions in the agreement and freely consents before accepting.[27]

6. **Non-discrimination and Equality**
    a. Platforms should ensure that all workers are not subjected to discrimination directly or indirectly on the basis of race, colour, sex, religion, political opinion, national extraction, social origin, or any other form of discrimination covered by national law and practice, such as age or disability.[28]
    b. Platforms should protect workers against discrimination by customers or users by excluding requirements which have the effect of discriminating directly or indirectly against workers on any of the grounds mentioned in a.
    c. Equality of treatment should be promoted in relation to remuneration, statutory social security protection, minimum age for admission to employment and maternity protection.[29]
    d. Workers should have access to information explaining any decision, including the criteria for automated decisions, affecting their access to work through the platform or the terms and conditions for the performance of work.

7. **Data**
    a. Processing of data by platforms should protect workers' personal data, ensure respect for workers' privacy, and be limited to matters related to the qualification and professional experience of workers and any other directly relevant information.[30] Data should only be collected with express and informed consent of the worker and should not be shared with third parties under any circumstances without the worker's express and informed consent.

8. **Representation**
    a. Platform workers should enjoy freedom of association and the effective recognition of the right to representation and to collectively negotiate on any terms and conditions affecting their work.[31]
    b. Platform workers should have the right to establish or join organizations of their own choosing and to participate in the activities of such organizations.[32]

r Platform workers should be adequately protected against acts of discrimination or any detrimental treatment based on their exercise of the right to freedom of association or collective representation.[33]

Notes

Introduction

1 Armstrong, S. (2017) The NHS is going to trial a gig economy app for nurses. Wired, 3 October. Available at: https://www.wired.co.uk/article/nhs-app-nurses-flexible-working-jeremy-hunt-gig-economy

2 For examples of some of our research on this topic, see Graham and Shaw (2017), Graham et al. (2017a, 2017b), Waters and Woodcock (2017), Graham and Anwar (2018, 2019), Graham and Woodcock (2018), Wood et al. (2018, 2019a, 2019b) and Woodcock (forthcoming).

3 For more on the research project, see Graham et al. (2017c) and Graham and Anwar (2018).

Chapter 1: Where did the gig economy come from?

1 https://www.wired.com/2013/12/uber-surge-pricing/

2 See https://www.itu.int/osg/csd/stratplan/AR2008_web.pdf

3 See https://www.itu.int/en/ITU-D/Statistics/Documents/facts/ICTFactsFigures2017.pdf

4 See https://www.change.org/p/save-your-uber-in-london saveyour
uber

5 The 'refusal of work' formed an important component of Italian
workerism. As Bifo has argued: 'refusal of work does not mean so
much the obvious fact that workers do not like to be exploited, but
something more. It means that the capitalist restructuring, the technological change, and the general transformation of social institutions
are produced by the daily action of withdrawal from exploitation, of
rejection of the obligation to produce surplus value, and to increase
the value of capital, reducing the value of life.' See http://www.
republicart.net/disc/realpublicspaces/berardi01_en.htm

6 https://www.koreatimes.co.kr/www/biz/2018/08/367_253635.
html

7 https://www.bls.gov/news.release/conemp.nr0.htm

Chapter 2: How does the gig economy work?

1 See https://www.gov.uk/employment-status/selfemployed-contractor

2 Employment law in the UK is slightly different, with three different employment categories, including 'the intermediate, but distinct,
"worker" status [which] has entitlements to the National Minimum
Wage, protection against unlawful wage deductions, statutory minimum rest breaks and paid holidays, a limit on 48 hours of work on
average per week (although worker can opt out), as well as protections against discrimination and for whistleblowing'. See https://
www.gov.uk/employment-status/worker

3 See https://assets.publishing.service.gov.uk/media/5a046b06e5274a
0ee5a1f171/Uber_B.V._and_Others_v_Mr_Y_Aslam_and_Others_
UKEAT_0056_17_DA.pdf

4 See https://www.sec.gov/Archives/edgar/data/1543151/00011931
2519103850/d647752ds1.htm

5 See https://dictionary.cambridge.org/dictionary/english/uberize

6 For 'the knowledge', prospective drivers must learn over 45,000
road names and points of interest in a six-mile radius drawn around
Charing Cross in London. To pass the tests (known as appearances),
drivers must be able to rapidly compute a route between any given
two points in order to pass.

7 See https://www.crunchbase.com/organization/uber/funding_rou nds/funding_rounds_list

8 See Isaac, M. (2017) How Uber deceives the authorities worldwide. *The New York Times*, 3 March. Available at: https://www.nytimes. com/2017/03/03/technology/uber-greyball-program-evade-auth orities.html

9 See https://www.sfgate.com/technology/businessinsider/article/ Billionaire-hedge-fund-manager-says-Uber-told-him-6271449.php

10 The taxi medallion is a system of transferable permits used in many US cities. See https://www.washingtonpost.com/news/wonk/wp/ 2014/06/20/taxi-medallions-have-been-the-best-investment-in-am erica-for-years-now-uber-may-be-changing-that/?noredirect=on& utm_term=.5c7c10ad134a

11 See https://www.uber.com/newsroom/bits-atoms-2

12 The role of machine learning as an instrument of labour control is also worth noting. Uber admits that its 'Marketplace team leverages a variety of spatiotemporal forecasting models that are able to predict where rider demand and driver-partner availability will be at various places and times in the future. Based on forecasted imbalances between supply and demand, Uber systems can encourage driver-partners ahead of time to go where there will be the greatest opportunity for rides.' https://eng.uber.com/scaling-michelangelo/

13 Because of Uber's reliance on venture capital, it is also worth noting not just the economic power that AI gives the company, but also the rhetorical power to promise to be profitable in the future.

14 See https://www.forbes.com/sites/kashmirhill/2014/10/03/god- view-uber-allegedly-stalked-users-for-party-goers-viewing-pleasure/ #75d855d03141

15 See https://techcrunch.com/2017/06/21/ubers-toxic-culture-risks- its-driverless-future-too/

16 That said, there are a few types of geographically tethered work which are essentially unrecognizable from traditional work processes. The South African platform M4JAM, for instance, pays workers to collect price data on products from nearby shops and supermarkets.

17 The argument in this section is expanded on in more detail in Graham and Anwar (2018).

18 Graham and Anwar (2019) show that 'Globally, less than seven percent of people who register for jobs are ever able to secure one.'
There is, however, significant regional variation in success rates.

19 For more on the index, see https://ilabour.oii.ox.ac.uk/online-
labour-index/. It is worth noting that the index ignores non-English-
speaking platforms and is therefore only a selective picture of 'online
labour'.

20 See World Trade Organization (2018) *World Trade Report 2018. The
Future of World Trade: How Digital Technologies Are Transforming Global
Commerce*. Available at: https://www.wto.org/english/res_e/publica
tions_e/world_trade_report18_e.pdf

21 Quoted in Solon (2018).

22 Not only do workers have no ability to individually set rates, but they
sometimes do not even know in advance what the rates that they are
accepting will be.

Chapter 3: What is it like to work in the gig economy?

1 Mumit, like the names of the gig workers that will be mentioned
subsequently in the book, is a pseudonym, chosen to protect their
identity.

2 See https://www.thenation.com/article/best-friend-lost-life-gig-
economy/

3 See https://www.arre.co.in/social-commentary/zomato-rider-reac
tion-twitter-delivery-boy/

4 1 rupee equals around US$0.014, meaning 60 rupees is around
US$0.86, and 30 rupees is around US$0.43.

5 See https://www.wired.co.uk/article/uber-employment-lawsuit-
gig-economy-leigh-day

6 See https://www.judiciary.uk/wp-content/uploads/2016/10/aslam-
and-farrar-v-uber-reasons-20161028.pdf

7 See https://www.wired.co.uk/article/uber-employment-lawsuit-
gig-economy-leigh-day

8 See https://www.iol.co.za/capetimes/news/taxi-driver-hijacked-in-
grassy-park-18801688

9 See https://www.news24.com/SouthAfrica/News/uber-drivers-
death-raises-fears-tension-20170722

10 See https://www.timeslive.co.za/news/south-africa/2018-07-04-this-is-why-im-striking--uber-driver-explains-how-petrol-hikes-have-nearly-crippled-him/

11 See Beres, D. (2014) What does it take to earn $90,000 as an Uber driver? *Huffington Post*, 4 December. Available at: https://www.huffingtonpost.com/2014/12/04/uber-driver_n_6249608.html

12 See https://www.wired.co.uk/article/uber-employment-lawsuit-gig-economy-leigh-day

13 See Doward, J. (2018) Uber drivers '£18,000 poorer' as firm appeals two-year-old tribunal order. *The Guardian*, 28 October. Available at: https://www.theguardian.com/technology/2018/oct/28/uber-drivers-owed-thousands-in-holiday-and-sick-pay

14 See https://ig.ft.com/uber-game/

15 See https://www.theguardian.com/commentisfree/2018/apr/26/gig-economy-flexibility-exploitation-record-employment-low-wages-zero-hours

16 See Capetalk (2016) [LISTEN] How much does Sweepsouth pay its domestic workers? Capetalk, 27 February. Available at: http://www.capetalk.co.za/articles/293620/listen-how-much-does-sweepsouth-pay-its-domestic-workers

17 Wood et al. (2019a) show that cloudworkers, for instance, spend an average of 16 hours per week just looking for work. Which is almost 40 per cent of the time that the average cloudworker spends working!

18 Quoted in Semuels (2018).

19 Limer, E. (2014) My brief and curious life as a Mechanical Turk. Gizmodo, 28 October. Available at: https://gizmodo.com/my-brief-and-curious-life-as-a-mechanical-turk-1587864671

20 Shontell, A. (2013) When Amazon employees receive these one-character emails from Jeff Bezos, they go into a frenzy. *Business Insider*, 10 October. Available at: https://www.businessinsider.com/amazon-customer-service-and-jeff-bezos-emails-2013-10?IR=T

21 Dynamo (2014) Dear Jeff Bezos. Available at: http://www.wearedynamo.org/dearjeffbezos

22 See http://www.wearedynamo.org/dearjeffbezos

23 https://www.freelancer.com/about

24 Despite having one of the smallest GDPs in the world (129th in

2017), Palestine is the world's 50th largest destination for online freelancing work.

Chapter 4: How are workers reshaping the gig economy?

1 See Roberts, Y. (2018) The tiny union beating the gig economy giants. *The Guardian*, 1 July. Available at: https://www.theguard ian.com/politics/2018/jul/01/union-beating-gig-economy-giants-iwgb-zero-hours-workers

2 See   https://en.labournet.tv/riders-across-europe-unite-form-trans national-federation-couriers

3 See Moyer-Lee, J. (2018) When will 'gig economy' companies admit that their workers have rights? *The Guardian*, 14 June. Available at: https://www.theguardian.com/commentisfree/2018/jun/14/gig-economy-workers-pimlico-plumbers-employment-rights

4 See https://www.medianama.com/2017/05/223-tanveer-pasha-ola-uber-drivers-association/

5 See   https://www.reuters.com/article/us-uber-ola-strike/uber-ola-drivers-strike-in-india-demanding-higher-fares-idUSKCN1MW 1WZ

6 Said, C. (2015) Could client poaching undercut on-demand companies? *San Francisco Chronicle*, 24 April. Available at: https://www.sfchronicle.com/business/article/Could-client-poaching-undercut-on-demand-6222919.php#photo-7874032

7 Quoted in Huet (2015).

8 Quoted in Said (2015).

9 Designed by the English philosopher and social theorist, Jeremy Bentham, the panopticon is an architectural design for a prison in which a single prison guard can watch all the inmates simultaneously without them knowing whether they are being watched, thus inducing self-regulating behaviour.

10 See Wiessner, D. (2018) US court revives challenge to Seattle's Uber, Lyft union law. Reuters, 11 May. Available at: https://www.reuters.com/article/us-uber-seattle-unions/u-s-court-revives-challenge-to-seattles-uber-lyft-union-law-idUSKBN1IC27C

Conclusion: What next for the gig economy?

1 For further information, see http://www.followthethings.com
2 See https://medium.com/@r44d/uber-the-world-s-largest-taxi-co mpany-owns-no-vehicles-facebook-the-world-s-most-popular-med ia-94a15186d020
3 Despite being a large and traditional trade union with roots in metal working, IG Metall has been at the forefront of thinking about how to respond to changes to working conditions wrought by the gig economy. They have set up an Ombuds Office for German crowdworking platforms and released a set of guidelines for decent platform-based work (IG Metall, 2016).
4 See https://citizen.co.za/news/south-africa/1454013/were-a-tech nology-company-not-a-taxi-service-says-uber/
5 See https://www.theguardian.com/business/2016/jul/20/uber-dri ver-employment-tribunal-minimum-wage
6 See https://www.judiciary.uk/wp-content/uploads/2016/10/aslam-and-farrar-v-uber-employment-judgment-20161028-2.pdf
7 See https://www.fwc.gov.au/documents/decisionssigned/html/20 18fwc6836.htm
8 See https://www.theguardian.com/law/2018/feb/07/couriers-carry ing-blood-for-nhs-win-full-employment-rights
9 We thank Darcy du Toit for his insightful suggestions in this section.
10 In addition to whatever beneficial tax arrangements it is able to bring about.
11 See https://iwgbunion.files.wordpress.com/2017/07/iwgb-respon se-to-taylor-review1.pdf
12 As explained in the report 'The ILO Minimum Wage Fixing Convention, 1970 (No. 131), provides for a minimum wage, taking into consideration: (a) the needs of workers and their families, taking into account the general level of wages in the country, the cost of living, social security benefits and the relative living standards of other social groups; and (b) economic factors, including the requirements of economic development, levels of productivity and the desirability of attaining and maintaining a high level of employment. Modalities for implementation can be designed to also address piece rates and hourly pay for self-employed workers' (ILO, 2019: 60).

13 The Movement is an organization that represents Uber drivers in South Africa.

14 There are a number of reasons why workers in some places are resistant to the idea of a trade union. In parts of India, for instance, trade unions are closely linked to political parties, many of which, in turn, are linked to ethnic and religious groups. In South Africa, many workers resent paying dues to unions that they suspect might not be transparent about how those funds are spent.

15 For more on this case, see the blog post by Valerio De Stefano: http://regulatingforglobalization.com/2018/12/10/collective-bargaining-of-platform-workers-domestic-work-leads-the-way/

16 See https://www.sagaftra.org/about/our-history/2000s

17 See https://platform.coop/

18 Following the Greek economic crash of 2011, the chemicals factory Viome became insolvent, leaving their workers without a stable source of income. The workers occupied the plant and re-opened it as a worker-run soap factory. All workers here know how to do every stage of the production process as knowledge is distributed to empower all that work there. See https://www.theguardian.com/commentisfree/2017/jul/18/cope-capitalism-failed-factory-workers-greek-workplace-control and http://www.viome.org

19 The Argentinian FaSinPat (Fábrica Sin Patrones – or Factory Without Bosses) is a worker-run factory producing ceramics, taken into worker ownership following the 2001 Argentinian crash. See https://www.newstatesman.com/south-america/2007/08/argentina-workers-movement

20 A document that went on to form a core part of the ILO's constitution.

Appendix: Draft Convention on Platform Work

1 Article 2, C181 – Private Employment Agencies Convention, 1997 (No. 181).

2 Regulations pursuant to the Maritime Convention 2006, regulation 2.2.

3 Article 11(c), C181 – Private Employment Agencies Convention, 1997 (No. 181)

4 Maritime Convention 2006, guideline B2.2.3.
5 Maritime Convention 2006, guideline B2.2.3.
6 Article 3(a), ILO Wage Fixing Convention 1970 (No.131).
7 Article 3(b), ILO Wage Fixing Convention.
8 Article 5, ILO Wage Fixing Convention.
9 Article 2, ILO Wage Fixing Convention; Article 3(2)(3), C026 – Minimum Wage Fixing Machinery Convention, 1928 (No. 26).
10 ILO guidance on how to define a minimum wage: https://www.ilo.org/global/topics/wages/minimum-wages/definition/lang--en/index.htm
11 Article 7 (e), C189 – Domestic Workers Convention, 2011 (No. 189).
12 See, mutatis mutandis, Article 3(c), Health and Safety Convention c155. (For example, the car driven by Uber drivers; or the home cleaned by domestic workers.)
13 Article 7, C177 – Home Work Convention, 1996 (No. 177).
14 Article 9, C155 – Occupational Safety and Health Convention, 1981 (No. 155).
15 Article 19, Occupational Safety and Health Convention.
16 Article 11(h), C181 – Private Employment Agencies Convention, 1997 (No. 181).
17 Article 13, Occupational Safety and Health Convention.
18 Article 15(c), Occupational Safety and Health Convention.
19 Article 21, Occupational Safety and Health Convention.
20 See: ILO Hours of Work (Industry) Convention, 1919 (No. 1); Hours of Work (Commerce and Offices) Convention, 1930 (No. 30). The aspiration should be to achieve a 40-hour working week (Forty-Hour Week Convention, 1935 c47).
21 Recommendation concerning the Employment Relationship (R198), paragraph 11(b).
22 Preamble, Recommendation concerning the Employment Relationship (R198).
23 Recommendation concerning the Employment Relationship (R198), paragraph 13(a).
24 Regulation 2.1 paragraph 1, Maritime Labour Convention 2006.
25 Article 15, Domestic Workers Convention (C189).
26 Article 7, Domestic Workers Convention (C189).

27 Regulation 2.1 paragraph 2, Maritime Labour Convention 2006.
28 Paragraph 5(1), Private Employment Agencies Convention, 1997 (No. 181).
29 Article 4(2), Homeworkers Convention C177.
30 Article 6, ILO Convention 181.
31 C087 – Freedom of Association and Protection of the Right to Organise Convention, 1948 (No. 87); C098 – Right to Organise and Collective Bargaining Convention, 1949 (No. 98).
32 Article 2, Convention 87 Freedom of Association Convention; Article 4(a), Homeworkers Convention, c177.
33 Article 2, Convention 87 Freedom of Association Convention; Article 4(a), Homeworkers Convention, c177.

References

Aloisi, A. (2018) Dispatch No. 13 – Italy – '*With great power comes virtual freedom*': A review of the first Italian case holding that (food-delivery) platform workers are not employees. *Comparative Labor Law and Policy Journal*, https://cllpj.law.illinois.edu/dispatches

Amabile, T.M. (1983) The social psychology of creativity: A componential conceptualization. *Journal of Personality and Social Psychology*, 45(2): 357–76.

Anderson, B. (2000) *Doing the Dirty Work? The Global Politics of Domestic Labour*. London: Zed Books.

Antunes, R. (2013) *The Meanings of Work: Essays on the Affirmation and Negation of Work*. Chicago, IL: Haymarket Books.

Badger, A. (2018) Reflections on writing conspiracy theories. *The Invisible Worker*, issue 1. Available at: https://theinvisibleworker.wordpress.com/reflections-on-writing-conspiracy-theories-by-adam-badger/

Balaram, B., Warden, J. and Wallace-Stephens, F. (2017) *Good Gigs: A Fairer Future for the UK's Gig Economy*. London: RSA.

Barbrook, R. and Cameron, A. (1996) The Californian ideology. *Science as Culture*, 6(1): 44–72.

Beck, U. (1992) *Risk Society: Towards a New Modernity*. London: Sage.

Benson, A., Sojourner, A. and Umyarov, A. (2015) 'Can reputation discipline the gig economy? Experimental evidence from an online labor market', IZA DP No. 9501. Available at: http://ftp.iza.org/dp9501.pdf

Bent, P. (2017) Historical perspectives on precarious work: The cases of Egypt and India under British imperialism. *Global Labour Journal*, 8(1): 3–16.

Berg, J., Furrer, M., Harman, E., Rani, U. and Silberman, M.S. (2018) *Digital Labour Platforms and the Future of Work: Towards Decent Work in the Online World*. Geneva: ILO.

Beynon, H. (1973) *Working for Ford*. London: Allen Lane.

Binfield, K. (2004) *Luddites and Luddism*. Baltimore, MD: The Johns Hopkins University Press.

Bosch, G. (2004) Towards a new standard employment relationship in Western Europe. *British Journal of Industrial Relations*, 42(4): 617–36.

Bourdieu, P. (1998) *Contre Feux*. Paris: Raisons d'agir.

Braverman, H. (1998) *Labor and Monopoly Capital: The Degradation of Work in the Twentieth Century*. New York: Monthly Review Press.

Bruns, A. (2008) *Blogs, Wikipedia, Second Life, and Beyond: From Production to Produsage*. New York: Peter Lang.

Cant, C. (2018) The wave of worker resistance in European food platforms 2016–17. *Notes from Below*, 1. Available at: https://notesfrombelow.org/article/european-food-platform-strike-wave

Cant, C. (2019) *Riding for Deliveroo: Resistance in the New Economy*. Cambridge: Polity.

Care.com (2018) Company overview. Available at: https://www.care.com/company-overview

China Labour Bulletin (2018a) Labour relations in China: Some frequently asked questions. *China Labour Bulletin*. Available at: https://www.clb.org.hk/content/labour-relations-china-some-frequently-asked-questions

China Labour Bulletin (2018b) '@chinalabour', Twitter, 5 June. Available at: https://twitter.com/chinalabour/status/1003933538855497728?s=19

China Labour Bulletin (2018c) Didi drivers in China protest pay cuts and restrictive work practices. *China Labour Bulletin*, 3 July. Available at: https://www.clb.org.hk/content/didi-drivers-china-protest-pay-cuts-and-restrictive-work-practices

Christie, N. and Ward, H. (2018) The emerging issues for management of occupational road risk in a changing economy. A survey of gig economy drivers, riders and their managers. London: UCL Centre for Transport Studies.

Cook, I. (2004) Follow the thing: Papaya. *Antipode*, 36(4): 642–64.

Countouris, N. and De Stefano, V. (2019) *New Trade Union Strategies for New Forms of Employment*. Brussels: ETUC.

Dalla Costa, M. and James, S. (1971) *The Power of Women and the Subversion of the Community*. Brooklyn, NY: Pétroleuse Press.

De Stefano, V. (2018) A more comprehensive approach to platform-work litigation. Regulating for Globalisation, 28 November. Available at: http://regulatingforglobalization.com/2018/11/28/a-more-comprensive-approach-to-platform-work-litigation/

Doogan, K. (2009) *New Capitalism: The Transformation of Work*. London: Polity.

du Toit, D. (2018) Uber the Border and Far Away? IR Network, LexisNexis.

Duffy, A.E.P. (1961) New unionism in Britain, 1889–1890: A reappraisal. *Economic History Review*, 14(2): 306–19.

Duménil, G. and Lévy, D. (2005) The neoliberal (counter-)revolution. In A. Saad-Filho and D. Johnston (eds.), *Neoliberalism: A Critical Reader*. London: Pluto Press.

Dynamo (2014) Dear Jeff Bezos. Available at: http://www.wearedynamo.org/dearjeffbezos

Eubanks, V. (2019) *Automating Inequality: How High-Tech Tools Profile, Police, and Punish the Poor*. New York: St. Martin's Press.

European Commission (2008) *Communication from the Commission to the European Council: A European Economic Recovery Plan*. Brussels: Commission of the European Communities.

Farr, C. (2015) Why Homejoy failed. Wired, 26 October. Available at: https://www.wired.com/2015/10/why-homejoy-failed/

Fear, C. (2018) 'Without our brain and muscle not a single wheel can turn': The IWW Couriers Network. *Notes from Below*, 3. Available at: https://notesfrombelow.org/article/without-our-brain-and-muscle

Fredman, S. (2003) Women at work: The broken promise of flexicurity. *Industrial Law Journal*, 33(4): 229–319.

Frey, C.B. and Osborne, M.A. (2017) The future of employment: How susceptible are jobs to computerisation? *Technological Forecasting and Social Change*, 114. 254–80.

Fudge, J. (2017) The future of the standard employment relationship: Labour law, new institutional economics and old power resource theory. *Journal of Industrial Relations*, 59(3): 374–92.

Gandini, A. (2016) *The Reputation Economy: Understanding Knowledge Work in Digital Society*. London: Palgrave Macmillan.

Gereffi, G., Humphrey, J. and Sturgeon, T. (2005) The governance of global value chains. *Review of International Political Economy*, 12(1): 78–104.

Goodwin, T. (2015) The Battle Is for the Customer Interface. TechCrunch, 3 March. Available at: https://techcrunch.com/2015/03/03/in-the-age-of-disintermediation-the-battle-is-all-for-the-customer-interface/

Goos, M. and Manning, A. (2007) Lousy and lovely jobs: The rising polarization of work in Britain. *Review of Economics and Statistics*, 89(1): 118–33.

Graeber, D. (2018) *Bullshit Jobs: A Theory*. London: Allen Lane.

Graham, M. and Anwar, M.A. (2018) Digital labour. In J. Ash, R. Kitchin and A. Leszczynski (eds.) *Digital Geographies*. London: Sage, pp. 177–87.

Graham, M. and Anwar, M.A. (2019) The global gig economy: Towards a planetary labour market? *First Monday*, 24(4). doi.org/10.5210/fm.v24i4.9913.

Graham, M. and Shaw, J. (eds.) (2017) *Towards a Fairer Gig Economy*. London: Meatspace Press.

Graham, M. and Woodcock, J. (2018) Towards a fairer platform economy: Introducing the Fairwork Foundation. *Alternate Routes*, 29: 242–53.

Graham, M., Hjorth, I. and Lehdonvirta, V. (2017a) Digital labour and development: Impacts of global digital labour platforms and the gig economy on worker livelihoods. *Transfer: European Review of Labour and Research*, 23(2): 135–162.

Graham, M., Lehdonvirta, V., Wood, A., Barnard, H., Hjorth, I. and Simon, D.P. (2017b) *The Risks and Rewards of Online Gig Work at the Global Margins*. Oxford: Oxford Internet Institute.

Graham, M., Ojanpera, S., Anwar, M.A. and Friederici, N. (2017c) Digital connectivity and African knowledge economies. *Questions de Communication*, 32: 345–60.

Gray, M.L. and Suri, S. (2019) *Ghost Work: How to Stop Silicon Valley from Building a New Global Underclass.* New York: Houghton Mifflin Harcourt.

Gray, M.L., Suri, S., Ali, S.S. and Kulkarni, D. (2016), The crowd is a collaborative network. In *CSCW'16: Proceedings of the 19th ACM Conference on Computer-Supported Cooperative Work & Social Computing, San Francisco, CA, 27 February–2 March.* New York: ACM Press, pp. 134–47.

Gupta, N., Martin, D., Hanrahan, B. and O'Neill, J. (2014) Turk-life in India. In *Proceedings of the ACM International Conference on Supporting Group Work (GROUP'14) Sanibel Island, 9–12 November.*

Hara, K., Adams, A., Milland, K., Savage, S., Callison-Burch, C. and Bigham, J.P. (2018) A data-driven analysis of workers' earnings on Amazon Mechanical Turk. In *CHI'18: Proceedings of the 2018 CHI Conference on Human Factors in Computing Systems,* Paper No. 449. New York: ACM Press.

Harvey, D. (1989) *The Urban Experience.* Oxford: Blackwell.

Harvey, D. (2007) *A Brief History of Neoliberalism.* Oxford: Oxford University Press.

Heeks, R. (2017) Decent work and the digital gig economy: A developing country perspective on employment impacts and standards in online outsourcing, crowdwork, etc. Paper No. 71. Manchester: Centre for Development Informatics, Global Development Institute, SEED.

Herman, S., Johnson, C., Hunter, R., Dunn, M. and Janse van Vuuren, P.F. (2019) Africa's digital platforms and financial services: An eight-country overview. Available at: https://www.i2ifacility.org/system/documents/files/000/000/086/original/DIGITAL_ADP_Focus_Note.pdf?1553833148

Heyes, J. (2011) Flexicurity, employment protection and the jobs crisis. *Work, Employment and Society,* 25(4): 642–57.

Hilfr (2018) Historic agreement: First ever collective agreement for the platform economy signed in Denmark. Available at: http://blog.hilfr.dk/en/historic-agreement-first-ever-collective-agreement-platform-economy-signed-denmark/

Hill, S. (2017) *Raw Deal: How the 'Uber Economy' and Runaway Capitalism Are Screwing American Workers.* New York: St Martin's Press.

Hochschild, A.R. (1983) *The Managed Heart: The Commercialisation of Human Feeling.* Berkeley, CA: University of California Press.

Hochschild, A.R. (1989) *The Second Shift: Working Families and the Revolution at Home.* New York: Penguin.

Howe, J. (2006) The rise of crowdsourcing. Wired, 1 May. Available at: http://www.wired.com/2006/06/crowds/

Huet, E. (2015) What really killed Homejoy? It couldn't hold on to its customers. Forbes, 23 July. Available at: https://www.forbes.com/sites/ellenhuet/2015/07/23/what-really-killed-homejoy-it-couldnt-hold-onto-its-customers/#22c9f5871874

Hunt, A. and Machingura, F. (2016) A good gig? The rise of on-demand domestic work. ODI Development Progress, Working Paper 7.

Hunt, A. and Samman, E. (2019) Gender and the gig economy. ODI Working Paper 546.

Huws, U. and Joyce, S. (2016) Crowd working survey: Size of the UK's 'gig economy'. Hatfield: University of Hertfordshire.

Huws, U., Spencer, N. and Joyce, S. (2016) Crowd work in Europe: Preliminary results from a survey in the UK, Sweden, Germany, Austria and the Netherlands. Hatfield: University of Hertfordshire.

Hyman, R. (1989) *Strikes*, 4th edn. Glasgow: Macmillan Press.

Iles, A. (2005) The insecurity lasts a long time. *Mute: Precarious Reader*, 2: 34–36.

International Labour Organization (ILO) (2011) *Policies and Regulations to Combat Precarious Employment.* Geneva: International Labour Office.

International Labour Organization (ILO) (2014) *Global Dialogue Forum on Employment Relationships in the Media and Culture Sector: Final report of the discussion.* Geneva: International Labour Office.

International Labour Organization (ILO) (2019) *Work for a Brighter Future.* Geneva: International Labour Office.

Irani, L. (2015) The cultural work of microwork. *New Media & Society*, 17(5): 720–39.

Irani, L. and Silberman, M.S. (2013) Turkopticon: Interrupting worker invisibility in Amazon Mechanical Turk. *Proceedings of CHI 2013, 28 April–2 May.*

IWGB (2018) Uber drivers to strike for 24 hours in London, Birmingham and Nottingham. IWGB, 8 October. Available at: https://iwgb.org.uk/post/5bbb3ff1bf94a/uber-drivers-to-strike-for

Jacoby, S.M. (2004) *Employing Bureaucracy: Managers, Unions, and the Transformation of Work in the 20th Century.* Mahwah, NJ. Lawrence Erlbaum.

Kaganer, E., Carmel, E., Hirscheim, R. and Olsen, T. (2013) Managing the human cloud. *MIT Sloan Management Review*, 54(2): 23–32.

Kalanick, T. (2013) Uber Policy White Paper 1.0. Uber. Available at: http://www.benedelman.org/uber/uber-policy-whitepaper.pdf

Kalanick, T. and Swisher, K. (2014) Uber CEO: We're in a political battle with an 'assh*le', Mashable, 28 May. Available at: http://mashable.com/2014/05/28/travis-kalanick-co-founder-and-ceo-of-uber/

Kalleberg, A.L. (2009) Precarious work, insecure workers: Employment relations in transition. *American Sociological Review*, 74(1): 1–22.

Kaplanis, I. (2007) *The Geography of Employment Polarisation in Britain.* London: Institute for Public Policy Research.

Kessler, S. (2018) *Gigged: The Gig Economy, the End of the Job and the Future of Work.* New York: St. Martin's Press.

Klein, N. (2008) *The Shock Doctrine.* London: Penguin Books.

Kuhn, J.W. (1961) *Bargaining in Grievance Settlement: The Power of Industrial Work Groups.* New York: Columbia University Press.

Lanier, J. (2014). *Who Owns the Future?* New York: Simon and Schuster.

Lee, M.K., Kusbit, D., Metsky, E. and Dabbish, L. (2015) Working with machines: The impact of algorithmic, data-driven management on human workers. In B. Begole, J. Kim, K. Inkpen and W. Wood (eds.), *Proceedings of the 33rd Annual ACM SIGCHI Conference.* New York: ACM Press.

McDowell, L., Batnitzky, A. and Dyer, S. (2009) Precarious work and economic migration: Emerging immigrant divisions of labour in Greater London's service sector. *International Journal of Urban and Regional Research*, 33(1): 3–25.

MacGregor, S. (2005) The welfare state and neoliberalism. In A. Saad-Filho and D. Johnston (eds.), *Neoliberalism: A Critical Reader.* London: Pluto Press.

McIlroy, J. (1995) *Trade Unions in Britain Today.* Manchester: Manchester University Press.

McKarthy, K. (2005) Is precarity enough? *Mute: Precarious Reader*, 2: 54–8.

McKinsey Global Institute (2017) Where machines could replace humans and where they can't (yet). London: McKinsey Global Institute.

Mankelow, R. (2017) The Port of London, 1790–1970. In S. Davies, C. J. Davis, D. de Vries, L.H. van Voss, L. Hesselink and K. Weinhauer (eds.), *Dock Workers: International Explorations in Comparative History, 1790–1970, Volume 1*. London: Routledge.

Manyika, J., Lund, S., Robinson, K., Valentino, J. and Dobbs, R. (2015) Connecting talent with opportunity in the digital age. McKinsey & Company. Available at: https://www.mckinsey.com/featured-insights/employment-and-growth/connecting-talent-with-opportunity-in-the-digital-age

Manyika, J., Lund, S., Bughin, J., Robinson, K., Mischke, J. and Mahajan, D. (2016), Independent work: Choice, necessity, and the gig economy. Available at: https://www.mckinsey.com/~/media/McKinsey/Featured%20Insights/Employment%20and%20Growth/Independent%20work%20Choice%20necessity%20and%20the%20gig%20economy/Independent-Work-Choice-necessity-and-the-gig-economy-Full-report.ashx

Marlow, J. (1971) *The Tolpuddle Martyrs*. London: History Book Club.

Marx, K. (1845) Theses on Feuerbach. Available at: https://www.marxists.org/archive/marx/works/1845/theses/theses.htm

Marx, K. (1955 [1847]) *The Poverty of Philosophy*. Moscow: Progress Publishers.

Marx, K. (1976) *Capital: A Critique of Political Economy Vol. 1*. London: Penguin Books.

Mason, P. (2016) *PostCapitalism: A Guide to our Future*. London: Penguin.

Massey, D. (1984) *The Spatial Divisions of Labour*. New York: Routledge.

Mitropoulos, A. (2005) Precari-Us. *Mute: Precarious Reader*, 2: 12–19.

Moody, K. (2017) *On New Terrain: How Capital is Reshaping the Battleground of Class War*. Chicago, IL: Haymarket.

Moulier-Boutang, Y. (2012) *Cognitive Capitalism*. Cambridge: Polity.

Munke, R. (2005) Neoliberalism and politics, and the politics of neo-liberalism. In A. Saad-Filho and D. Johnston (eds.), *Neoliberalism: A Critical Reader*. London: Pluto Press.

Nedelkoska, L. and Quintini, G. (2018) Automation, skills use and training. OECD Social, Employment and Migration Working Papers

No. 202. Available at: https://www.oecd-ilibrary.org/employment/automation_skills_use_and_training_jodt4loaa en

Noble, S.U. (2018) *Algorithms of Oppression: How Search Engines Reinforce Racism.* New York: NYU Press.

OECD (2019) Measuring platform mediated workers. OECD Digital Economy Papers No. 282.

Ojanperä, S., O'Clery, N. and Graham, M. (2018) Data science, artificial intelligence and the futures of work. Alan Turing Institute Report, 24 October. Available at: http://doi.org/10.5281/zenodo.1470609

O'Neil, C. (2017) *Weapons of Math Destruction: How Big Data Increases Inequality and Threatens Democracy.* London: Penguin.

Pasquale, F. (2015) *The Black Box Society: The Secret Algorithms That Control Money and Information.* Cambridge, MA: Harvard University Press.

Peck, J. (2013) Explaining (with) neoliberalism. *Territory, Politics, Governance,* 1(2): 132–57.

Peck, J. (2017) *Offshore: Exploring the Worlds of Global Outsourcing.* Oxford: Oxford University Press.

Pollert, A. and Charlwood, A. (2009) The vulnerable worker in Britain and problems at work. *Work, Employment and Society,* 23(2): 343–62.

Pollman, E. and Barry, J. (2016) Regulatory entrepreneurship. *Southern California Law Review,* 90: 383–442.

Ravenelle, A. (2019) *Hustle and Gig: Struggling and Surviving in the Sharing Economy.* Oakland, CA: University of California Press.

Raw, L. (2009) *Striking a Light: The Bryant and May Matchwomen and their Place in History.* London: Continuum Books.

Richey, L.A. and Ponte, S. (2011) *Brand Aid: Shopping Well to Save the World.* Minneapolis, MN: University of Minnesota Press.

Roberts, S.T. (2016) Commercial content moderation: Digital laborers' dirty work. In S.U. Noble and B. Tynes (eds.), *The Intersectional Internet: Race, Sex, Class and Culture Online.* New York: Peter Lang.

Rosenblat, A. (2018) *Uberland: How Algorithms are Rewriting the Rules of Work.* Oakland, CA: University of California Press.

Rosenblat, A. and Stark, L. (2016) Algorithmic labor and information asymmetries: A case study of Uber's drivers. *International Journal of Communication,* 10: 3758–84.

Ryan, B. (2005) *Labour Migration and Employment Rights*. Liverpool: Institute of Employment Rights.

Salehi, N., Irani, L.C., Bernstein, M.S., Alkhatib, A., Ogbe, E., Milland, K. and Clickhappier (2015) We are Dynamo: Overcoming stalling and friction in collective action for crowd workers. *Proceedings of CHI'2015, 18–23 April.*

Scholz, T. (2015) Think outside the boss. Public Seminar, 5 April. Available at: http://www.publicseminar.org/2015/04/think-outside-the-boss

Scholz, T. (2017a) *Uberworked and Underpaid: How Workers are Disrupting the Digital Economy.* Cambridge: Polity.

Scholz, T. (2017b) Platform cooperativism vs. the sharing economy. In N. Douay and A. Wan (eds.), *Big Data & Civic Engagement.* Rome: Planum Publisher.

Scott, W.R. (2001) *Institutions and Organizations.* Thousand Oaks, CA: Sage.

Semuels, A. (2018) The Internet is enabling a new kind of poorly paid hell. The Atlantic, 23 January, Available at: https://www.theatlantic.com/business/archive/2018/01/amazon-mechanical-turk/551192/

Silver, B.J. (2003) *Forces of Labor, Workers' Movements and Globalization since 1870.* Cambridge: Cambridge University Press.

Slee, T. (2015) *What's Yours Is Mine: Against the Sharing Economy.* London: OR Books.

Smith, A. (2016) Gig work, online selling and home sharing. Pew Research Centre, 17 November. Available at: http://www.pewinternet.org/2016/11/17/gig-work-online-selling-and-home-sharing/

Solon, O. (2018) The rise of 'pseudo-AI': How tech firms quietly use humans to do bots' work. *The Guardian,* 6 July. Available at: https://www.theguardian.com/technology/2018/jul/06/artificial-intelligence-ai-humans-bots-tech-companies

Srnicek, N. (2017) *Platform Capitalism.* Cambridge: Polity.

Standing, G. (2011) *The Precariat: The New Dangerous Class.* London: Bloomsbury.

Standing, G. (2016) *The Corruption of Capitalism: Why Rentiers Thrive and Work Does Not Pay.* London: Biteback Publishing.

Sundararajan, A. (2017) *The Sharing Economy: The End of Employment and the Rise of Crowd-Based Capitalism.* Cambridge, MA: MIT Press.

Susskind, R. (2018) AI, work and outcome-thinking. *British Academy Review*, 34: 30 1.

SweepSouth (2018) Report on pay and working conditions for domestic work in SA 2018. SweepSouth, 13 May. Available at: https://blog.sweepsouth.com/2018/05/13/report-on-pay-and-working-conditions-for-domestic-work-in-sa-2018/

Taylor, F. (1967) *The Principles of Scientific Management*. New York: Norton.

Taylor, P. and Bain, P. (2005) 'India calling to the far away towns': The call centre labour process and globalization. *Work, Employment and Society*, 19(2): 261–82.

Taylor, B. and Li, Q. (2007) Is the ACFTU a union and does it matter? *Journal of Industrial Relations*, 49(5): 701–15.

Taylor, M., Marsh, G., Nicol, D. and Broadbent, P. (2017) Good work: The Taylor Review of modern working practice. Available at: https://assets.publishing.service.gov.uk/government/uploads/system/uploads/attachment_data/file/627671/good-work-taylor-review-modern-working-practices-rg.pdf

Thompson, P. and Ackroyd, S. (1995) All quiet on the workplace front? A critique of recent trends in British industrial sociology. *Sociology*, 29: 615–33.

Tillett, B. (1910) *A Brief History of the Dockers' Union*. London: Dock, Wharf, Riverside & General Workers' Union.

Ticona, J. and Mateescu, A. (2018) Trusted strangers: Carework platforms' cultural entrepreneurship in the on-demand economy. *New Media & Society*, 20(11): 4384–404.

Tucker, J. (1993) Everyday forms of employee resistance. *Sociological Forum*, 8(1): 25–45.

van Doorn, N. (2017) Platform labor: On the gendered and racialized exploitation of low-income service work in the 'on-demand' economy. *Information, Communication & Society*, 20(6): 898–914.

Vandaele, K. (2018) Will trade unions survive in the platform economy? Emerging patterns of platform workers' collective voice and representation in Europe. Working Paper. Brussels: European Trade Union Institute.

Waters, F. and Woodcock, J. (2017) Far from seamless: A workers' inquiry at Deliveroo. *Viewpoint Magazine*, 20 September. Available at: https://www.viewpointmag.com/2017/09/20/far-seamless-workers-inquiry-deliveroo/

Webster, E., Lambert, R. and Bezuidenhout, A. (2008) *Grounding Globalization: Labour in the Age of Insecurity*. Oxford: Blackwell.

Weightman, G. and Humphries, S. (2007) *The Making of Modern London: A People's History of the Capital from 1815 to the Present Day*. London: Random House.

Williams, E. (1994) *Capitalism and Slavery*. Chapel Hill, NC: University of North Carolina Press.

Williams, S. and Adam-Smith, D. (2009) Web case: Trade unions and the prospects for unionization in the service sector. In S. Williams and D. Adam-Smith (eds.), *Contemporary Employment Relations: A Critical Introduction*, 2nd edn. Oxford: Oxford University Press.

Wood, A.J. (2015) Networks of injustice and worker mobilisation at Walmart. *Industrial Relations Journal*, 46(4): 259–74.

Wood, A.J., Lehdonvirta, V. and Graham, M. (2018) Workers of the Internet unite? Online freelancer organisation among remote gig economy workers in six Asian and African countries. *New Technology, Work and Employment*, 33(2): 95–112.

Wood, A., Graham, M., Lehdonvirta, A. and Hjorth, I. (2019a) Good gig, bad big: Autonomy and algorithmic control in the global gig economy. *Work, Employment and Society*, 33(1): 56–75.

Wood, A., Graham, M., Lehdonvirta, A. and Hjorth, I. (2019b) Networked but commodified: The (dis)embeddedness of digital labour in the gig economy. *Sociology*, https://doi.org/10.1177/0038038519828906

Woodcock, J. (2014a) The workers' inquiry from Trotskyism to Operaismo: A political methodology for investigating the workplace. *Ephemera*, 14(3): 493–513.

Woodcock, J. (2014b) Precarious work in London: New forms of organisation and the city. *City: Analysis of Urban Trends, Culture, Theory, Policy, Action*, 18(6): 776–88.

Woodcock, J. (2017) *Working the Phones: Control and Resistance in Call Centres*. London: Pluto.

Woodcock, J. (2018a) Changes in employment: Role of the state and its reconfiguration in the liberalization of employment policies. In O. Fedyuk and P. Stewart (eds.), *Inclusion and Exclusion in Europe:*

Migration, Work and Employment Perspectives. London: ECPR Press, pp. 17 34.

Woodcock, J. (2018b) Digital labour and workers' organisation. In M. Atzeni and I. Ness (eds.), *Global Perspectives on Workers' and Labour Organizations.* Singapore: Springer, pp. 157–73.

Woodcock, J. (forthcoming) The algorithmic Panopticon at Deliveroo: Measurement, precarity, and the illusion of control. *Ephemera.*

Woodcock, J. and Johnson, M.R. (2018) Gamification: What it is, and how to fight it. *The Sociological Review,* 66(3): 542–58.

Yin, M., Gray, M.L., Suri, S. and Vaughan, J.W. (2016), The communication network within the crowd. *Proceedings of the 25th International World Wide Web Conference (WWW), Montreal, Canada, 11 April.*

Index